Exploring the
Yellowstone Backcountry

The Sierra Club Totebooks®

A Sierra Club Totebook®

EXPLORING THE YELLOWSTONE BACKCOUNTRY

A Guide to the Hiking Trails of Yellowstone with Additional Sections on Canoeing, Bicycling, and Cross-country Skiing

by Orville Bach, Jr.

SIERRA CLUB BOOKS
San Francisco

The Sierra Club, founded in 1892 by John Muir, has devoted itself to the study and protection of the earth's scenic and ecological resources—mountains, wetlands, woodlands, wild shores and rivers, deserts and plains. The publishing program of the Sierra Club offers books to the public as a nonprofit educational service in the hope that they may enlarge the public's understanding of the Club's basic concerns. The point of view expressed in each book, however, does not necessarily represent that of the Club. The Sierra Club has some sixty chapters coast to coast, in Canada, Hawaii, and Alaska. For information about how you may participate in its programs to preserve wilderness and the quality of life, please address inquiries to Sierra Club, 730 Polk Street, San Francisco, CA 94109.

Library of Congress Cataloging-in-Publication Data

Bach, Orville E.
    Exploring the Yellowstone backcountry : a guide to the hiking
trails of Yellowstone with additional sections on canoeing,
bicycling, and cross-country skiing / by Orville Bach.
        p.   cm.
    Includes index.
    ISBN 0-87156-628-1
    1. Hiking—Yellowstone National Park—Guide-books.   2. Trails—
Yellowstone National Park—Guide-books.   3. Outdoor recreation—
Yellowstone National Park—Guide-books.   4. Yellowstone National
Park—Guide-books.   I. Title.
GV199.42.Y45B33   1991
917.87'52—dc20   91–35111
                                                                CIP

Production by Amy Evans
Cover design by Bonnie Smetts
Book design by Mark Ong
Illustrations by Margaret C. Bach

Printed in the United States of America on acid-free paper containing a minimum of 50% recovered waste paper, of which at least 10% of the fiber content is post-consumer waste.

10 9 8 7 6 5 4 3 2 1

Contents

TRAIL DESCRIPTIONS BY REGION

TRAVEL BY CANOE, BIKE, & SKI

Foreword

Yellowstone . . . land of hissing steam and tumbling streams, of bison and bugling elk, stronghold of the grizzly bear, justifiably precious as the world's first national park.

But Yellowstone National Park, in all its splendor, is but the core and the cornerstone of something more complex and even more precious than the park alone. For surrounding the park's 2.2 million acres are some 12 million more acres of wildland, collectively called the Greater Yellowstone Ecosystem. Intricate and whole, the Greater Yellowstone is considered by many to be the largest essentially intact ecosystem in the temperate zones of the earth. And it is on the health and integrity of the Greater Yellowstone Ecosystem that the future of the great Yellowstone National Park depends.

The term "Greater Yellowstone Ecosystem" was first coined by biologists Frank and John Craighead, whose pioneering studies of grizzly bears in the 1960s revealed that the Great Bear ranged over an area nearly three times as large as the political area defined as Yellowstone Park. The boundaries of occupied grizzly habitat became the first loose borders of what is now called the Greater Yellowstone Ecosystem.

The boundaries of Greater Yellowstone have since been refined to encompass the totality of the plants and animals, the physical features and ecological processes that, like the grizzly bear, reach beyond the political boundaries of Yellowstone National Park and function as a whole, dynamic, ever-changing system. The migration routes and winter ranges of Greater Yellowstone's renowned ungulates, the extent of its unique geothermal systems, the watersheds of the three major rivers whose origins lie high in its pristine mountains, the mountain ranges themselves ringing this high plateau, and other geologic, hydrologic, vegetative, and wildlife characteristics that make this region distinct from the plains and basins that surround it . . . all feed into our current understanding of the "what" and "where" of the Greater Yellowstone Ecosystem.

Unfortunately, though "Greater Yellowstone: The Concept" is reasonably whole, "Greater Yellowstone: The Management Unit" is not so unbroken. Encompassing two national parks, seven national forests (about 40 percent of which are designated Wilderness), three national wildlife refuges, BLM lands, state lands from three different states, and over a million acres of privately owned land, the ecosystem involves a total of some 30 different political jurisdictions whose management goals and missions often conflict. Consequently, the management of the ecosystem to date has been fragmented, often uncoordinated, rarely recognizing the ecological values of the system as a whole.

Compounding and fueling the fragmented management are burgeoning threats from inside and outside the ecosystem's borders. Development in the national forests and private lands for timber, oil and gas, hard-rock mining, recreation, and housing nibble away at the threads that bind the system together. Soils and spawning streams, wildlife habitat and wondrous views, and regional community economies are all at risk from uncontrolled exploitation of the ecosystem's natural treasures.

And Yellowstone National Park, an island within an island, is especially at risk. Increasing development around park boundaries fragments wildlife habitat, interrupts critical migration routes for wildlife that must leave park boundaries in winter, and threatens to degrade the soils, air, and water that transcend park limits. Burgeoning recreational use both in summer and winter within the park itself threatens wildlife populations, as traffic, introduction of exotics, trampling and overuse, poaching, vandalism, simple disturbance during sensitive periods, and other human activities take their cumulative toll.

And always, overriding biological and ecological considerations, always there is politics—politics that allows the development to continue, politics that refuses to acknowledge the ecological and biological realities of the ecosystem, politics that influences and too often drives the resource planning, management, and protection efforts of the public agencies into whose hands most of the ecosystem is entrusted.

The effort to reintroduce the wolf into Yellowstone National Park is a perfect example of the kind of biopolitics at work. Despite extensive scientific studies confirming that Yellowstone, where wolves once were an important component of its fauna, is world-class wolf habitat; despite exhaustive studies demonstrating that there is an abundant prey base for wolves in Yellowstone and that the reintroduction of a viable wolf population would have minimal effects on the size of Greater Yellowstone's wildlife herds or privately owned livestock; despite the acknowledgement that returning this predator to the ecosystem would restore a missing link in its ecological web—still, there are no wolves in Yellowstone National Park. Still, politics prevails.

In large part to counter these political strangleholds on Greater Yellowstone's future, the Greater Yellowstone Coalition (GYC) was formed in 1983 to preserve and protect the Greater Yellowstone Ecosystem. Thanks to the efforts of GYC members and thousands of other committed individuals and organizations, changes are coming slowly but surely to Greater Yellowstone's protection and management. After much prodding, for example, the Park Service and Forest Service together recently produced a new set of common goals for managing their Greater Yellowstone lands.

Much remains to be done to ensure that the diversity and wildness of Yellowstone National Park and the Greater Yellowstone Ecosystem stay intact for future generations. As you explore the Yellowstone backcountry with this guide, soak yourself in its spirit, and join in the effort to keep the Greater Yellowstone great, forever.

Mary Carr, Communications Director
Greater Yellowstone Coalition
P.O. Box 1874
Bozeman, MT 59771
August 1991

Preface

This new edition represents a complete revision of *Hiking the Yellowstone Backcountry*. Information on the fires of 1988, as well as changed trails, have been incorporated into the trail descriptions. Several new topics have been added in the pre-hiking section, especially regarding safety and bears. A new Overview of Yellowstone Hikes section makes it easier for you to find the information you need to select and plan a trip into the backcountry.

While hiking may be the primary mode for exploring Yellowstone's backcountry, there are other means of travel. In an attempt to create a truly comprehensive guide to the Yellowstone backcountry, sections on canoeing, bicycling, and cross-country skiing have been added. Thus the title of this new edition has been changed to *Exploring the Yellowstone Backcountry*.

Since I first began exploring the Yellowstone backcountry in the 1960s, I have observed a number of changes—some positive and some negative. A positive development involves the tight permit system the National Park Service has instituted in the face of increased backcountry use, which for the most part ensures the same quality wilderness experience today that I enjoyed back in the sixties. In order for this to continue to be the case, each one of us who ventures out into Yellowstone's backcountry must treat the resource with the utmost respect and care. (On the negative side Yellowstone is threatened by external development and biopolitics. Mary Carr, Communications Director of the Greater Yellowstone Coalition, addresses some of these concerns in the Foreword.)

Safety should be the most important consideration of a backcountry trip in Yellowstone. Today there are certainly many more footbridges and well-marked trails, and much more information about bear activity than existed when I first began exploring. However, travel in the backcountry is not without risk. There are no guarantees of safety. Yellowstone contains some truly *wild* country. I trust that this book will help you to plan, prepare for, and enjoy a rewarding experience in Yellowstone's wilderness, but please remember that you are individually responsible and accountable for your own safety. There are no substitutes for being well-prepared and using good judgement.

In order to achieve a greater degree of consistency and accuracy, each trail and trip in this book has been traveled by yours truly. Of course, I do not make any claims regarding infallibility, so if you find information you feel is inaccurate or misleading, please write me in care of Sierra Club Books, 100 Bush Street, San Francisco, CA 94104. I will do my best to investigate your information and incorporate changes where appropriate in the next printing. In the meantime I sincerely hope your visit to Yellowstone's wild and diverse backcountry will not only be safe and enjoyable, but will inspire you to join those who are working to preserve and protect the integrity of the Greater Yellowstone Ecosystem for our children and grandchildren.

Orville E. Bach, Jr.
Old Faithful, Yellowstone National Park
June 1991

Acknowledgements

There is no way I could have written this book without the encouragement, assistance, and companionship of numerous people. First and foremost I am deeply indebted to my wife, Margaret, who has accompanied me on many trips through the park and endured my absences during others. Margaret's outward show of love of nature in Yellowstone—especially for the wildflowers—has stirred my emotions on so many occasions. I am also indebted to my good friends Rod and Kathy Busby. Rod and I have been exploring wild country, including most of the park's trails, since 1968. John and Deb Dirkson are true Yellowstone backcountry explorers who possess the savvy of early-day pioneers. They taught me how to slow down and truly make the wilderness a comfortable home away from home. Park Geologist Rick Hutchinson has been my friend over the years, and has joined me in some rugged areas of Yellowstone's wilderness. Jim Lenertz has worked in Yellowstone since the late 1960s, and has shared a great deal of his backcountry know-how with me on our many backpacking and canoeing trips. Some of my favorite backcountry memories stem from lengthy September excursions with good friend Al Duff into Thorofare and Lamar country. Tom Caples and Tom Gerrity are long-time Yellowstone friends who both possess great skills in capturing Yellowstone's wild beauty on film. Hank Barnett and I had some great trips through Yellowstone before he headed to Crater Lake to work as a ranger. Bill Millar around a campfire is a gem.

And I am indebted to Glen Wells: Glen, you were the best naturalist and interpretive ranger I ever knew. You revealed so many of nature's wonderful secrets to me and so many others.

You left us so early, with so much left to share. So this book is dedicated to your memory, Yellowstone Park Ranger Glen Wells, and to your wife, Parthenia, and your two fine sons, Devin and Logan.

About the Author

Orville Bach received his undergraduate and graduate degrees from Auburn University, specializing in resource economics. He and his wife, Margaret, began working as seasonal employees in Yellowstone and Glacier national parks during the late 1960s. From 1970 through 1974 they were stationed at Malmstrom Air Force Base in Great Falls, Montana.

Bach has traveled the Yellowstone backcountry extensively during all seasons, including an 18-day cross-country winter ski trip, an account of which appeared in *Backpacker* magazine. He has worked as a seasonal National Park Service interpretive ranger in Yellowstone every summer since 1974, except for two summers during which he worked in Great Smoky Mountains National Park.

The rest of the year Bach, his wife, and their daughters, Caroline and Alison, live in Morristown, Tennessee, where Bach teaches at Walters State Community College.

BEFORE YOU SET OUT

How to Use This Book

My primary objectives for this book are to help you (1) select and plan a backcountry trip in Yellowstone, (2) adequately prepare for your trip regarding gear and safety considerations, and (3) enhance your enjoyment of the backcountry once you are there.

There are sections on canoeing, bicycling, and cross-country skiing as well as hiking. The Overview of Yellowstone Hikes section allows you to select a hike that fits your desired distance and difficulty. The pre-hiking information concerning such items as safety, clothing and equipment, weather and climate, and backcountry regulations is designed to help you prepare for your hike. A handy Backpacker's Checklist is included under the Clothing and Equipment heading to help you remember to bring the items you will need to make your trip comfortable and enjoyable. Much of this information is based on my own personal experience in the field, and reading through this material *before* you head out will help you avoid making some of the mistakes I have made over the years. You want your backcountry experience to be memorable, but for reasons that are pleasant.

The section on Natural History will help you better understand and appreciate Yellowstone country. Specific trip/trail descriptions are organized according to each of the park's seven wilderness regions and further subdivided according to park areas within each region (see map on page 80). A foldout topographic map allows you to negotiate the park's maintained trails.

Overview of Yellowstone Hikes

To the first-time visitor Yellowstone's backcountry can be somewhat overwhelming since the park encompasses nearly 3,500 square miles. Selecting a hike or overnight backcountry trip usually depends on the following variables: (1) distance and difficulty desired, (2) time of year, (3) personal preferences regarding scenery, and (4) trail restrictions. Hopefully, this book will help you in making your selections for variables 1, 2, and 3. Variable 4 can be determined only by checking at a ranger station. *Never* embark on a hike without first ascertaining trail conditions and restrictions at a ranger station, preferably one in the vicinity of your desired trip.

To help you select a trip with the desired distance and difficulty, many of the destinations in this book have been sorted into three categories: Short, Medium-distance, and Recommended Extended Backcountry Trips. The short hikes are appropriate for excursions lasting a half-day or less. Medium-distance trips include hikes that may be taken in a full day or as a 2- to 3-day overnight trip. Extended backcountry trips require three days and longer.

Information on variables 2 and 3 (time of year and scenery) can be found in the Weather section on page 44 and in the specific trail descriptions. But remember that weather conditions vary from year to year and, in turn, affect trail conditions and stream crossings—another reason to check in at a ranger station prior to heading for the trailhead!

SHORT HIKES (ROUNDTRIP DISTANCES OF 2 TO 8 MILES)

Hike	Nearest Location	Miles Round-trip	Difficulty (Easy–Hard: 1–5)	Page No.
Artist Paintpots	Norris	1	1	150
Avalanche Peak	Fishing Bridge	4	5	220
Beula Lake	South Entrance	5	2	96
Beaver Ponds Loop	Mammoth	5	1	170
Bunsen Peak	Mammoth	5	3	182
Bechler Falls via Union Falls Trail from Cave Falls	Bechler Ranger Station	2	1	98
Bechler Meadows via Bechler River Trail	Bechler Ranger Station	7	1	92
Cascade Lake	Canyon	5	1	180
Clear Lake–Ribbon Lake Loop	Canyon	4.2*	2	228
Canyon Rim	Canyon	4	1	227
Divide Lookout	Old Faithful	3.4	3	114
Elk Point Bay via Thorofare Trail	Fishing Bridge	6	1	124
Elephant Back Loop	Fishing Bridge	3.5*	3	150
Fairy Falls–Imperial Geyser	Old Faithful	6.8	1	108

*These distances are one-way since they involve a loop or traveling from one trailhead to another. **NOTE:** To convert miles to kilometers, multiply the number of miles by 1.62.

SHORT HIKES *(continued)*

Hike	Nearest Location	Miles Round-trip	Difficulty (Easy–Hard: 1–5)	Page No.
Glen Creek to Mammoth via Howard Eaton Trail	Mammoth	6	1	171
Grebe Lake	Canyon	6	1	178
Glacial Boulder to View of Silver Cord Cascade via Seven-Mile Hole Trail	Canyon	2.6	1	231
Grizzly Lake	Norris	4	2	167
Gneiss Creek Trail to open valley	Madison	4	2	167
Hellroaring Creek	Tower	8	3	193
Harlequin Lake	Madison	1	1	169
Ice Lake	Norris	0.5	1	179
Lamar River Trail to Cache Creek	Lamar Ranger Station	6	2	206
Lost Lake & Lost Falls	Tower	1	1	182–3
Lone Star Geyser	Old Faithful	5	1	113
Lower Blacktail Trail to Yellow-stone River	Mammoth	8	4	192
Mystic Falls Loop	Old Faithful	3.2*	3	107

*These distances are one-way since they involve a loop or traveling from one trailhead to another. **NOTE:** To convert miles to kilometers, multiply the number of miles by 1.62.

SHORT HIKES (continued)

Hike	Nearest Location	Miles Round-trip	Difficulty (Easy–Hard: 1–5)	Page No.
Mallard Lake	Old Faithful	7	2	111
Mt. Washburn	Canyon	6	4	232
Monument Geyser Basin	Norris	2	4	168
Observation Point– Solitary Geyser Loop via Upper Geyser Basin Trail	Old Faithful	1*	2	104
Osprey Falls	Mammoth	4	3	181
Pelican Valley via Pelican Creek Trail	Fishing Bridge	4	2	212
Purple Mountain	Madison	6.6	4	169
Queen's Laundry Spring & Sentinel Meadows	Old Faithful	6	1	113
Rescue Creek Trail	Mammoth	8*	2	190
Riddle Lake	Grant	5	1	141
Shoshone Lake via DeLacy Creek Trail	Old Faithful	7	3	103
Shoshone Lake via Dogshead Trail	Grant	9	2	104

*These distances are one-way since they involve a loop or traveling from one trailhead to another. **NOTE:** To convert miles to kilometers, multiply the number of miles by 1.62.

SHORT HIKES (continued)

Hike	Nearest Location	Miles Round-trip	Difficulty (Easy–Hard: 1–5)	Page No.
Slough Creek Meadows via Slough Creek Trail	Tower	4	2	197
Solfatara Creek to Whiterock Springs via Cascade Lake to Beaver Lake Trail	Norris	7	2	175
Yellowstone River Overlook	Tower	4	2	220
Storm Point Loop	Fishing Bridge	2*	1	221
Tower Falls Trail	Tower	1	2	220
Trout Lake Trail	Northeast Entrance	0.6	1	201
Upper Geyser Basin–Biscuit Basin Loop	Old Faithful	5*	1	104
Upper Pebble Creek Meadows via Pebble Creek Trail	Northeast Entrance	5	3	198
Undine Falls via Lava Creek Trail	Mammoth	6	2	191
Wraith Falls	Mammoth	0.6	1	182

*These distances are one-way since they involve a loop or traveling from one trailhead to another. **NOTE:** To convert miles to kilometers, multiply the number of miles by 1.62.

MEDIUM-DISTANCE HIKES (ROUNDTRIP DISTANCES OF 10 TO 24 MILES, APPROPRIATE FOR FULL-DAY HIKES AND/OR 2- TO 3-DAY OVERNIGHT TRIPS)

Hike	Nearest Location	Miles Round-trip	Difficulty (Easy to Hard: 1–5)	Page No.
Buffalo Plateau Loop	Tower–Roosevelt	21*	4	194
Bighorn Pass	Mammoth	17	4	162
Blacktail Trail to Knowles Falls	Mammoth	11	3	192
Bliss Pass via Pebble Creek Trail from Warm Creek Picnic Area	Northeast Entrance	15	4	198–9
Bighorn Peak	West Entrance	12	5	153
Cache Lake via Sportsman Lake Trail from Glen Creek Trailhead	Mammoth	11	3	157
Cascade Lake Trail to Ice Lake	Canyon	10.5*	2	180
Colonnade and Iris Falls via Bechler River Trail	Bechler Ranger Station	18	3	87
Crescent Lake— High Lake loop from Specimen Creek	West Entrance	22*	4	157
Dunanda Falls via Boundary Creek Trail	Bechler Ranger Station	18	2	92

*These distances are one-way since they involve a loop or traveling from one trailhead to another. **NOTE:** To convert miles to kilometers, multiply the number of miles by 1.62.

MEDIUM-DISTANCE HIKES *(continued)*

Hike	Nearest Location	Miles Round-trip	Difficulty (Easy to Hard: 1–5)	Page No.
Electric Peak via Sportsman Lake Trail from Glen Creek Trailhead	Mammoth	18	5	158
Fairy Creek Trail	Old Faithful	13*	3	110
Fawn Pass	Mammoth	24	4	160
Gneiss Creek Trail	West Entrance	14*	2	167
Heart Lake and Geyser Basin	Grant	16	3	135
Heart Lake Trail to South Entrance	Grant	23.5*	3	135
Hellroaring Trailhead to Blacktail Trailhead via Yellowstone River Trail	Tower	14*	3	188, 192
Mallard Lake Loop via Mallard Lake and Mallard Creek Trails	Old Faithful	11.5*	2	111
Mary Lake via Mary Mountain Trail	Canyon	22	2	145
Mt. Holmes	Norris	21.6	5	165
Mt. Sheridan via Heart Lake Trail	Grant	22	5	135, 142

*These distances are one-way since they involve a loop or traveling from one trailhead to another. **NOTE:** To convert miles to kilometers, multiply the number of miles by 1.62.

MEDIUM-DISTANCE HIKES (*continued*)

Hike	Nearest Location	Miles Round-trip	Difficulty (Easy to Hard: 1–5)	Page No.
Mt. Washburn via Dunraven Pass to Glacial Boulder Trail	Canyon	12	4	233
Observation Peak via Cascade Lake Trail	Canyon	11	4	180
Park Point via Thorofare Trail	Fishing Bridge	14	2	124
Pebble Creek Trail	Northeast Entrance	13*	3	198
Pelican Cone via Pelican Creek Trail	Fishing Bridge	11	4	212
Pelican Valley Loop via Pelican Creek Trail	Fishing Bridge	16*	2	212
Seven-Mile Hole	Canyon	11	4	231 .
Shoshone Lake via DeLacy Creek to Lewis Lake Trail	Grant	12.5*	2	103
Shoshone Lake Loop via Lewis Channel Trail to Dogshead Trail	Grant	11*	2	104
Skyrim Trail Loop via Daly Creek– Skyrim Trail	West Entrance	21*	5	164

*These distances are one-way since they involve a loop or traveling from one trailhead to another. **NOTE:** To convert miles to kilometers, multiply the number of miles by 1.62.

MEDIUM-DISTANCE HIKES *(continued)*

Hike	Nearest Location	Miles Round-trip	Difficulty (Easy to Hard: 1–5)	Page No.
South Pitchstone Plateau Trail	Grant	18.5*	3	94
Sportsman Lake	West Entrance	22	4	157
Summit Lake	Old Faithful	15	4	109
Sepulcher Mountain	Mammoth	10	4	170
Shoshone Lake and Geyser Basin via Shoshone Lake Trail from Lone Star Geyser	Old Faithful	18	3	101
Snake Hot Springs via South Boundary Trail	South Entrance	10	2	130
Specimen Ridge Trail	Tower–Roosevelt	17.5*	4	217
The Thunderer Saddle	Northeast Entrance	10	4	211
Trilobite Lakes via Mt. Holmes Trail	Norris	17	3	166
Union Falls from Grassy Lake	South Entrance	15	3	100
Union Falls from Cave Falls	Bechler Ranger Station	23	2	98
Upper Slough Creek Meadows via Slough Creek Trail	Tower–Roosevelt	22	2	197
Yellowstone River Trail	Tower–Roosevelt	19*	2	188

*These distances are one-way since they involve a loop or traveling from one trailhead to another. **NOTE:** To convert miles to kilometers, multiply the number of miles by 1.62.

RECOMMENDED EXTENDED BACKCOUNTRY TRIPS (DISTANCES OF OVER 20 MILES)

These trips combine different trails. Please refer to topo maps as well as trail descriptions when making trip plans.

Bechler Region

Shoshone Lake Trail: *Kepler Cascades to Lone Star Geyser–Grants Pass–Shoshone Geyser Basin–Moose Creek–Lewis River Channel Trail and out at Dogshead trailhead. Distance: 25 miles. Pages: 101; 104.*

Bechler River Trail: *Kepler Cascades to Lone Star Geyser–Three River Junction–Bechler Canyon–Bechler Meadows and out at Bechler Ranger Station. Distance: 30 miles. Pages: 115; 87.*

Shoshone Lake Canoe Trip. *Page: 238.*

Thorofare Region

Heart Lake–Thorofare Loop: *Heart Lake trailhead to Heart Lake (p. 135)–South and Southeast arms of Yellowstone Lake–Yellowstone River Trail (p. 138) down to Thorofare Ranger Station (p. 124), then east on Lynx Creek–Mariposa Lake–South Boundary Trail over Big Game Ridge–Harebell Creek–Snake River Hot Springs and out at South Entrance (p. 130). Distance: 80 miles.*

Yellowstone Lake Canoe Trip. *Page: 241.*

Gallatin Region

Northwest Corner: *Daly Creek to Skyrim Trail (p. 164)–Bighorn Peak–Shelf Lake–High Lake (p. 153) and out at Specimen Creek (p. 157). Distance: 20 miles.*

Sportsman Lake Trail–Fawn Pass Trail Loop: *Begin at trailhead on Glen Creek to Fawn Pass (p. 160), take the Fan Creek Trail north (p. 162) to connect with the Sportsman Lake Trail (p. 157), to Sportsman Lake, over Electric Divide and out from where you began, Glen Creek. Distance: 42 miles.*

Fawn Pass–Bighorn Pass Loop: *Glen Creek trailhead near Mammoth to Fawn Pass (p. 160) to cutoff trail over to Bighorn Pass Trail (p. 162)–Bighorn Pass and out at Indian Creek Campground. Distance: 31 miles.*

EXTENDED TRIPS *(continued)*

Washburn Region

Cascade Lake Picnic Area to Beaver Lake: *Cascade Lake–Grebe Lake–Wolf Lake–Ice Lake–Solfatara Creek to Beaver Lake. Distance: 18 miles. Page: 175.*

North of Yellowstone River Region

Yellowstone River Trail: *Roosevelt to Hellroaring Creek–Crevice Lake–Knowles Falls and out at Gardiner. Distance: 24 miles. Page: 188.*

Buffalo Plateau Trail: *Hellroaring Creek trailhead across the Yellowstone River bridge, up the Buffalo Plateau to the north park boundary, then to Poacher's Trail to Buffalo Fork Meadows, then south down to Slough Creek and out at the campground. Distance: 22 miles. Page: 194.*

Bliss Pass Loop: *Warm Creek Picnic Area near Northeast Entrance to Pebble Creek (p. 198)–Bliss Pass (p. 199)–Slough Creek (p. 197) and out at Slough Creek Campground. Distance: 20 miles.*

Mirror Plateau Region

Lamar River Trail to Pelican Valley: *Lamar River Trail down to Cold Creek Junction (p. 206), over Mist Creek Pass to Pelican Valley (p. 209) and out trailhead near Fishing Bridge. Distance: 34 miles (side trips from Cold Creek Junction to Frost Lake and Upper Lamar River add 12 miles each).*

Pelican Valley Loop: *Pelican Valley up Pelican Creek to Wapiti Lake (p. 212) then south to Fern Lake–Astringent Creek (p. 215) and back out in Pelican Valley. Distance: 35 miles.*

Hoodoo Basin and Parker Peak: *Lamar River Trail (p. 206) to Miller Creek Trail (p. 210) up to Parker Peak and Hoodoo Basin, across the park boundary and out at Sunlight Creek in Sunlight Basin (p. 222). Distance: 43 miles.*

Safety

The wilderness naturally presents some hazards, but traveling through the backcountry is not a perilous venture—if you use your head. To a large extent, safety is common sense and logic.

Before You Go

Stop at the park ranger station before you take off into the wilderness. The rangers will issue you a backcountry use permit (no charge). Permits have become necessary as more and more people are attracted to the wilderness. Such a system might seem overly restrictive at first, but it is necessary to prevent overuse and overcrowding in the backcountry. Without it, much wilderness would be destroyed. It's for your own benefit.

It's also for your safety. When you obtain permits for a series of campsites you are, in effect, filing an itinerary. Park personnel are then aware of your whereabouts should an emergency develop. Be sure to leave your itinerary with a trusted friend and follow it as closely as possible.

Before leaving, discuss your trip plans with one of the rangers. The ranger will fill you in on current conditions, warn you away from areas that are, at that moment, dangerous or otherwise unappealing, and supply you with a variety of helpful tips. Aside from your traveling companions, the park rangers are the best friends you have in the wilderness.

The ranger will also provide you with a pamphlet containing backcountry rules and regulations. They are the outgrowth of decades of park management, and all of them are designed to protect both you and the park. Don't flout them—violators will be fined by a United States Magistrate.

There may be a few other items of special business between you and the rangers. If canoeing or boating is on your agenda, you'll need a boat permit. Fishermen must also obtain a permit and a copy of the backcountry fishing regulations. The use of firearms is prohibited on all park lands.

The Park Service has designated a set number of backcountry campsites, and permits are issued only for those locations. With few exceptions, they are issued on a first-come, first-served basis. If the sites in an area fill for a particular night, no more permits are given out.

Backcountry campsite locations change so it is not possible to include them in this book. Write Backcountry Information, P.O. Box 168, Yellowstone National Park, WY 82190, and request a publication listing current campsite locations.

Brief junkets are a good alternative if there are no permits left for the area you want to explore on the day you would like to leave. Even though your primary goal may be a deep penetration of the interior, short hikes act as a sort of decompression chamber from the "civilization" you've left behind. If, like most people, you are an urban dweller, you probably screen out much of the world around you. Some short hiking can help you slow down, open your lungs, tune up your deadened sensitivity, and make you aware of the sights and scents and textures of the natural universe. A day trip or two helps you to get the "feel" of the land, work up to the big plunge.

Don't wait until you're halfway up a mountain to open your map. Familiarize yourself with it and the trail descriptions in this book before you leave.

You will find that distances shown on the map are no indication of how long it will take to get from point A to point B. You will also find that climbing steep trails above 7,000 feet with a heavy pack is a slower process than you had imagined. Don't exhaust yourself by trying to travel too far or too fast.

Backpacking is a *leisure* activity. A slow, steady, measured pace is preferable to short bursts of speed followed by long rests. Rest when you feel the need, but try not to dally more than 10 minutes each time. Lunchtime should be your long break.

After You Get Lost

Trails in Yellowstone are, for the most part, well-marked (unlike trails in some nearby national forests). Look for bright orange squares of metal nailed to trees at regular intervals. These markers are always helpful, but on snow-covered trails and meadows where the trail is barely visible, they are indispensable. In many backcountry meadows, tall poles mark the route.

A reasonably good system of trail signs indicates routes and distances. They can be helpful, but it is never wise to depend solely on them for directions. That's why you have a topo map and a compass.

Do *not* leave designated trails unless you're a *very experienced hiker.* Cross-country travel can be rewarding, but only if you know what you're doing. Even if you do, you *must* be given permission to travel off established trails, and the use permit you carry must indicate those plans.

Almost any trail can become difficult to follow at times. If it does, stop to consider the rate of climb or descent that it has been following. Most trails are pretty consistent. Yours will almost certainly continue at the same up or down rate that it has been maintaining. To relocate it, move along the same contour you were following without making any major changes in your elevation.

Vegetation may hide the trail. Push the underbrush aside and check for human and animal tracks on the ground. If you can't find it nearby, look for a post on the horizon. Other signs to watch for include wooden poles, branches and willow limbs sawed or cut from trees, and excavated stream crossings.

When you reach an unmarked trail junction, take the fork that most closely follows the grade and general direction of the trail you've been following. If you're still doubtful, hunt for footprints. You want the fork that shows the most signs of human traffic, not animals. Most unmarked junctions occur at points where hiking paths are intersected by outfitter and game trails. The latter can be identified by the fact that they follow much steeper grades, and the route tends to be a straight line rather than one that moves along contours. Because such trails may be heavily traveled by horses and other animals, they can give you the idea that they are the most used and, therefore, the most desirable to follow. Don't be misled. Search for signs of other hikers and follow them.

Any one of the above strategies should have you back on the proper trail within a quarter-mile or so.

If you do get to a point where you find yourself saying, "I am lost, hopelessly lost," the first thing to do is nothing. Sit down. Reconnoiter. Reconstruct your previous movements on the topo map and find your general location. The solution to your problem will probably become obvious. In any case, don't rush around frantically—you will get more lost, if that's possible. Plan first, then act.

Look for water. Small streams eventually flow into larger ones that parallel trails or roads. All major drainages eventually lead back to civilization.

Remember, also, that trails were laid out with a reasonable amount of logic. Though there are many acres in the park, there are many trails criss-crossing them.

Watching Your Step

There are certain areas and certain times that require extra caution. Be wary of loose rock. Remain alert for falling dead snags, especially when traveling through burned areas. Do not stop in the path of such snags. Never travel at night or in a blinding storm.

The thermal areas in Yellowstone can be hazardous. The Park Service has erected boardwalks and placed warning signs around boiling hot springs in heavily visited areas. There is no such protection in the backcountry. The ground around these areas is often only a thin crust. It can easily crack open under your weight. More than one unwary wild animal has been parboiled this way.

Stream Crossings

Although numerous footbridges have been added to the park's trail system over the years, there are still many fords to cross. Following are some suggestions on how to deal with Yellowstone's streams.

First of all, plan your trip carefully to avoid stream crossings during early summer when the snow melt is at its peak. Then be sure to pack along an old pair of tennis shoes to wear; unless you spend months at a time running through the woods barefoot, you do *not* want to subject your tender feet to a cold, slippery, rocky streambed. Never cross a stream in your boots for this will invite blisters. Wear shorts or roll up your pants. Keep your clothes dry even if you have to ford the stream in your undies. Use a stout branch as your "third leg" to increase balance and stability during a fording. Keep your backpack's waist belt unfastened in the event that you slip during the crossing. Sometimes a logjam can be found near a ford and can serve as a bridge, but use your good judgement; a slippery log may prove to be more dangerous than the stream crossing. Face sideways to reduce the force of the current pushing against you. If the stream is swift and deeper than your thighs, use a safety rope to avoid being swept away. If there are at least two members in your party, tie a rope to a tree before crossing the stream. Hold onto the rope while crossing. When you reach the other side tie the rope onto *another* tree. The last person to cross will need to untie the rope before crossing so the rope can be retrieved. Better yet, if the stream is high leave this trail for a later date when the stream has subsided.

Drinking and Treating the Water

Because of Yellowstone's very low humidity, your body will tend to lose moisture quickly. If you do not drink enough water, dehydration will lower your energy level and thus your enjoyment of the trip. A full, active day requires consumption of at least three quarts of water. Keep your water bottle handy and sip on it frequently as you travel along.

In recent years a severe intestinal disorder called giardiasis has become rather widespread throughout the Rocky Mountains. The symptoms generally appear one to three weeks after exposure and include such unpleasantries as diarrhea, cramps, and nausea. In order to eliminate the risk of contracting giardia or other troublesome waterborne organisms, bring your water to a boil for one minute or use a good-quality filter system. Select a filter system with a pore size of 0.2 microns. Keep your filter clean and replace it according to the manufacturer's recommendations.

Many long-time backcountry travelers in Yellowstone have fared well without treating the water, but given the severity of the symptoms, why take the risk? Try boiling your water after supper and setting it out to cool so it will be more palatable for drinking the next day.

Weather Hazards

In Yellowstone, weather patterns tend to be extremely variable, so don't place too much faith in glowing forecasts. Summer comes late and leaves early, and any summer day may begin as calm, bright, and sunny, only to deteriorate into a cold, rainy (or even snowy) mess. For this reason you must be prepared for the worst weather conditions, even on a day hike, and no matter how nice the day appears to be at the outset.

Exposure to cold weather conditions can result in rapid loss of body heat, referred to as hypothermia, which can be life-threatening. To avoid hypothermia, keep warm and dry (see the Backpacker's Checklist on page 142). Victims of hypothermia display such symptoms as stumbling, slurred speech, and shivering. *If you suspect that you or your companion is becoming hypothermic, take immediate action!* Get out of the rain and wind by taking shelter under trees or behind a rise in the terrain. Get out of your wet garb and don some dry clothes (the importance of proper preparation: a backup of warm and dry clothes!). Put on your stocking cap. Build a fire. Quickly heat up a cup of soup and drink it. Climb into your sleeping bag. Hypothermia is a killer of the unprepared and an insidious kind of danger. Even if you are fully prepared, you must remain alert to its possible approach. For more information on hypothermia be sure to read the informative pamphlets available at any visitor center or ranger station.

Of course not all days are cold and wet; many are bright and sunny. But in the highcountry of Yellowstone, the sun can quickly damage your skin. Wear a hat that protects your ears and neck as well as your face. Bandanas are helpful, as is a lightweight, long-sleeved shirt to protect your arms. Don't forget to wear sunscreen. If the weather is hot and dry be sure to drink at least three quarts of water per day (see Drinking and Treating the Water).

Lightning storms have killed and injured backcountry travelers in Yellowstone. If you see an electrical storm approaching, quickly get off summits and exposed ridges. If you are canoeing on a stream or lake, paddle to shore immediately. Avoid standing in water, under isolated trees, or in open meadows. Crouch low with only your boots touching the ground if you are caught out in the open. Remove metal objects, such as your pack and climbing hardware.

Blisters and Burns

Blisters are the most common complaint requiring first aid on a hike. The possibility of developing them can be minimized if you do a thorough job of breaking in your shoes before you begin. At the *first* sign of rubbing or tenderness, place some molefoam over the sore areas. If you wait too long, a blister will form. If one does develop, don't apply the molefoam directly over it. Cut a hole in the molefoam to fit the size and shape of the blister and place it around the area. At the end of the day, check the amount of fluid in the blister. If there's a lot, sterilize a needle with a match, prick the blister, and drain it. Cover it with a piece of adhesive tape, then moleskin or molefoam.

Ticks can be a problem on early summer hikes. Take the time to thoroughly check for them on your body each night in camp. If you find one imbedded in your skin, a little alcohol applied to the spot should send him packing. When there is no alcohol handy, a steady hand holding a burning match near the spot serves the same purpose.

Sunburn can be a problem at high altitudes. Apply sunscreen frequently. A wide-brimmed hat will protect your nose and ears.

Your first-aid kit should include:

- Molefoam or moleskin.
- Needle.
- Band-aids (large, medium, small).
- Alcohol (optional).

Obviously that won't take care of serious injuries, but for the commonplace, you have everything else you need in your pack. Clean handkerchiefs or bandanas can serve as bandages. Soap cleans minor wounds.

Maps

Among all the paraphernalia you're taking, no item is more important than a map. The foldout topographic map (approx. ¹¹⁄₁₆ inch = 1 mile) included with this book should be sufficient for hiking the park's maintained trails, which are indicated by heavy dashed lines. Other trails visible on the map represent old trails that may still be marked but in most cases are no longer maintained. If you are hiking around the park's boundary or if you plan any off-trail travel, you may want to obtain some additional topo maps. During the 1950s the United States Geological Survey (USGS) published a series of 15-minute maps (minutes of latitude and longitude) for the Yellowstone region. Each map covers a quadrangle of about 13 by 17 miles, on a scale of 1 inch to 1 mile, with contour intervals of 40 to 80 feet. Although these maps may still be available in stores in and around the park, the USGS is replacing them with the more detailed series of 7½-minute maps. The maps should be available to the public in the early 1990s. The 7½-minute maps contain great detail; in fact, it takes four 7½-minute maps to comprise a single 15-minute map. You would need to purchase over 100 of these maps to view the entire park. When using a single 7½-minute map (or a copied excerpt from a 15-minute map) it is not possible to identify from your map distant peaks, ridges, and mountain ranges because the features are prominent only on the horizon, not on this scale of map.

If you obtain the old 15-minute maps, keep in mind that some trails and roads have changed, as have forest cover patterns (trees have replaced some meadows and forest fires have created new openings in old forests). USGS topographic maps are available at the Old Faithful Visitor Center in the park and at outdoor gear stores in the communities surrounding the park. To order by mail contact the Map Distribution Center, USGS, Denver, CO 80225. Allow several weeks for your order to be processed.

Camping and Hiking in Bear Country

Hiking and, especially, camping in grizzly country tend to add a distinct amount of excitement, wildness, and perhaps even fear to your backcountry experience. Just the thought of sharing the Yellowstone wilderness with grizzlies can be exhilarating. However, encountering a grizzly at close range is anything but fun. It happened to me once, as I will describe shortly, and I do not recommend it to anyone.

To avoid an encounter with a bear, minimize the risks. First of all, never camp in an area where you have observed a bear or his fresh signature: droppings (similar in appearance to the human variety, only larger), diggings, or tracks (a large paw print with long, pointed clawmarks). Move to another campsite, even if you do not have it reserved on your permit. Report the activity to a ranger as soon as possible.

In setting up your campsite, keep in mind that the grizzly has an extraordinary sense of smell, so the thing most likely to bring you trouble is food. Where fires are permitted, burn leftover scraps from all meals. Burn empty food containers to remove lingering odors. After you have a clean camp, place all other food supplies in your pack and tote it well away from your sleeping area—100 yards if possible.

The National Park Service (NPS) provides bear poles at many campsites. Hoist your foodpack up at least 12 feet high and

Bear Identification

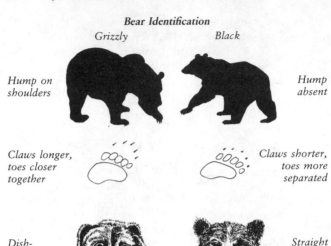

Grizzly   Black

Hump on
shoulders

Hump
absent

Claws longer,
toes closer
together

Claws shorter,
toes more
separated

Dish-
faced

Straight
facial
features

5 feet from the sides. If there is no pole present, locate a tree, preferably a dead one with no foliage, and pull your foodpack over a stout branch. Select your tree and toss your rope long before dark.

In setting up your tent, take care to select a site away from any trails (established or game) or ridgetops, as bears tend to travel on both. All of your meal preparations should be done at your fire ring. Freeze-dried meals are handy in grizzly country because there is little mess to clean up. However, if you prefer to fry up a tasty—and odorous—meal, clean and wash up thoroughly. It is even a good idea to change out of your "cooking clothes" before retiring.

Never leave any food unattended around your camp. If you

decide to take a stroll away from camp during the day, hang your food up before you leave. Also keep in mind that there is some evidence, though not conclusive, that menstruation, sexual intercourse, and perfumes, deodorants, and other cosmetic odors may attract bears.

When hiking the trails, certain precautions are in order as well. If possible, hike in a group of at least four people. Serious bear encounters are quite rare with larger groups. *Never* hike at night. Bears are more active after dark, and the chances of surprising one are greater then. One of the worst things you can do is surprise a grizzly, especially a sow with cubs.

A bear will normally smell you coming down the trail and move away. However, if you are hiking into the teeth of a strong breeze, the bear may not smell you coming, even if you've been out for several bathless days! In such a case make noise. A bear's sense of hearing is thought to be roughly equivalent to that of a human. If the trail heads over a hill or into a patch of timber take a bearbell (available at stores in the park) out of your pocket and ring it well ahead of the blind spot. This method is preferable to suffering the mental anguish of listening to the constant clanging of a bell.

My one serious bear encounter involved my failure to adequately announce my presence on the trail. Rod Busby and I were hiking in the Gallatins in an area where the trail winds in and out of meadows and small islands of trees. The wind was in our faces and though we were talking a lot the sounds of our voices were probably muffled by the groaning of the trees swaying back and forth. As the trail entered a patch of timber and made a 90-degree turn, we surprised a grizzly cub, which let out a frightened wail. Just as we had shed our backpacks the big sow charged around the bend in the trail heading straight for us. Luckily, we were close to some good climbing trees, and we were perched on top with the squirrels in short order. While

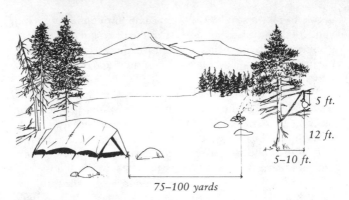

5 ft.

12 ft.

5–10 ft.

75–100 yards

Situating Your Camp in Grizzly Country
Pitch your tent at least 75 to 100 yards (upwind if possible) from your cooking area and your food and garbage storage. Try to place your tent door near climbable trees. Suspend food and garbage in sealed plastic bags at least 12 feet above the ground, 5 to 10 feet from the tree trunk and 5 feet below the limb (or rope or pole) on which they hang. A clean campsite without tempting or strange odors will best ensure a night's sleep untroubled by bear visits.

this story has been fun to tell around the campfire, it was a harrowing, life-threatening encounter at the time—an encounter which in all probability could have been avoided had we been making adequate noise! The grizzly only displayed its normal motherly instincts.

Suppose you've taken all the precautions and one day you round a bend in the trail and find yourself looking at a grizzly. Hopefully, the bear will be at some distance from you. If the bear is not aware of you, quickly leave the area by either backing away or making a very wide detour. If the grizzly bear is a sow with cubs, the situation is potentially more dangerous. If a wide detour is not possible, turn back and leave this trail to the bear for the day. If the bear detects your presence it will probably leave the area or stand up in an attempt to recognize what you are. Bears have poor eyesight. In this case slowly leave the area. Look for climbable trees as you go in case the bear charges.

If, on the other hand, you surprise a bear at close range, as I did, your reaction will basically depend on what the bear does. Let the bear make the first move, not you. The last thing you want to do is turn and run, because it may trigger the bear's natural predatory instinct to pursue, and you cannot outrun him. He can clip along at 40 mph! Try to remain calm and do not look the bear squarely in the eyes. Hopefully, the bear will leave.

If the bear charges you, your next move depends on how close you are to some climbable trees. Drop an object such as a jacket to distract the bear (do not drop food as this would reinforce the bear's charge), then if there is a tree nearby, climb up at least 15 feet. If the bear is able to climb up after you, protect yourself by staying above the bear. If there are no climbable trees nearby, you are down to your last resort: playing dead. Lie down on the ground and curl up with your knees tucked against your chest, hands behind your head and neck, and pray. The grizzly may do nothing more than sniff you, satisfy its curiosity, and depart in peace. It is important that you remain still and silent until you are certain the bear has left the area, because you are trying to convince the bear that you are no threat to it or its cubs. Clearly, this sort of strategy will require more guts than you ever thought you had, but people have survived encounters with grizzlies in this manner.

Perhaps the most frightening scenario involves a bear that comes into your camp at night. Be ready to climb some trees if the bear does not leave. If and when the bear leaves, *do not* retire for the evening. If, heaven forbid, a bear invades your camp while you are asleep and tries to come after you in your tent, *do not play dead*. This situation may be a predator-prey event. Fight back with whatever you have. One of my hiking companions carries a cannister of Capsaicin Bear Repellent into his tent in case of such an attack. It is an irritant derived from cayenne peppers and has provided some promising results in laboratory tests on captive grizzlies. However, its use should be limited to a last resort, such as the above-mentioned situation. Clearly, your chances of survival in such an incident would be greatly improved if your group size is four or more.

Now that you are on the verge of cancelling your trip into the Yellowstone backcountry, let's try to put things into perspective. Realistically, just how much danger do grizzlies pose to a backpacker? If you meet one, a lot of danger. But the chances are extremely low. There are perhaps only about 250 grizzlies in the entire Greater Yellowstone Ecosystem. A noisy hiker who keeps a clean, odor-free camp is not likely to have bear problems in the backcountry. In fact, statistically, you are much safer traveling the trails than you are the roads in the park. However, there is a risk, slight as it may be. All the cautionary measures mentioned here come endorsed and tested, but there are no guarantees.

One of the things that makes a grizzly dangerous is its unpredictability. To quote Stephen Herrero from his excellent book *Bear Attacks,* "If grizzly bears readily attacked people then there would be far more injuries and I, for one, wouldn't care to try to coexist with them. The challenge of continued coexistence, however, does require that we accept some small chance of injury, and even death."

Actually, most injuries resulting from animals involve the bison, which can weigh up to 2,000 pounds and sprint 30 mph (thrice as fast as you can run). All animals are dangerous if approached too closely, especially bull elk, moose, and bison during the mating season or when young offspring are present. Mountain lions and coyotes inhabit the park, but they tend to stay away (unless they have become accustomed to human handouts, in which case you want to keep a wide distance).

Backcountry Etiquette

Regulations

One thing you must bring with you is your manners. There was a time when wilderness explorers could be casual about matters like garbage and campfires. That time has passed. More and more people crowd into the backcountry. A few thoughtless ones can spoil it for everyone. The wilderness is fragile.

When you look for a campsite, find a *naturally* level spot for your sleeping bag and tent. There's no need to shovel or flatten earth. Don't dig a trench around your tent. The scars you leave would take years to heal. Beavers are the only engineers allowed to practice here.

No one relishes somebody else's bathwater. Remember that when you wash yourself, your kitchen utensils, or anything else. Don't use soap directly in any of the lakes, pools, streams, or other natural running waters. Don't rinse anything in them. Fill a cookpot with water and carry it away from the stream to do all your bathing and camp cleanup. Make sure you tote it some distance away from the stream so when you empty the dirty water it doesn't drain back. Be not a polluter of wild waters.

In Yellowstone, it is strictly forbidden to swim or bathe in any of the natural hot springs or pools — no matter the temperature of the water.

If you're camping in an area where fires are allowed, use the designated fire ring. Remember, the only fuel you're permitted is wood that has already fallen. Use it with discretion. The next party will want a fire too. Put out the fire before you retire. When you leave camp, be absolutely certain your fire is dead out. If the ashes are still warm, wet them down.

A toilet is the only thing you are allowed to dig in the wilderness and, if you do it right, nobody should know but you. Nature's own disposal system is at your service. Biological action within the top 6 to 8 inches of soil decomposes organic materials.

Carry out all garbage: cans, bottles, plastics, aluminum foil, etc. Burying won't do. Eventually your trash will be unearthed by sharp-nosed animals or frost action, and the campsite will turn into a garbage dump. Flatten all cans and drop them into one of the plastic sacks you brought along. The containers you packed in full will weigh a lot less as you pack them out empty.

Don't shortcut switchbacks. It only accelerates erosion and scars the land forever. If you are a smoker, don't discard any cigarettes or matches. Smokey the Bear is watching you. Don't roll or throw rocks down mountains or into canyons. Somebody might be down there. Don't toss objects into springs, pools, or vents. Don't pick the wildflowers. Don't collect souvenirs. All the above are subject to fines.

Pack animals have the right-of-way on trails. (If you are planning a backcountry trip by horseback, write in advance to the Chief Ranger's Office in the park. Ask for a copy of current regulations and a list of campsites approved for horse parties.)

You are not allowed to operate motorized vehicles on the trails or in any area of the park that isn't a proper roadway or parking area. Nor can you ride a bicycle on the hiking trails. (See the section on bicycling on page 256.)

No dogs, cats, or pet monkeys are allowed on any trail in the park, not even if you have them on a leash. Bears and other native beasts do not like domestic pets. And it's *their* park.

Nesting Waterfowl

Studies have shown that several species of waterfowl, notably the trumpeter swan, are *very* easily disturbed by approaching hikers and may temporarily leave their nests, thus greatly reducing the chance for a successful hatch. Please use extreme caution and give a wide berth (more than 75 yards) when in the area of nesting waterfowl.

Bear Management Areas

Several portions of Yellowstone's backcountry are designated as Bear Management Areas. The National Park Service describes the purpose of these areas this way: "To reduce human related impacts on bears in high density grizzly bear habitat. Eliminating human entry and disturbance in specific areas prevents human/bear conflicts and provides areas where bears can pursue natural behavioral patterns and other social activities free from human disturbance. Types of restrictions include area closures, trail closures, a minimum party size of four or more people, and travel limited to daylight hours or to established trails."

The grizzly is a true symbol of wildness, but it is indeed a threatened species south of Canada. If you are denied access to a favored backcountry spot, it may seem painful at first, but most backcountry travelers willingly concede the majestic grizzly some room to roam and feed in peace without human interference. Research in Yellowstone documents just how easily grizzlies can be disturbed by passing hikers. Grizzlies have been known to leave trout-spawning streams, winter-killed carcasses, and prime open meadows because of human activity near them.

Since Bear Management Areas and restrictions occasionally change, I do not attempt to list them here. A document containing current closures and other restrictions can be obtained from most visitor centers and ranger stations or by writing the National Park Service, P.O. Box 168, Yellowstone National Park, WY 82190.

Clothing and Equipment

Your Wilderness Wardrobe

Underfoot: For day hikes over relatively smooth, well-traveled trails, a light trail shoe is sufficient. But where you will encounter rocky terrain, snow, and ice, a heavier boot is advisable. Whatever the weight, certain specifications are in order:

- Sturdy, rock-resistant leather throughout.
- Rubber lug soles.
- Reinforced heel and toe.
- Protective padding of soft leather around the ankle for support, warmth, and comfort. (Be sure there's enough room for heavy socks inside.)
- A long, padded tongue.
- Waterproofing. (Remember to re-waterproof between backpacking expeditions.)

Once you have the boots, break them in gradually. Wear them around the house; take walks outdoors. Always wear the socks you're taking on the trip. The boots are broken in when you can walk all day with a full pack over all kinds of terrain without sore feet. Clearly, this isn't something you wait to do until two days before the trip.

If your projected route includes streams without bridges, it's advisable to have along a pair of sneakers. A change before fording saves your boots and keeps your feet dry. Before you bed down for the night, remember to turn your boots upside-down to keep the moisture out.

Inside the boots, traditionalists prefer good old heavy woolen socks—warm and cushiony. You may want a light inner sock if the wool is scratchy. New terry-stitched socks made of synthetic fiber and cotton can equal wool in warmth and cushioning. The air pockets in the looser weave also insulate better, keep feet dryer, and eliminate the need for inner socks. Terry-stitched thermal socks are available in wool.

Inside: You may find yourself a bit less fastidious in the wilderness, but if you insist on changing underwear every day, accept the fact that you'll have to do more laundry along the trail. Consider taking a set of long johns (cotton or wool) in colder weather.

Outside: Wear warm, long pants made of wool or cotton twill. Be sure the legs fit loosely. Tight legs get hot and bind up— awful if they get wet. Walking shorts—also loose-fitting—are a nice option when the weather heats up.

You'll probably want to spend most of the day in a cotton or light wool shirt. For cooler temperatures you'll need something more. Wool sweaters are not such a hot idea. They are too bulky and don't offer enough options to adjust for changing temperatures. A heavy wool shirt or a light down jacket is better. A good wool sheds water and stays warm even when wet, but it adds weight and bulk. A zippered nylon/down jacket insulates well and lets moisture escape; and it's light and compressible. However, if it should get soaked, it takes a long time to dry out. For early and late in the season, a heavier down jacket is recommended.

Take wool mittens and a cap if you're going early or late in the season. A hat will protect you from rain, cold, and sun.

A poncho is the world's greatest portable shelter and one of the most essential items on your list. If you're caught in heavy rains or wicked winds, you can poke your head through the center, drape the big waterproof rectangle over you, and either wait till the weather blows over or flap along the trail like a big bat. Your poncho does multiple duty: a rainfly for your tent, an emergency tent along the trail, a ground cloth, a cover for your sleeping bag on extra-misty nights. Spend the money for a poncho made of tough, lightweight nylon coated with plastic resin. The inexpensive sheet-plastic variety won't hold up through many trips. Get one big enough to cover your pack frame as well as yourself (100 by 70 inches). A good rainsuit also works well.

Backpacks

On day hikes, you can use a summit pack or rucksack. For a longer trip, you should have a pack mounted on a metal frame. Make sure the frame is the right length to fit comfortably on your torso. It should curve along your spine. Get one with a padded waist belt and test it with a loaded pack. A proper frame will hold the load high so the weight is directed down through your hips to your legs. Padded shoulder straps are more comfortable than unpadded.

The best packs are made of waterproof, nylon duck. The easiest to organize have strips of fabric inside that divide the pack into vertical or horizontal compartments. Look for plenty of zippered pockets on the outside to stow maps and other small items you want to get at quickly.

Sleeping Bags

In this part of the world, any summer night can be cold. The lightweight summer sleeping bag that kept you cozy in the Catskills will not serve you so well out west. The minimum you should figure on for Yellowstone and Grand Teton is a bag that will keep you warm in 30°F. That should suffice for the latter part of June through most of August. From mid-May to mid-June and the last week of August to mid-September you will need a bag for 20°F. Earlier or later, a 10°F bag is necessary.

These are general standards. What you choose naturally depends on your own ability to adjust to cold. For the sake of long-range flexibility, it may make sense to get the 10°F bag (for which you will pay more). Unzipped, it can be comfortable up to 60°F. When it's warmer than that, you can open the bag over you like a blanket instead of crawling inside.

The critical element in your comfort is the guts of the bag: the filler. The type that offers the best combination of insulation, light weight, and compactness is goose down, an excellent insulator. Its fluffiness traps warm air more efficiently than any other filler.

Synthetic fillers combine a reasonable alternative with a much lower price. Such fillers tend to continue to insulate even when wet and are quicker to dry out than down, which becomes useless when wet. So if your backcountry trips consist mainly of canoe trips, this is the best choice. On the other hand, synthetic-filled bags are heavier and bulkier than down.

The factor that contributes most to warmth is the *loft* of the down, meaning the thickness of the sleeping bag after you fluff it out and lay it on a flat surface. That thickness creates insulating power. A six-inch loft is proper for a bag that has a 10°F rating. The finest quality goose down is the most expensive because it holds its loft longer than the cheaper grades. Warm toes are worth almost any price. Figure on spending a lot for a good quality goose-down bag.

The other major considerations in your choice of a bag are lightness (four pounds maximum) and outer material (get tightly woven, water-repellent, rip-stop nylon). Also look for a heavy-duty zipper.

The exact type of construction is not vital as long as the down is spread evenly through the bag by a series of baffles, or tubes, sewn around the circumference of the bag (not lengthwise). Without the baffles, the filler will shift and settle in one spot.

Style is a matter of personal preference. The mummy bag with its hood is the snuggest. If that's too confining for you, get a semi-rectangular bag that spreads out more.

Having invested in a good sleeping bag, take good care of it. Put something between it and the ground, or it will soak up moisture. Down dries *very* slowly. Freshen it with sun and air every morning before you repack. For added comfort bring an inflatable foam pad to put under your sleeping bag.

Tents

In this region a tent is not a luxury. Heavy rain, snow, sleet, and high winds can occur with little warning. Obviously, you want a tent that burdens you as little as possible, while supplying maximum protection. A two-person tent shouldn't add more than five pounds to your load. Plan on eight pounds as the maximum weight for a three-person shelter.

The tent's rainfly should fit tautly over the frame and not touch the tent itself. Otherwise, moisture will condense on the inside of the tent. Your tent should be equipped with a completely enclosed mosquito netting.

Cameras

In high mountain country there are sharp lighting contrasts. Forests are full of shadows. Use a light meter, preferably one that measures spot as well as average readings. Snow and ice will fool your meter into giving readings that are wrong for your subject. Open the diaphragm two stops more than the meter indicates in order to compensate for glare. Above timberline there is so much sky that the extra light will confuse your meter.

For more realistic readings, aim the meter more toward the ground than you normally would. If your camera has a through-the-lens meter, that device will do the job, but it lacks the flexibility—and probably the accuracy—of a separate meter. When you depend on an attached meter, you stand a better chance of getting the photo you want if you bracket the shot with several exposures.

You won't need filters for color film, but it's always worth-while to keep a skylight filter over your lens to protect it against scratches. Use a medium yellow filter if you're shooting black and white.

In this sort of country, a wide-angle lens is generally the most useful, particularly in the vicinity of high peaks and deep canyons. New panoramas present themselves every time you look in another direction. For a 35mm camera, a 28mm or even a 21mm lens is advisable. A 35mm lens doesn't expand the scope of your camera much more than its standard 50mm.

Ninety mm or 135mm telephoto lenses rank next in terms of usefulness and are great for capturing details of the scenic wonders around you. A 200mm lens will certainly help, but without a tripod you need a pretty steady hand, or a shoulder brace. A conveniently positioned rock with a fairly level surface will also do, but don't count on one always being where you want it. Any lens with a focal length longer than 200mm definitely requires a tripod, and probably a cable release. They're strictly for serious wildlife photographers though. The opportunities are sensational *if* you're willing to lug the extra weight.

Nature buffs interested in closeups of wildflowers and butterflies might also consider macro lenses, particularly those with a focal length longer than 50mm.

There are even some situations where the normal 50mm lens that came with your camera is the most suitable. For almost every occasion on this backpacking excursion, you will be well prepared if you take along a wide-angle, a normal, and a medium telephoto. If three is too many, take a wide-angle and a telephoto.

There is no such thing as too much film for the camera buff. Allow at least a roll a day. It takes a lot of shooting—even for professionals—to come up with a few really superb pictures.

The abundance of lighting variables raises questions about what kind of color film to take. A medium-speed film should handle most situations you're likely to encounter. It gives you more latitude in dark forests and handles all lighting with more color warmth than high-speed film.

Food

Fires in the backcountry can be dangerous and—without special permit—illegal. If you want to cook you will need a stove. Compact, butane-cartridge stoves are easy to operate, but may stall in cold weather. Gasoline stoves are the better all-around choice.

Your Kitchen:

- 1½- or 2-quart pot. The lid can double as a frying pan or plate.
- Plastic or metal cup.
- Spoon.
- Bowl for mixing or eating (optional).
- Bottle to mix powdered drinks.
- Spatula if fried foods are on the menu.
- Scouring pads for cleanup.
- Waterproof stick matches in a waterproof container.

Breakfast: Remember what your mother told you: Eat a good breakfast. Her advice was never truer than on the trail. For juices, Tang is the best combination of taste and low cost. Orange and tomato juice crystals taste good but cost much more. To warm yourself, freeze-dried or instant coffee or instant cocoa are good. Mixed together, they make a pleasant mocha drink.

On cold mornings instant oatmeal or other hot cereals make a nutritious breakfast. Granola is filling in the stomach but heavy in the pack. Raisins, dates, and various freeze-dried fruits flavor up any cereal, hot or cold.

Lunch: As a foundation for most trail lunches, depend on jerky and gorp, that unfortunately named but highly palatable and nutritious blend of raisins, seeds, dried fruits, nuts, and chocolate.

You can vary your lunches with hard cheese and unsliced salami. (On lengthy trips, salami may get a little ripe.) Try breads and crackers. Canned butter will keep without refrigeration. Or spread your bread with dehydrated cheese or peanut butter. Dehydrated salads are available: tuna, potato, or egg.

Wash it all down with tea or lemonade or other fruit drinks.

Dinner: Soup helps to replace liquid you've lost during the day. It's also nourishing and takes the chill off the evening.

There are many possibilities for the main course with today's wide variety of freeze-dried entrees, as well as vegetables and desserts.

Many people enjoy harvesting fruit that grows along the trail at various times during the summer: blueberries, huckleberries, raspberries, serviceberries, thimbleberries. It means expending extra time and energy but, if you find them, they make delightful desserts and delicious additions to breakfast. Know what you're picking. Not every bright berry is edible.

Snacks: This is one time you *should* nibble between meals. Your nibbles should have food value to supply extra protein, recharge your energy quickly (with easily assimilated sugars), and replenish water you've lost through perspiration.

The ever-popular gorp is your most likely trail snack. Also helpful are nuts, dried fruits, seeds, fruit sticks, hard candy, and drink mixes.

The feeding schedules you normally follow go out the door when you do. In the wilderness eat when you're hungry.

At all times throughout the day, drink plenty of liquid. During the hottest part of the summer, a supply of salt tablets is

THE BACKPACKER'S CHECKLIST

Note: Capitalized items represent ESSENTIAL GEAR that should be carried at all times, even when day hiking.

FOOD/COOKING
___ Stove/Fuel
___ Cook Kit/Drinking Cup
___ Eating/Cooking Utensils
___ FIRE STARTER KIT
___ Seasonings
___ Powdered Milk/Sugar
___ Drink Mixes
___ Cooking Oil
___ Dehydrated Food
___ EMERGENCY TRAIL SNACKS
___ Plastic Bags for food storage and to carry out garbage
___ Backpacker's Grill where permitted

NECESSITIES
___ TOPO MAP & COMPASS
___ FLASHLIGHT
___ Fresh Alkaline Batteries and Spare Bulb
___ KNIFE
___ Lightweight nylon rope (50 ft.)
___ Candle Lantern/Candles
___ Needle/Thread
___ Nylon Repair Tape
___ WATER BOTTLE

SHELTER
___ Tent

___ Ground Cloth
___ Sleeping Bag
___ Pad

TOILETRIES
___ Toothbrush/Toothpaste
___ Biodegradable Soap
___ Toilet Paper
___ Towel and Face Cloth

CLOTHING
___ Socks (heavy wool & light liners)
___ Cotton Underwear
___ HAT for sun protection
___ Polypropylene Underwear*
___ DOWN VEST, LIGHT SWEATER, OR FLEECE JACKET
___ Parka*
___ Windbreaker
___ RAIN GEAR and EXTRA SET OF CLOTHES
___ Wool Shirt*
___ Bandanas
___ Swimsuit*
___ Gloves*
___ HIKING SHORTS/PANTS
___ Shirt
___ Hiking Boots
___ Tennis Shoes for camp and stream crossing

---

*Optional depending on season

THE BACKPACKER'S CHECKLIST *(continued)*

___ Insulated Booties*
___ STOCKING CAP for
warmth

MEDICAL

___ FIRST-AID/SURVIVAL KIT
___ Vaseline
___ Sunglasses
___ Lip Salve
___ Sunscreen
___ Insect Repellent
___ Water Treatment (tablets or
filter)

PERMITS/ID

___ Backcountry Use Permit
___ Fishing Permit
___ PERSONAL ID

OPTIONAL

___ Camera/Film
___ Notebook/Pen
___ Field Guide(s)
___ Fishing Gear

---

advisable to help minimize water loss. Nutritional needs are an individual thing. If you have any doubts, talk to your doctor. A small container of multi-vitamin capsules or vitamin C capsules might be in order.

In General: Any dish that needs more than 30 minutes of preparation should be left behind. The repeated emphasis on speed is especially pertinent on trips to Yellowstone and the Tetons. The higher you go, the lower the boiling point of water. When you hit 8,000 feet, it takes twice as long to cook as it does at sea level. Remember also that food digests more slowly at high altitudes. Frequent small meals are better than a lot of food at once.

Plan ahead. If you average out to a pound or a pound-and-a-half of dry food for each day, you're on target. Become a food packager. Pack each item in the quantity desired for each meal. Many main courses are already packed in suitable single-meal containers.

Don't forget the salt and pepper.

Weather

Month to month, the climate is rather similar in Yellowstone and Grand Teton, but the latter generally takes you to higher elevations. Once you've passed timberline, there are few places to hide. Even after clear, sunny days, the nighttime temperature at these heights dips close to freezing.

June

Each month has its advantages and disadvantages. If the high country is your goal, better wait till midsummer. Winter weather persists above 6,500 feet through May. June is still wintry above 8,500 feet. At slightly lower elevations, the bulk of the wilderness is frequently too soggy to do extensive hiking for at least the first three weeks of June; slushy snow and high water make it inaccessible.

June can be ideal for traveling the shorter trails of the two parks. Newly blossoming wildflowers line paths through the valleys. Waterfalls, refreshed by melting snows, are at the peak of their beauty. The mountains are still capped with white. Most of the migratory birds are back, and there's a flurry of nest building. Mule deer fawns are usually born in June. It's easier to see wildlife in general. Perhaps the best reason for going is that few tourists have arrived. June is wonderfully unpredictable. Every day of your visit could be clear and sunny. It might rain every day. It could snow.

July

July is more inviting to the backpacker. Days are generally brighter, brisk, seldom chilly. Nights are cold, particularly in the Tetons. In the mountains there are thunderstorms and stiff winds almost every afternoon, sometimes snow. But it should all pass in one or two hours. Have patience.

When the water level drops late in July, fishing is at its best. Wildflowers are blooming at higher elevations. As the weather warms, some of the wildlife retreats up the slopes to mountain meadows. There are still many elk in the river valleys and moose in the bogs. The pelicans and gulls on the Molly Islands are scooping up fish for their newborn chicks. This is the month when fledglings of almost every bird species try their wings, and trumpeter swans lead their young to water.

July is also the time when the bugs wake up. There are clouds of mosquitoes around marshes, lakes, meadows, any place where the snow has just melted. And they bite and bite and bite. Colder temperatures make them inactive. So they rest up at night for the next day's feast. If the mosquitoes neglect any part of you, an assortment of other insects are ready to help. It's imperative that you carry the proper repellent, creams, clothing, and netting for your tent.

August

In many ways, August is the prime month for backpacking excursions. Weather is dependable except for occasional thundershowers, especially high in the Tetons. Days are hot, nights are refreshingly cool, sometimes cold. The snow is gone, the water has receded, trails are in great shape. The mosquitoes and their pestiferous brethren have subsided considerably. Above timberline, alpine vegetation flowers briefly. In the forests, young birds declare their independence from the nest.

September and Later

For many backpackers, September is the *only* time for Yellowstone and Grand Teton. Wildflowers are disappearing but the trees are touched with color. Scarlets and golds appear on the high slopes and seem to drift down toward the valleys as the month goes on. The groves of aspen acquire their golden glow.

Ponds and lakes are filled with ducks and geese stopping over on their way south. Flocks of songbirds pause here on their migrations. The insects are gone. So are most of the people.

The large animals are at their best. The ones that moved into the mountains for the summer, like the bison, return to the valleys. The grizzly is especially handsome, bundled in its heavy winter coat. With a lot of luck you may spot a mature "silvertip." Its fur has a frosty appearance, the result of light coloration on the tips of the hairs. Deer, elk, and moose are living trophies, their racks of antlers matured to magnificence, their coats thick as they glisten with a new sheen in the autumn sunlight. For the elk, this is the time of the rut or mating season. The bull elk announces his intentions by bugling a high, piercing shriek that descends to a booming, low grunt—a sound you won't forget.

In September, the wilderness is wild. So is the weather, which becomes unpredictable. Rain is common, snow is likely. But while caution is necessary with snow, it isn't quite the same problem as early in the season because it hasn't had time to accumulate in great depths.

Fishing

The pristine waters of Yellowstone and Grand Teton—lakes, rivers, streams, ponds, brooks—offer some of the most spectacular trout fishing in the American West. Sport species include cutthroat (named for the red mark on its jaw), rainbow, brown, brook, and lake (also called mackinaw) trout, Arctic grayling, and mountain whitefish. Only the cutthroat trout, grayling, and whitefish are natives.

A policy of artificial stocking has been abandoned, but the damage has been done. To a person whose primary interest is the quality of the fishing—it is terrific—"damage" may seem like a peculiar word; and the question of native versus introduced species may appear to be over-concern with ecological esthetics. But if a wilderness is to remain truly wild, it must be maintained in its original state with minimal meddling by humans.

Native fish that were interesting in their own right, both as battlers and as food, are fewer. Their decline has forced the adoption of stringent regulations on park fishing so that what remains may be preserved. There may be many cutthroat trout, but they are not there simply for humans to consume. Numerous other creatures—the grizzly, otter, mink, pelican, osprey, kingfisher, heron, and others—all prey on this fish: It is a vital link in the ecosystem. It has been estimated that pelicans alone—most of them from the Molly Islands colony—consume many thousands of cutthroat each year.

You can pick up a copy of fishing regulations at visitor centers or ranger stations. They will tell you where and how you can fish, and which fish you can keep. Generally, fishing with bait is prohibited. In some streams, only fly fishing is permitted.

That's because you must not keep (and eat) depleted "wild" fish like the grayling, and studies show that about 48 percent of all fish caught on bait and then released eventually die. For those hooked on lures and flies the death rate goes down to about 4 percent after release.

Because of increased fishing in the backcountry, park officials are initiating the policy of "catch and release." You can still have your fun, if not a meal. To do so, remove barbs from the hooks on your lures and flies. When you catch a fish, unhook it carefully so you don't tear its mouth, then drop it back into the water. Make sure you wet your hands before you touch the fish. Dry hands may cause a fungus that could wind up killing it anyway.

You must obtain a permit to fish anywhere in the park. You may obtain a permit and current regulations from any visitor center or ranger station in the park.

Mountain Climbing
in Yellowstone

Technical climbers should head a few miles south to the Tetons' granite peaks, for Yellowstone's mountains primarily consist of loose, crumbly rock—unsuitable for the use of technical gear. Most prominent peaks in Yellowstone are accessible by trail or can be reached via some off-trail scrambling. A few peaks in the Absaroka Range are, for the most part, inaccessible, but several can be reached. Trails lead to the summits of Mt. Holmes, Mt. Washburn, Mt. Sheridan, Observation Peak, Bighorn Peak, Sheep Mountain, and Pelican Cone.

Electric Peak (10,992 ft.), a very popular climb, can be reached by three different routes: (1) following the North Boundary Trail (marked by boundary posts) from Electric Creek to near the north face; (2) ascending the southwest ridge from the saddle on the Sportsman Lake Trail; and (3) via the *very steep* southeast ridge from Cache Lake. Electric Peak has a false summit (10,943 ft.) 0.4 miles west of the actual summit that is easily climbed from the north and southwest; the true summit requires some scrambling over loose, steep, and *potentially dangerous* rocky slopes. The true summit has a register box permanently affixed to it. This knife-edged summit has room for only a few people.

Before climbing mountains in the park it is recommended that you stop by a ranger station to ascertain trail and snow conditions.

Off-Trail Travel

This book is certainly not a guide to *all* of Yellowstone's backcountry. In fact, the park's 1,000 miles of trails traverse only a portion of its 3,472 square miles. Those who enjoy traveling cross-country with compass and topo map have the opportunity of exploring seldom-visited mountaintops, lakes, waterfalls, streams, and thermal areas.

It is the opinion of this writer that such areas should be excluded from the pages of a trail guide, in order to preserve the mystique and feeling of discovery that accompany present-day explorers in much the same fashion that they did Colter, Bridger, and other early explorers of the Yellowstone.

It must be emphasized that off-trail travel is for the expert backpacker only, and special permission must be received from park rangers before embarking on such a trip.

A Natural History of the Yellowstone–Teton Region

If animals could vote, there would be more places like Yellowstone National Park. Take the ducks, for instance. Flocks of mallards approach the park by riverway, hugging the water, refusing to become airborne targets. Then they reach the boundary. Invisible though that line may be, the birds lift off and fly into the peace they know is on the other side. It is there for us, too.

The land of Yellowstone (3,472 square miles) is mostly high, rolling, forested plateau bounded by mountains — the Gallatin and Madison ranges to the west, the Absarokas along the east. Six miles south of the Yellowstone border lies the northernmost entrance to Grand Teton National Park (484 square miles) and the sky-high spires that gave the mountain range its name and a reputation as a climbers' paradise. Most visitors arrive in their four-wheeled prisons, checking off a list of postcard sights as if they were touring a version of Disneyland. Pity. Because beyond the limited viewpoint of looping scenic roads stretch thousands of acres of wilderness — enough spectacular scenery to keep even the most dedicated explorers busy for years. It takes time.

It took time. Billions of years went into the creation of these unique landscapes. Yet many of the wilderness wonderments you walk among today have been there for only a few ticks on the geologic clock.

The Making of the Mountains

The Tetons are among the youngest mountains in the Rockies—less than 10 million years old (most of the others go back 50 million years). The crystalline peaks gleaming in today's sun had their origin deep under the earth's crust in Precambrian times. During the Early Precambrian, sedimentary and volcanic rock accumulated down there in great heat and under intense pressure. This material was recrystallized into gneiss and schist (or mica schist) and repeatedly folded into enormous, multicolored layers. As the strata settled, fractures developed. The underground heated up again and volcanic action poured molten streams of pegmatite and pink and light-gray granite up into the cracks. This mixture ultimately cooled and solidified in those fractures to form cross-hatchings and rocky wriggles called dikes.

Eons passed, and the mountains eroded away to a rolling plain on the earth's surface—until some 600 million years ago when shallow seas swept over the area to deposit the sedimentary rock that still covers much of the range. During the next 500 million years the waters receded and returned periodically, each time leaving behind additional crusty layers of limestone and sandstone. As the climate slowly changed, the region stabilized into luxuriant jungles so that, about 50 million years ago, the area that is now Grand Teton National Park resembled the Florida Everglades.

In mid-Pliocene, the whole rocky melange that had been brewing for eons began an upward movement. The Teton fault shifted and colossal blocks of gneiss, schist, and granite arose, breaking through the crust of limestone and sandstone that had covered them for centuries. The tilted blocks gradually lifted. Since that time, the forces of erosion have carved the Tetons we see today.

As the rock mass uplifted along the whole 40-mile-long fault, myriad dikes were exposed. Perhaps the most intriguing that are visible today are the enormous, nearly vertical dikes of diabase, shaded from dark green to black. The biggest of these, on Mt. Moran, ranges from 100 to 120 feet in thickness and extends 7 miles in length. Grand Teton's black dike is 40 to 60 feet thick, and the one on Middle Teton is 20 to 40 feet thick.

Volcanic Activity

The formation of Yellowstone came somewhat later and with considerably more violence. A series of volcanic eruptions — the first 2 million years ago, the second about 1.2 million years ago — blasted pumice and ash over several hundred cubic miles. A third cycle of eruptions began 600,000 years ago. Molten rock, or magma, churned upward into underground basins, creating on the surface a domelike mountain 50 to 75 miles across. As surface stone cracked, some of the lava spilled out across the landscape. Finally, after preliminary rumbling and smoking, a massive explosion of gas spewed tons of debris over the land as far as what is now Kansas and Nebraska, destroying every vestige of life in its path. Modern geologists estimate the force of this blast at 200 times that of Krakatoa, the modern record-holder, and 2,500 times that of Mt. St. Helens.

Gas pressure eventually subsided and the flow of molten ash and pumice halted. The giant earth dome that had risen over the lava collapsed and became an elliptical crater, or caldera. The crater, measuring 50 miles in diameter (just short of a world's record), has eroded and become overgrown with vegetation, but is still visible below Mt. Washburn.

Volcanic activity continued with leaks rather than blowouts. The material that trickled over the earth — sometimes cutting a path 30 miles across — was mostly rhyolite, a blend of quartz and feldspar that still covers much of Yellowstone. Some of the rhyolite solidified into a black or brown glass known as obsidian. Thus, today's backpackers sometimes find themselves walking over black glass, as on the Shoshone Trail.

Eruptions continued with diminishing force until about 75,000 years ago. Between each of these cycles, trees sprouted in the new volcanic soil, only to be destroyed by the next series of subterranean upheavals. During some of the less violent blasts, nearby trees were buried—and preserved—under clouds of ash, dust, and other debris. Their death was the birth of Yellowstone's 40 square miles of fossil forest—the world's largest. Many of the trees, like some on Specimen Ridge, remain upright, a unique departure from the fallen logs of other petrified forests around the world.

New watercourses opened across the land where those early forests were taking root, and a lake welled up inside the giant crater. Its waters spilled over the rim to become the Yellowstone River, which in turn cut a 26-mile gash known as the Grand Canyon of Yellowstone. In one section the river has long been (and still is) heated by magma deep below the surface. The scalding water has boiled the canyon walls for century after century, transforming the brown and gray rhyolite into vivid yellow rock.

A Glacial Facelift

It remained for ice to finish the work, giving Yellowstone and Grand Teton their more or less final shape. In the Pleistocene, temperatures dropped, great masses of snow and ice accumulated, and, ultimately, enormous glaciers pushed forward and altered the landscape. The glaciers arrived in three major and several minor waves over a period extending from 350,000 to 9,000 years ago. Each time, Yellowstone was almost completely submerged under these ice oceans, in some places as deep as

3,000 feet. On several occasions, sheets of ice flowing south from the Yellowstone plateau met and joined sheets moving from the east into Jackson Hole.

Over these thousands of years, the climate warmed periodically, causing the glaciers to melt and retreat, but when the temperatures dropped, the glaciers returned once more. Each time they left their mark. The ice runoff branched into the canyons, grinding the edges of those chasms and rounding out their floors. Yellowstone's Madison River Canyon was transformed from a sharp cleft into a U-shaped valley. About 30,000 years ago, ice that was several thousand feet thick filled Jackson Hole and gouged out more of the great dip of flat plain that is walled by the towering Tetons. In valley after valley, a combination of glacial battering, frost, and avalanches chiseled gentle slopes into sharp inclines. The same abrasive action sharpened mountain peaks and ridges above.

During the last major advance, approximately 9,000 years ago, glaciers streamed through the Teton valleys, depositing great masses of rock, gravel, sand, and other debris into terminal moraines. When the glaciers eventually melted, these moraines remained as natural dams to form several of the Teton area's major lakes: Jackson, Leigh, Jenny, Bradley, Taggart, and Phelps.

Glaciers are still to be seen in Grand Teton National Park. But they are small, essentially dormant. They are probably recent arrivals, not remnants of the ice monsters that once dominated this part of the earth. Backpackers can hike trails to both Teton and Schoolroom glaciers for a glimpse of the past.

Firewater

Hot magma remains under Yellowstone, ready to take advantage of faults in the surface. The most apparent manifestations of such thermal activity are the geysers and hot spring and sulfur pools and fumaroles, spouting, hissing, and bubbling throughout the area. Mention Yellowstone and most people instantly conjure up an image of Old Faithful. It, and the more than 200 other geysers in Yellowstone, are the products of water from above meeting fire down below.

Yellowstone gets a great deal of rain and snow, particularly at higher elevations. The Upper Geyser Basin's annual precipitation is 18 to 20 inches. Millions of acre-feet of this water run off in the park's rivers and streams, but a great deal of it first seeps into the earth through the porous volcanic rock. Some of it stops at the water table and returns to the surface through cold springs. Much water keeps going deeper, possibly to 2 miles. Contact with hot rocks at these depths plus pressure from water above sends its temperature soaring over the boiling point, perhaps to more than 500°F. But down there it can't boil. Nor can it turn to steam because there is too much pressure. It has to go somewhere.

The escape route is an extremely complicated subterranean plumbing system. As water rises through the rocky channels, pressure goes down and the water begins to boil vigorously.

Whether or not this overheated liquid bursts forth in fountain fashion or emerges with a hiss and a gurgle as a garden variety hot spring depends on a delicate balance among several factors; temperature, pressure, the nature of the conduits through which it is passing, and how much steam energy is left after the cooling-off process on the way up. The same variables determine what kind of a geyser it becomes: a gusher like Old Faithful—with 4,000 to 7,000 gallons per eruption—or a quiet splash.

There is no shortage of geysers in Yellowstone, and some of the most intriguing are for the backpacker only, reachable by trail to some remote region, such as the Shoshone Geyser

Basin. Despite popular mythology about the park's star attraction, Old Faithful is neither the most punctual nor the most powerful. The interval between its discharge times can vary from 33 to 148 minutes. Old Faithful shoots its watery plume up 100 feet, occasionally 160.

Name a color, and there's a pool to match it. Sometimes rings of several colors occur within a single pool. A blue color is produced in a hot pool over 167°F (algae can only survive under 167°F) as the water absorbs the red rays from sunlight and reflects blue. The colors of algae beds range from yellow to dark brown. A few pools are colored by mineral particles in the water, including Sulfur Cauldron and Black Dragon's Cauldron (iron oxide). Perhaps the most spectacular is Mammoth Hot Springs, not because of the color, but for what it has left behind. The water there has a high concentration of calcium carbonate. For centuries, it has percolated up through layers of limestone and deposited extensive travertine terraces that look like relics of some ancient marble castle.

Mud pots are the comedians of the thermal world. They offer as much variation in sound as they do in color—a cacophony of bloops and belches, wheezes and gurgles, and resounding splats as mud flops back into the natural vats after being spit as high as 6 feet in the air. Sulfuric acid—hot spring water mixed with sulfur in the escaping gases—breaks down rhyolites to create the muddy "paint" that fills these holes. The colors—whites, pastel pinks, grays, yellows—come from sulfur and iron compounds mixing with the clay.

Flora

Of the two park areas, Yellowstone is the more heavily wooded. About 80 percent of it is forest, and 80 percent of that is lodgepole pine. Apparently, the lodgepole took over because forest

COMMON YELLOW AND WHITE FLOWERS

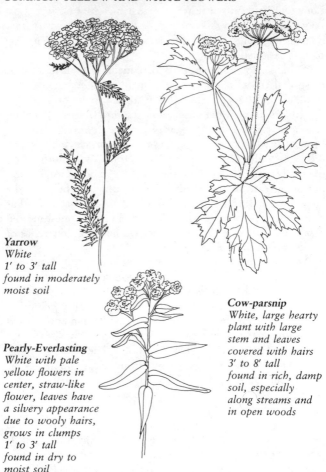

Yarrow
White
1' to 3' tall
found in moderately
moist soil

Pearly-Everlasting
White with pale
yellow flowers in
center, straw-like
flower, leaves have
a silvery appearance
due to wooly hairs,
grows in clumps
1' to 3' tall
found in dry to
moist soil

Cow-parsnip
White, large hearty
plant with large
stem and leaves
covered with hairs
3' to 8' tall
found in rich, damp
soil, especially
along streams and
in open woods

COMMON YELLOW AND WHITE FLOWERS

Shrubby Cinquefoil
*Yellow flowers,
shrub
1' to 5' tall
found often near
sagebrush*

**Arrowleaf
Balsamroot**
*Golden yellow,
arrow-shaped
leaves are large
and covered with
silvery gray hairs,
grows in clumps
8" to 24" tall
found in dry soils*

Glacier Lily
*Yellow, two large
shiny oblong leaves
4" to 10" tall
found in rich, moist
soil following
melting snowline*

COMMON RED AND PINK FLOWERS

Fireweed
Bright pink
1' to 4' tall
prevalent in
burned areas

Indian Paintbrush
Red to red-orange,
deep rosy red,
many species
8" to 12" tall
found in dry to
moist soil
throughout
Yellowstone

Sticky Geranium
Pink to lavender,
can be white,
deeply lobed leaves
1' to 2' tall
found throughout
Yellowstone

COMMON RED AND PINK FLOWERS

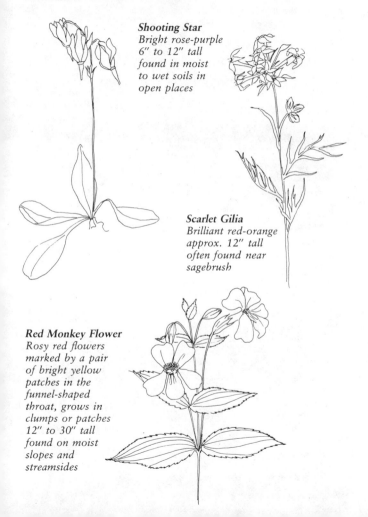

Shooting Star
Bright rose-purple
6" to 12" tall
found in moist
to wet soils in
open places

Scarlet Gilia
Brilliant red-orange
approx. 12" tall
often found near
sagebrush

Red Monkey Flower
Rosy red flowers
marked by a pair
of bright yellow
patches in the
funnel-shaped
throat, grows in
clumps or patches
12" to 30" tall
found on moist
slopes and
streamsides

COMMON BLUE AND PURPLE FLOWERS

Bluebells
*Blue with pinkish
buds
1' to 4' tall
found in damp areas*

Larkspur
*Almost metallic blue
6" to 10" tall
frequently seen in
the geyser basins
in June*

Harebell
*Bell-shaped violet-
blue flowers, grows
in clumps
8" to 20" tall*

COMMON BLUE AND PURPLE FLOWERS

Blue Flax
*Sky blue flowers
12" to 15" tall
found in dry
places among the
sagebrush*

Forget-me-not
*Sky blue with
yellow center
4" to 12" tall
found in moist soil*

Lupine
*Blue pea-like flower
4" to 12" tall
found in the
lodgepole forest,
open meadows and
hillsides*

COMMON BLUE AND PURPLE FLOWERS

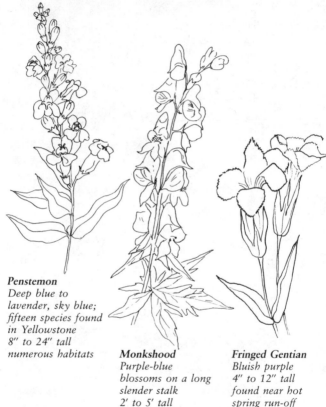

Penstemon
*Deep blue to
lavender, sky blue;
fifteen species found
in Yellowstone
8" to 24" tall
numerous habitats*

Monkshood
*Purple-blue
blossoms on a long
slender stalk
2' to 5' tall
found along
streams, and near
springs and wet
meadows*

Fringed Gentian
*Bluish purple
4" to 12" tall
found near hot
spring run-off
channels, common
in the geyser basins*

fires were good for them—up to a point, that is. It takes fiery heat to pry open the cones the lodgepole deposits on the ground. The cones can then eject their seeds for sprouting. While fire wiped out other tree species, it helped the lodgepole to reproduce and move in where the others had fallen. Also, the lodgepole tends to grow well in Yellowstone's nutrient-poor volcanic soil.

Conifers are now dominant in both parks, but no one is sure how most of the trees and plants got to this region. The experts think that at least some of the species traveled a circuitous route, riding the breeze and the glaciers.

A trek through the wild places of present-day Yellowstone and Grand Teton is like an excursion through a series of gardens, the more charming for their lack of formality. You can meander over a meadowland trail edged with a blue and purplish bouquet of larkspur, lupine, gentian, and elephanthead, patches of cinquefoil and buttercups, and fields of lilies sprinkled with sage. A wooded path will lead you past trees garlanded with pale lavender clematis, stands of tall monkshood and blue harebells, starry asters, and brilliant fireweed. Luminescent mosses cloak the rocky banks of a mountain stream and, under an archway of shady alders, the soft earth yields a colorful congregation of pink monkeyflowers, scarlet paintbrush, mountain bluebell, ivory columbine, red and yellow coralroot, and yellow senecio. If you want to be sure of the name of that blossom beside the trail, take along a field guide to flowers.

Fauna

Man has always been lured to the Yellowstone–Teton region more by animals than by anything else. Ancestors of many of today's wild species probably arrived via the land bridge that once spanned the Bering Strait to Asia. During the Ice Age, primitive hunters followed the mammoth to this area. Later, the Indians pursued bison, elk, and deer along the slopes and through the valleys. The first full-time human residents we know of were mountaineering Indians who stalked bighorn sheep. The earliest white men were obsessed with the beaver, whose luxurious fur made it a natural resource to be exploited.

Most people today regard this part of the world as bear country. Small wonder. There are several hundred bears inhabiting the Yellowstone country in and around the park. The black bear used to be a familiar sight along park roads. However, due to a change in bear management policy and stricter enforcement of regulations, the clownish roadside alms-seeker is a thing of the past.

Then there are the others the tourists have no desire to meet: the grizzlies. Actually, there are only about 200 to 250 spread around Yellowstone (each requires a lot of space) and a mere handful south of the park in the Teton Wilderness. Fierce and fearless, the grizzly has all the equipment necessary to be king in these parts: bone-crushing jaws, razor-sharp six-inch claws, and amazing speed for a bulky, lumbering, 600-pound animal. There is nothing subtle about a grizzly bear, yet there is nothing quite so winsome as the springtime sight of a grizzly leading her cubs across Yellowstone's Hayden Valley in a search for roots and berries.

One of the best places to see wildlife, grizzlies included, is on Yellowstone's central plateau: Hayden Valley and the meadows along the banks of the Firehole, Madison, and Gibbon rivers. These grasslands are home to the elk, or wapiti, which are certainly the most numerous of the region's large animals. In the summer, there are up to 31,000 in Yellowstone alone.

The smaller mule deer is also here, grazing the valleys and forest edges. The pronghorn, America's only antelope, prefers the plains but occasionally ventures into the open slopes of the valleys. Seeing one for more than a few seconds may take some doing since they are as speedy as they are skittish.

In the high meadows lives the bison. This shaggy, bearded beast is a symbol both of human folly and enlightenment. At their peak, vast herds totaling 60 million animals ranged across the continent from western New York to Oregon and from Canada to Mexico. The Indians always hunted them, but without seriously depleting the population. When white explorers and settlers opened the West, the buffalo suddenly fell victim to hungry railroad workers, hunters (a good "professional" could bring down 250 a day), and the U.S. Army, which embarked on a campaign to exterminate troublesome Indians by exterminating their food. By the late 1850s the 60 million had dwindled to an estimated 540—most groups owned by conservation-minded individuals. A few remained in Yellowstone.

In 1905 a group of concerned conservationists founded the American Bison Society to lobby for rigid protection laws, to arouse the public, to establish preserves, and to set up the nucleus of a breeding herd. The society was successful on all fronts and was eventually able to restock protected refuges at several points in the West. Now there are about 20,000 bison in the U.S., including Yellowstone's 3,000.

Moose, the only other really large creature hereabouts, is to be found mostly in the wetlands, occasionally feeding along hillsides. Look for them on the Yellowstone River downstream from Yellowstone Lake, or at Avalanche Canyon in the Tetons.

Marshlands also supply food and nesting grounds for the North American trumpeter swan. Like the bison, these birds were once on the verge of extinction. Although the situation improved, a recent decline in nesting pairs in the park is cause for concern.

Mountain marshes, ponds, and lakes are home as well to muskrat, mink, otter, beaver, sandhill crane, great blue heron, osprey, and a variety of ducks, geese, and coots. The Molly Islands in the Southeast Arm of Yellowstone lake are the only breeding grounds in a national park for the white pelican. Gulls, terns, and cormorants also nest on these rocky islets.

A climb to higher elevations—say, to Yellowstone's Mt. Washburn—may be rewarded by the sight of bighorn sheep along the ridges. And bald and golden eagles may also be seen launching themselves from rocky crags to soar over the valleys in search of food.

Any visit to the park interior is a birdwatcher's delight. More than 200 species have been identified: warblers, juncos, king-fishers, nuthatches, goldfinches, flycatchers, swallows, hum-mingbirds, tanagers, chickadees . . . . This is another cataloging operation that is better done on foot with the help of a pocket-sized field guide.

The unjustly maligned coyote patrols valleys, mountains, for-ests, meadows, or marshes keeping things tidy. If it weren't for coyotes, the park would be overrun with mice, gophers, and rab-bits. Smaller carnivorous critters—red fox, lynx, mink, wolverine, badger—are a secretive lot, difficult but not impossible to spot.

Park animals are protected from humans but not from each other. The aim now is to give equal rights to predators and re-store the balance of life.

An early misguided policy held that eliminating predators would be good for the ungulates, such as the elk, deer, and moose. However, it wasn't. Hundreds of wolves and mountain lions were killed in the early 1900s, and the ecosystem has not been in balance since. Today there are perhaps 25 to 30 moun-tain lions in the north area of the park—too small a number to have a significant impact on the ecosystem.

The stirring howl of the wolf is missing from the Yellowstone country. The gray wolf was completely exterminated from Yel-lowstone when 134 known wolves were killed in the park be-tween 1912 and 1926. The wolf is referred to as the "missing link" since it is the only animal both native to and absent from the Yellowstone ecosystem. Without the presence of wolf packs, elk and bison herds tend to reach higher populations. Also, weak and diseased animals are not efficiently removed from the ecosystem.

For example, during the winter of 1981–82 Yellowstone's herd of bighorn sheep was inflicted with pinkeye, a highly contagious disease that causes blindness. With no wolves present to efficiently remove the infected bighorn, the disease continued to spread and eventually decimated the herd, killing over 60 percent of the population.

Grizzlies are also hurt by the lack of wolves. Studies in Alaska and Canada document that grizzlies frequently displace wolves from fresh kills. Thus the grizzly in Yellowstone is being denied a dependable and critical source of protein through the spring, summer, and fall seasons.

Since the wolf is an endangered species and the absence of a viable wolf population in Yellowstone represents the greatest single departure from the park's mission of maintaining a natural ecosystem, there are serious efforts and studies underway to reintroduce the wolf to Yellowstone. As of this writing, opposition from politicians in Wyoming, Idaho, and Montana is holding up reintroduction efforts. The overwhelming majority of Yellowstone visitors surveyed favor reintroduction of the wolf, as do the majority of citizens polled in the states of Wyoming and Montana. This is another example of biopolitics, where what is best biologically for the park takes a back seat primarily due to the political considerations of the three members of the Wyoming Congressional delegation. Of course Yellowstone National Park belongs to all Americans. You may want to write your representatives in your home state and let them know how you feel about Yellowstone's biopolitics.

Sights and Sounds of the Yellowstone Forest

Since 80 percent of Yellowstone is forested, chances are you will spend at least part of your time hiking through the woods. If your forest hike seems boring, try waking up your senses. Nature is at work all around you. Take a closer look at your surroundings and listen to the sounds of the forest. The ability to identify trees, plants, and flowers adds to the enjoyment of a hike, so bringing along a field guide to the park's plants is recommended.

As you take a closer look while in the forest you are apt to discover several interesting sights. The bright green growth along tree branches is called wolf lichen, supposedly named for its use many years ago by superstitious Europeans in warding off werewolves. The black growth in trees that looks almost like animal hair is also a lichen and is called old man's beard. The different colors in lichens are due to the different chemicals and pigments contained in them. Colorful lichens also may be found growing on rocks and boulders, where they are considered to be pioneer plants as they aid in the breaking-down process that eventually leads to soil conditions capable of supporting a variety of plants.

Frequently you will spot trees containing a small but very dense tangled growth of small tree branches. This growth is called witch's broom and may be caused by a variety of natural conditions (such as the parasite mistletoe) that disturb the reproductive process within a tree, thus causing this unusual formation.

You undoubtedly will notice many fallen trees, for the lodgepole pine has a very shallow root system and is vulnerable to heavy winds and snows (see p. 88). Take a close look at the tree bark. If you are in a lodgepole forest, chances are you will occasionally spot trees with many small dots of sap protruding from the bark. This is where pine-bark beetles have entered the trees. Many lodgepoles in Yellowstone are dead or dying due to this insect. The larvae of the beetle bore under the bark in all directions and may eventually girdle the tree, which shuts off the flow of nutrients in the tree, thus killing it. Look at dead tree trunks and branches and you will notice the larvae patterns on many.

The pine-bark beetle is considered a natural part of the Yellowstone ecosystem and is important in providing forest openings and homes for birds that favor dead trees. However, the infestation is probably unnaturally high due to the suppression of forest fires over the years. This has resulted in a forest composed of mostly mature trees, which are especially susceptible to the beetles' attack. Young trees, on the other hand, tend to flush out the beetles with a heavy flow of sap. Natural fires are now allowed to burn in most of the park (see p. 74).

If you are in the northern section of the park and notice dying spruce and fir trees, it is most likely due to the spruce budworm, which feeds on the new needles that emerge from buds in the spring. In some areas of a lodgepole forest you may notice many knots and knars on the trees; these are called burls and are due to abnormal cell growth within the trees. Some of the older buildings in the Old Faithful area contain many interesting burled logs.

In Yellowstone, where large wildlife is abundant, it is interesting to look for the "signatures" of animals on trees. If you travel through an area frequented by bison, look for light-colored rubbed rings around and horn marks on tree trunks, along with long, brown, somewhat kinky bison hairs clinging to the bark. You may also see bison wallows, where they roll and produce depressed bare spots on the ground, and bison chips or droppings.

Yellowstone is elk country, with summer herds numbering

more than 31,000, so their signs are common in the forest. A bull likes to rub his antlers on small trees in order to rub off the velvet and polish them. Often the saplings are girdled in the process and die. The elk's pelletlike droppings are seen practically everywhere.

If you notice a tree with gnawed patches up and down the trunk, this is the work of the porcupine. The patches are distinguished from other animal barking by the neatly gnawed edges, irregular outlines, and many small tooth marks.

Curious about the raised tunnels of dirt seen in some open areas? These are mud cores formed by pocket gophers tunneling underneath snow. When the snow melts, the earth cores that had been pushed behind in the snow tunnels are left as evidence of the gophers' travels. Large excavations in such open areas may be the work of a grizzly, as it tries to locate pocket gophers or their caches of roots a few inches underground. Other bear signs include overturned rocks, old logs torn apart or turned over, and clawed trees (see p. 23). With Yellowstone's varied and abundant wildlife, a field guide to animal tracks is recommended.

If your hike takes you over lingering patches of snow, you probably will notice places where the snow is pink. This is due to a red algae that lives in the melting water on the snow. The fiberlike substance that appears on the ground following the melting of snow is a fungus that also thrives in the cold water from the snow melt.

The sounds of the Yellowstone forest are as varied and interesting as its sights. If you are walking near a rocky slope (in the forest or especially above timberline) and you hear a high-pitched "Eek!" follow the sound and see if you can find a little brownish-gray animal that looks like a guinea pig sitting among the boulders. This is a pika, a member of the rabbit family. The pika, which does not hibernate, is usually busy collecting plants and drying them on stones. The little "haystacks" are then cached deep among the loose boulders to sustain the pika through winter.

Another sound to listen for along rocky slopes is the loud, musical "chirp" of the yellow-bellied marmot. The marmot is a true hibernator, as it goes into a deep sleep during the winter.

When approaching large meadows you may be lucky enough to hear a shrill, musical rattle. This is the call of the sandhill crane, and there is no other sound quite like it. If hiking during the fall you probably will hear one of Yellowstone's wildest sounds—the bugling of a bull elk, which starts with a low note, ascends to a high-pitched bugle, then ends with a few low-toned grunts. It is a sound you will not soon forget. Cow elk and calves occasionally emit high-pitched squeals, especially when in danger. Of course, one of the true symbols of wilderness is a sound not heard in too many parts of the country anymore: the crying bark and howl of the coyote, an unjustly maligned animal referred to by Indians as God's dog.

The Yellowstone forest is vibrant and alive. Allow your senses to come alive in this wilderness.

Fire in Yellowstone

The human perspective tends to view forest fires as an evil and destructive force of nature. Our view of a healthy forest is often one that consists of dense stands of lush, green trees. However, if we could interview the true permanent residents of Yellowstone—the animals—we would receive a very different perspective on fire and the forest. In fact, during the great fires of 1988 it was rather fascinating to note that the wildlife was almost completely indifferent to the presence of fires around them. The animals continued to casually feed in the meadows despite the proximity of flames and smoke only a short distance away. Very few large animals were killed by the fires. The notion that forest fires cause large herds of animals to stampede was proven a myth, at least as far as Yellowstone is concerned.

For a period of 100 years, from the time the park was established in 1872 through 1971, official park policy had been to suppress all fires, whether caused by man or lightning. But biologists began to recognize that this policy was causing great harm to the ecosystem. Yellowstone's forests were losing their diversity since there were more old trees and fewer young ones. The thick forest canopy was depriving the lower plants of sunlight. These plants died and began to pile up on the forest floor as litter. As the abundance and variety of plants decreased, so did the wildlife. The beautiful aspen tree, which depends upon fire for its existence, declined in number. As the number of aspen declined, so did the beaver. The nutrient level in the park's streams and lakes was declining; one study found that the nutrient level in Yellowstone Lake had declined 68 percent between 1884 and 1970. Fewer nutrients meant less food for the

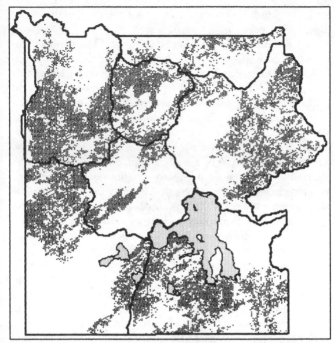

PARK ROADS - *heavy black lines*

What Burned in Yellowstone in 1988?

The shading represents areas that were in some way affected by the fires. The forest fires burned in a spotted or mosaic pattern; less than half the vegetation burned within fire perimeters. Satellite photographs have revealed that 36 percent of the park was burned by the fires. Of that, 15 percent was canopy burn in which the tops of the trees were consumed by fire.

Map produced by GIS Lab, Yellowstone National Park, Wyoming, George McKay, Chief Cartographer.

cutthroat trout, and so fewer cutthroat for the grizzly, eagle, osprey, and pelican.

In 1972 park officials initiated a "natural burn" policy under which lightning-caused fires were allowed to burn in designated backcountry areas of Yellowstone. However, 16 fire seasons produced only 34,000 acres of burn, or about 1.5 percent of the park. Then came the summer of 1988, in which Yellowstone experienced the peak of a forest-fire cycle as great as a 100- or 150-year great flood or hurricane. Severe drought conditions, an accumulation of fuel in the forest, low humidity, numerous lightning strikes, and gale-force winds up to 70 mph all combined to create a fire season the likes of which the Yellowstone country had not experienced in over 150 years. Some 48 fires burned, some lightning-caused and some human-caused.

Yellowstone's fire policy had always dictated that any human-caused fire be immediately suppressed. As fire conditions worsened, suppression efforts began on the fires that had been started by lightning. Despite the efforts of 25,000 firefighters and an expense of over $120 million, Mother Nature prevailed. The firefighters managed to save many buildings, including the historical and unique Old Faithful Inn, but it took the rain and snow of September to bring the fires to a standstill. Several critics in Congress and elsewhere blamed the National Park Service's "let burn" policy for the fires; however, given the fire conditions of 1988, such accusations were akin to blaming South Carolina's "let blow" policy for Hurricane Hugo in 1989.

The fires of 1988 burned in a mosaic, or spotted, fashion. At first it was thought that over half the park had burned; however, satellite photographs later revealed that only 36 percent had, and just 15 percent of that consisted of canopy burns — where fire consumed the treetops.

In the fire's aftermath members of the Wyoming delegation stood on the floor of Congress to proclaim that "Yellowstone's soils had been sterilized by the fires." At first the burn areas did look bleak, but as of this writing in 1991, it is now apparent that practically none of the soil was sterilized. The forest is revegetating nicely with tree seedlings and an abundance and variety of plants. Wildflowers such as fireweed and lupine provide spectacular displays and offer a beautiful contrast to blackened tree snags.

A healthy forest consists of trees of various ages. Forest fires are basically nature's way of providing this diversity. The fires of 1988 were actually a tremendous blessing to the greater Yellowstone ecosystem.

Assuming that we are able to take the long view to understand the benefits of fire to the ecosystem, what practical applications have the fires had on backcountry travelers? Very few, actually. Most trails have been remarked and rehabilitated and burned footbridges replaced. As the burned areas continue to revegetate there are usually enough grassy spots to find one to sit on during rest stops.

On hot days you may find shade lacking in a burned area. In other words, some forest hikes have become open-area hikes. Of benefit to hikers are the many views of mountain ranges and plateaus that had previously been blocked by dense forest foliage.

The most likely danger is falling snags. Based on previous burns in Yellowstone, about 35 percent of the snags will fall within 10 years of the burn, and 70 percent within 15 years.

Some have said that Yellowstone has experienced a rebirth. Actually, she never died. Nature has produced fires in the Yellowstone country as long as there have been trees there. As of this writing Yellowstone's natural burn policy has been suspended pending a review. If science prevails, rather than politics, the natural burn policy will be reestablished.

Trees in Black Sand Basin *(Photo by Tom Caples)*

TRAIL DESCRIPTIONS
BY REGION

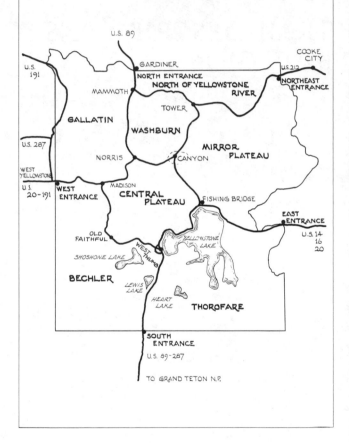

YELLOWSTONE'S WILDERNESS REGIONS

U.S. 89

COOKE CITY

GARDINER

U.S. 191

U.S. 212

NORTH ENTRANCE

NORTHEAST ENTRANCE

MAMMOTH

NORTH OF YELLOWSTONE RIVER

TOWER

GALLATIN

WASHBURN

U.S. 287

MIRROR PLATEAU

NORRIS

CANYON

WEST YELLOWSTONE

U.S. 20-191

WEST ENTRANCE

MADISON

CENTRAL PLATEAU

FISHING BRIDGE

EAST ENTRANCE

U.S. 14 16 20

OLD FAITHFUL

WEST THUMB

YELLOWSTONE LAKE

SHOSHONE LAKE

BECHLER

LEWIS LAKE

HEART LAKE

THOROFARE

SOUTH ENTRANCE

U.S. 89-287

TO GRAND TETON N.P.

MAP LEGEND

RANGER STATION	✪
LAKE	⬭
RIVER OR CREEK	〰
PARK BOUNDARY	——
PAVED ROAD	▬▬
ONE WAY ROAD	—→ —→ —→
TRAIL	– – – – – –
SPRING	♀
WATERFALL	〜┿
CONTINENTAL DIVIDE	•••••••••••••••••
MOUNTAIN SUMMIT	• 10,334
PATROL CABIN	■
PASS	⟝⟞

This legend is the key for all maps that follow.

Union Falls (260 ft.)

Bechler Region

The Bechler area or Cascade Corner of Yellowstone is truly magnificent. No other region in the park better exemplifies the park's gentle and serene wilderness. In fact, it was one of the few regions in the park to escape the great fire season of 1988 unscathed.

Bechler is appropriately known as "waterfalls country." The volcanic lava flows that formed the Pitchstone Plateau some 70,000 years ago produced a rim of steep-edged ridges. This region is also the wettest in the park, with annual precipitation of up to 80 inches per year. These two ingredients, abundant surface water and abrupt-edged plateaus, combine to produce 21 of the park's 41 waterfalls.

The Pitchstone Plateau acts as a huge sponge, soaking up the substantial precipitation that falls, mainly in the form of snow. Rivulets gush forth out of the plateau to form the major streams of the region—the Bechler and Falls rivers, and the Boundary and Mountain Ash creeks, all tributaries of the Snake River.

During June and early July when the streams are at their maximum flow, the numerous waterfalls here are absolutely spectacular. Unfortunately, travel can be a problem at this time due to high fords. From mid-June through early August, mosquitoes and biting flies are a heavy menace.

Besides the waterfalls, many of which are over 100 feet high, several other attractions draw backpackers to the Bechler's 100 miles or more of trails. Because of the lower altitude and warmer, moister climate, the area contains rich vegetation. The forests include large spruce and fir and tall white-barked aspen. Undergrowth includes raspberry, thimbleberry, buffalo berry, and

BECHLER REGION

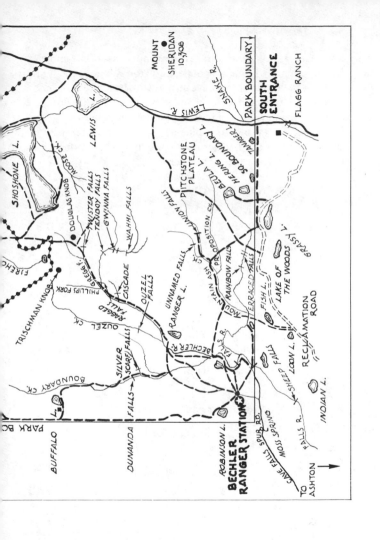

huckleberry, along with various ferns and mosses. The immense Bechler Meadows, with the majestic Teton Range to the south, are some of the most impressive meadows to be found in the park.

Wildlife common here includes black bear (they love the abundance and variety of berries), moose, elk, mule deer, sandhill crane, osprey and great blue heron. Due to increased pressure, fishing in the Bechler country is not what it once was. Catch-and-release rules apply here.

BECHLER REGION TRAILS

Bechler River Trail (to Three River Junction)	14.0 mi.
South Boundary Trail (Calf Creek Meadows to Cave Falls)	7.0 mi.
South Boundary Trail (South Entrance to Grassy Lake)	7.6 mi.
Boundary Creek Trail	15.5 mi.
West Boundary Trail	36.0 mi.
South Pitchstone Plateau Trail	18.5 mi.
North Pitchstone Plateau Trail	2.0 mi.
Grassy Lake to Beula Lake	2.5 mi.
Fish Lake Road to Union Falls	7.8 mi.
Cave Falls to Union Falls	11.5 mi.
Grassy Lake to Union Falls	7.5 mi.
Shoshone Lake Trail	22.5 mi.
DeLacy Creek Trail	12.0 mi.
Shoshone Lake North Shore Trail	7.0 mi.
Dogshead Trail	4.5 mi.

Lewis Channel Trail	7.0 mi.
Upper Geyser Basin–Biscuit Basin Loop	5.0 mi.
Mystic Falls Loop Trail	3.0 mi.
Fairy Falls–Imperial Geyser Trail	3.4 mi.
Summit Lake Trail	7.5 mi.
Fairy Creek Trail	13.0 mi.
Fern Cascades Loop Trail	3.0 mi.
Mallard Lake Trail	3.5 mi.
Sentinel Creek and Meadows Trail	3.0 mi.
Lone Star Geyser Trail	2.5 mi.
Divide Lookout Trail	1.7 mi.
Observation Point Trail	0.8 mi.
Bechler River Trail (Kepler Cascades to Three River Junction)	15.5 mi.

BECHLER AND FALLS RIVER AREA

Bechler River Trail to Three River Junction

Bechler Ranger Station to:

Boundary Creek	3.5 mi.
Bechler River	5.5 mi.
Colonnade Falls	8.7 mi.
Iris Falls	9.0 mi.
Three River Junction	14.0 mi.

From Bechler Ranger Station (where a ranger is stationed throughout the summer months), this trail winds 3.5 mi. through dense forest before reaching Bechler Meadows at Boundary Creek. The dominant tree here, as throughout the park, is lodge-pole pine. Although 80 percent of the park is forested, there are relatively few species of trees; almost all are conifers, and three-quarters of these are lodgepole pine. The lodgepole can grow to an elevation of between 7,000 and 8,500 ft., although the Bechler area is somewhat lower (approx. 6,400 ft.). For this reason the plant growth in this forest is much more dense and varied than in other lodgepole forests at higher elevations throughout the park. You will notice numbers of dead trees and branches scattered on the forest floor. This is because the lodge-pole pine has a very shallow root system and is unable to with-stand strong winds and heavy snows. Do not make camp under a group of dead and swaying lodgepoles on a windy evening.

Approximately 1.5 mi. from the ranger station, to the left of the trail, is a small pond framed by aspens. Immediately be-hind it lies a meadow that is occasionally a feeding spot for moose, especially during early morning and late afternoon.

At 3.5 mi. from the ranger station the trail emerges from the forest into Bechler Meadows and Boundary Creek. Bechler Meadows are home to a variety of birdlife. You can usually see the sandhill crane flying low over the meadows. Many years ago, before the whooping crane reached a tragically low level, sightings were made of that majestic bird. Note that the mead-ows, being located below the plateaus of the area, receive a great deal of spring runoff and as a result are quite swampy early in the summer. During the height of the spring runoff they are prac-tically inaccessible, so it is best to plan your trip for no earlier than July 1. A new trail skirts east of the meadows.

As you cross the bridge over Boundary Creek and start over the meadows, Ouzel Falls appears about 4 mi. to the north, plunging over the edge of the plateau. This giant 230-ft. water-fall remains impressive throughout the summer, although it is most spectacular when much runoff is still present. Two miles across the meadows lies the Bechler River (named for Gustavus R. Bechler, topographer on the Snake River Division of the Hayden Expedition in 1872). You are now 5.5 mi. from the Bechler Ranger Station.

A bridge crosses the Bechler River here. Leaving the river, you walk a short distance through trees before emerging into another meadow, the last to be crossed before entering Bechler Canyon, already clearly visible in the distance.

The scenery is superb as the trail winds up Bechler Canyon. The forest consists of spruce and fir, with an assortment of ferns and mosses, and innumerable huckleberry bushes. Shortly after entering the canyon, a rockslide area extends all the way down into the river. Tip your hat to the trail crew who cleared it. Horse parties must ford the river and go around this area.

In the heart of Bechler Canyon lies Colonnade Falls, a terraced waterfall consisting of two plunges of the Bechler River totaling 102 ft. Upstream 0.3 mi. from Colonnade lies Iris Falls, similar to Colonnade Falls in appearance but dropping only 45 ft. Once past Iris Falls, the trail continues to climb steadily up the canyon, with many small falls and cascades along the way. You old-timers who are grimacing at the thought of the many fords can relax. In 1976, trail crews relocated the trail on the south side of the river, thus eliminating numerous fords. Expect some mud though.

About 1 mi. southwest of Three River Junction Campground, to the right of the trail, is a very steep cascade. Although less than 0.2 mi. from the trail, it is located in dense forest, and it is worth a side trip since it is at least 200 ft. high. Three River Junction lies in a flat, open area surrounded to the north and south by steep canyon walls. The increased use of this area, particularly by large horse parties, has resulted in some deterioration of the fragile beauty found here.

There are numerous hot pools and springs at Three River Junction, causing both hot and cold streams. In some pools, color is produced when water absorbs the red rays from sunlight and reflects blue. Often this combines with yellow-red shades of mineral deposits and algal growths to produce emerald greens. The temperature of the pool itself may help determine the color, as different forms of algae thrive at different temperature levels.

At the foot of the canyon walls on both sides of the campground the scattered rocks and boulders are frequently covered by yellow-bellied marmot (also called groundhogs, woodchucks, or roundchucks).

The actual junction of the three rivers lies about 0.5 mi. upstream from the campground. Here the Phillips, Gregg, and Ferris forks unite to form the Bechler River. As the trail crosses Ferris Fork, Three River Junction lies just off to the left (N); to the right (S) on Ferris Fork is Ragged Falls, a 50 ft. drop. There are numerous hot springs and pools upstream along Ferris Fork. The beauty is special here since many of the pools are surrounded by a lush, verdant growth of grass rather than the customary sinter deposits. Please walk lightly here. One runoff channel leads to a small spouting geyser surrounded by yellow sinter deposits.

South Boundary Trail
(Calf Creek Meadows to Cave Falls)

Calf Creek Meadows on Reclamation Road to:

Falls River	2.6 mi.
Fish Lake Trail Junction	3.2 mi.
Winegar Lake	4.2 mi.
Cave Falls Road	7.0 mi.

If you are looking for a less frequented route, the South Boundary Trail definitely qualifies. For scenic value this section is the best choice. The trail begins from Calf Creek Meadows (about 4 mi. west of Grassy Lake) along Reclamation Road, a very rough and primitive dirt road. After descending Calf Creek through a densely forested arroyo, the trail enters a beautiful meadow along the Falls River. An old wooden bridge was still in place in 1990, allowing you to traverse the marshy area. With all of the willow brush here, you may shake hands with a moose before you see him! From the west end of the meadow there are nice views of Pitchstone Plateau to the north. Shortly after leaving the meadow you will come to Fish Lake Trail, which provides access to Union Falls (see p. 97). Be careful not to follow this trail across the Falls River. The trail you want heads into an area so thickly vegetated it is quite obvious that more moose than people walk here. The trail passes just north of Junco and Winegar lakes. A sidetrip to each will probably produce some sightings of bird activity. The required ford of the Falls River is wide and deep, so plan to take this trip late in the summer.

South Boundary Trail
(South Entrance to Grassy Lake)

South Entrance to:

Tanager Lake	1.0 mi.
Polecat Creek	3.0 mi.
South Boundary Lake	5.0 mi.
Beula Lake Trail Junction	7.0 mi.
Grassy Lake	7.6 mi.

Most sections of this route are strictly for boundary patrol, as the linear characteristic of the trail suggests. Nevertheless, South Boundary Lake and Tanager Lake provide quiet, peaceful settings to observe birds, and occasionally deer and moose.

Boundary Creek Trail
(Bechler Ranger Station to Buffalo Lake)

Bechler Ranger Station to:

Bechler Meadows	3.0 mi.
Boundary Creek	5.0 mi.
Silver Scarf Falls	7.5 mi.
Dunanda Falls	9.0 mi.
Buffalo Lake	15.5 mi.

This trail takes you through interesting wilderness scenery past one of the park's most beautiful waterfalls. The first 1.4 mi. coincide with the Bechler Ranger Station–Three River Junction Trail, but at that point our trail forks off to the left. Just beyond this fork, to the left, is a small pond covered with lilypads. It is a watering spot often visited by deer early in the morning. The trail crosses the heart of Bechler Meadows, affording fine views of the surrounding country and of the plateaus to the north and east.

After crossing Bechler Meadows, the trail enters a forest (chiefly lodgepole) but continues along many open areas and meadows providing fine views and opportunities for wildlife sightings. Blue and ruffed grouse are sometimes observed here.

During the last 4 mi. to Dunanda Falls, there is only one cold stream from which to drink (at the 6.5-mi. mark; all other streams are warm, due to nearby thermal activity). Another mile brings you to Silver Scarf Falls, not a sheer drop, but a sloping cascade of some 250 ft. Continuing across a hill the trail passes above the brink of Dunanda Falls on the east and affords a breathtaking view. However, the most spectacular and satisfying view of the 150-ft. drop of Boundary Creek is from the foot of the falls. A steep grassy slope from the trail permits easy access to this area. Along the stream below the falls are hot pools that contain algae.

There are not very many travelers beyond Dunanda Falls, although the wilderness scenery to Buffalo Lake is very beautiful. The trail continues 2.5 mi. before crossing Boundary Creek and emerging into a meadow with a steep canyon wall rising to the east. The wall is actually the edge of Madison Plateau, and its continuation can be seen to the north for quite some distance. From Buffalo Lake, meadows extend away from the northern and southwestern shores (favorite feeding spots for elk, moose, and deer, especially in early morning and late afternoon). There are no fish in Buffalo Lake, but its shores are home to numerous species of birds. Beyond Buffalo Lake the trail continues for 1 mi. before it joins the West Boundary Trail, which parallels the park boundary.

West Boundary Trail
(Bechler Ranger Station to West Yellowstone)   (36.0 mi.)

The West Boundary Trail from Bechler Station to West Yellowstone is not recommended because the land is dry and the scenery monotonous. This trail is used by park rangers for border patrols, primarily to ensure that hunters respect the park boundary.

The first 2 mi. take you to Robinson Lake, which is surrounded by meadows. Birdlife is abundant here, and chances are good for spotting moose and elk. Rock Creek, which rises from Robinson Lake, contains only small populations of pan-sized cutthroat and rainbow trout. Beyond this lake, the attractions on the West Boundary Trail become few and far between. In numerous places the U.S. Forest Service has clearcut right to the park boundary. At South Riverside patrol cabin the trail passes along a pretty meadow from which several springs flow on the north end. Young lodgepoles are encroaching on the meadow. North of the meadow the trail re-enters the familiar lodgepole forest, which burned here in 1988. Notice the numerous chunks of obsidian here, common on the volcanic Madison Plateau.

South Pitchstone Plateau Trail

Trailhead on South Entrance Road to:

Phantom Fumarole	4.5 mi.
Springs (cold)	5.5 mi.
BM 8715	8.0 mi.
Proposition Creek	15.0 mi.
Falls River	17.0 mi.
Grassy Lake	18.5 mi.

For those interested in Yellowstone's geology, the trip across the Pitchstone Plateau is highly recommended. The trailhead is on the west side of South Entrance Road, 8 mi. from the entrance station and 2 mi. south of Lewis Falls.

The trail climbs 450 ft. in the first mile, then through lodgepole forest. At 4.5 mi. it passes Phantom Fumarole. (A fumarole differs from a hot spring only in that there is no surface water.)

Yellowstone's geological history is most apparent from high on the Pitchstone Plateau. You are actually standing on a huge lava flow that oozed across the land almost like a glacier, and then quickly cooled to freeze the flow lines and swirls. Today, these lava flow lines are accentuated by many stands of timber, which have grown up right along their edges. (Seen from the air, much of the Pitchstone Plateau looks like a great glacier.) In exploring the area you will find some rhyolite lava flows that appear to be very recent. The Pitchstone Plateau is mostly an open, grassy region dotted with rhyolite and obsidian and wonderful views of the Tetons to the south.

From the high point at 8,715 ft. the trail begins its descent, and at 8,400 ft. (the 11-mi. mark) re-enters the forest. The descent continues to the Falls River at 6,920 ft. Just before crossing the river, the trail intersects the Grassy Lake–Union Falls Trail. At the Falls River you will have come 17 mi. Another mile brings you to Reclamation Road. Note: In late summer, water is scarce beyond Phantom Springs.

North Pitchstone Plateau Trail (2.0 mi.)

This trail begins from the Bechler River Trail in a small meadow about 1 mi. south of Douglas Knob. The trail crosses Gregg Fork then climbs 650 ft. as it winds through the forest to reach the open plateau above treeline. Here the maintained trail ends.

For a number of years several experienced backpackers have attempted some very difficult cross-country loops of the Bechler country. With this relatively new trail, those who are *experienced in traveling cross-country with map and compass and who have obtained permission from Bechler rangers* can make such a loop. Your topo map shows the highest point on the plateau at "VABM 8977" where a USGS benchmark is located. It is possible to shoot for this high point then proceed south until you hit the South Pitchstone Plateau Trail. Note that the Pitchstone Plateau receives heavy snow, so this trip is best beginning in late July. Also, it is advisable to travel from the north trail to the south trail, rather than vice versa, to avoid missing the trail connection.

Grassy Lake to Beula Lake (2.5 mi.)

The trailhead is located at the east end of Grassy Lake on Reclamation Road south of the park. (For directions on how to locate this road, see *Grassy Lake to Union Falls.*) The first 0.5 mi. requires a 400-ft. climb, ending in a superb view of the full length of Grassy Lake.

The remaining 2 mi. pass through dense lodgepole. The lake itself is completely surrounded by forest. Beula Lake, at 7,377 ft., is the ultimate lake source for the Falls River. It contains a population of cutthroat trout.

TRAILS TO UNION FALLS

At a height of 260 ft., Union Falls is one of the park's most impressive waterfalls, especially when viewed in early to mid-July. Most people visit in late summer after the trails have dried out, the bugs have diminished, and the streams have subsided (remember, the waterfalls subside too). As a result, the area receives heavy use at this time. Unfortunately, the National Park Service has established a multiparty campsite near Union Falls, so don't expect to find much solitude if you camp here in late summer. Also, with Boy Scout Camp Loll located nearby off Reclamation Road, the Union Falls area has become a popular spot among scout troops. A Bechler ranger recently counted 165 boy scouts at one time in the area. The increased use of this area led to the establishment of the Union Falls Ranger Station on the trail 1.5 mi. west of the falls.

There are three routes to Union Falls, all of which are actually in the Bechler and Falls River area. Two begin from Reclamation Road at Fish Lake or Grassy Lake and the third begins from Cave Falls. Descriptions of these three trails follow.

Fish Lake Road to Union Falls

Fish Lake Road to:

Fish Lake	0.6 mi.
Falls River	1.5 mi.
Mountain Ash Creek	3.0 mi.
Union Falls	7.8 mi.

This trail is the easiest route to Union Falls in terms of distance and level terrain, but getting to the trailhead may be a tough part of the trip. The 1.6-mi.-long Fish Lake "road" begins from Reclamation Road at a point about 7.5 mi. west of the Grassy Lake dam. Fish Lake Road is not maintained and is *very* rough with *deep* potholes. Your vehicle should have high clearance; still the road may not be passable after a heavy rain.

If you make it to the trailhead in one piece, the trail will prove very rewarding. Soon after entering the Winegar Hole Wilderness Area, you will approach Fish Lake in a beautiful setting with meadows, aspen, and steep volcanic bluffs as a backdrop. Nearby Loon Lake is appropriately named as loons are often seen (or heard) in this region. Just beyond Fish Lake the trail enters Yellowstone National Park and then turns west toward the Falls River ford. Just before crossing the river notice the trail junction with the South Boundary Trail leading west to Cave Falls. The overgrown vegetation here suggests that this is perhaps the least-traveled trail in Yellowstone. The Falls River ford is knee to mid-thigh deep after midsummer.

Now the trail enters an interesting mixed forest with beautiful aspen dotting the landscape. Look for a giant aspen on the west side of the trail containing bear-claw marks all the way up into the tree where a black bear must have climbed. With all the berry bushes this trail is prime black bear country. Look for dead logs that bears have torn apart in search of insects.

At the 3-mi. mark, Mountain Ash Creek is reached. This ford is deeper and the water is much colder than the Falls River ford, so be careful. In the meadow just beyond this ford, Mountain Ash Creek Trail connects. From here it is 4.7 mi. to Union Falls (see *Cave Falls to Union Falls*).

Cave Falls to Union Falls

Cave Falls to:

Bechler River	0.25 mi.
Bechler Falls	1.0 mi.
Rocky Ford	3.2 mi.
Mountain Ash Creek	8.2 mi.
Grassy Lake Trail Junction	9.5 mi.
Union Falls	11.5 mi.

Cave Falls, the starting point for this hike, is located at the end of the spur road that extends into the Bechler country. To get there you have to take a 56-mi. drive south from West Yellowstone on U.S. 191 to Ashton, Idaho. From Ashton, you drive east on Cave Falls Road for 25 mi. There is a picnic area and campground near Cave Falls. The name is derived from a large cave at the base of the falls on the west side of the Falls River.

The impressiveness of Cave Falls is not in its height, but in its width and volume. The river is quite wide and there are some additionally impressive falls and cascades both upstream and downstream.

After 0.25 mi. you reach the point where the Bechler River empties into the Falls River. Here the Falls River bends to the east and disappears from view. The trail continues above the Bechler River for several miles through a dense spruce and fir forest. The vegetation is quite rich, with various ferns and mosses and many berry bushes—primarily huckleberry. Keep a close watch along the river banks for moose and deer feeding. At 1.0 mi. you reach Bechler Falls, a 20-ft. drop. Within the next mile you will notice two other trails. Both lead westward to Bechler Ranger Station a short distance away. If you are leaving a vehicle behind, plan to begin your trip from the ranger station rather than Cave Falls for security.

At 3.2 mi. you come to Rocky Ford. Here the trail fords the Bechler River and continues eastward to Union Falls. As the name indicates, there is a good solid rockbed on which to ford the river, and the water is not very deep during mid- to late summer. Nevertheless, the going can get quite slippery here, so be very careful. After fording the Bechler River, you will actually be on the old Marysville Road, from Marysville, Idaho, to Jackson Hole, built in the 1880s by the Mormons. Wagon marks are still visible in places, although trees have grown up between the tracks.

From Rocky Ford to Union Falls the trail continues to wind in and out of forest and meadow. The meadows provide beautiful views, especially of the plateau to the north, and wonderful opportunities for sighting wildlife. You may well be able to spot some deer along this stretch, and possibly moose. Five miles from Rocky Ford (8.2 from Cave Falls), the trail crosses Mountain Ash Creek, which it continues to follow most of the rest of the way. After crossing the creek and traveling 1.3 mi., you will come to a trail junction. Here the old Marysville Road forks to the right, and a trail follows it most of the way to Grassy Lake, 5.2 mi. away (see *Grassy Lake to Union Falls*). Walking 0.5 mi. beyond the trail junction, you will see a fairly large (unnamed) stream flowing into Mountain Ash Creek from the north. If you stand at the junction of these streams facing upstream, you will see Mountain Ash creek on your right and the unnamed stream on your left. There is a large pool where these streams join.

You will be able to hear Union Falls long before you see it. The last 50 yds. of the trail climb to an overlook that provides a spectacular view of these magnificent falls. Two streams unite at the brink to form the 260-ft. drop, hence the name "Union."

Grassy Lake to Union Falls

Grassy Lake to:

Proposition Creek	5.0 mi.
Mountain Ash Creek	5.75 mi.
Union Falls	7.5 mi.

This route to Union Falls is shortest but least scenic.

Grassy Lake lies just south of the park boundary line. It is reached via Reclamation Road, which travels some 45 mi. from just below the park boundary at the South Entrance westward to Marysville, Idaho. Reclamation Road begins a few miles south of the South Entrance at the turnoff from U.S. 89–287 to Flagg Ranch. Grassy Lake is a 10-mi. drive from there. You should be warned, however, that this is a very primitive dirt road, which may be difficult to travel in wet weather.

The trailhead to Union Falls is at the picnic area on the east side of the Grassy Lake dam. The trail runs for the first mile through a marshy area full of willows. This is ideal moose country, and deer are also frequently sighted. After 0.7 mi. you reach the Falls River, where it is necessary to ford the ice-cold water. Though shallow, the current is rather swift and the rocks are slippery, so go carefully. Another 0.5 mi. brings you to the junction of the Pitchstone Plateau Trail.

After swinging away from the Falls River, the trail climbs steadily through a typical lodgepole pine forest for 2 mi. before dropping sharply to Proposition Creek. Here you can have a refreshing drink and rest for a while as you ponder the climb required when hiking out. However, the hill will not seem so steep when you consider that in the 1880s the Mormons hauled their wagons over this very terrain. (The wagon tracks are still visible in some places.) For the most part, the trail follows the old Mormon road from Grassy Lake to the junction of the Cave Falls–Union Falls Trail, and from there to Rocky Ford on the Bechler River.

From Proposition Creek it is 0.75 mi. to Mountain Ash Creek, where you join the Cave Falls–Union Falls Trail. And from there it is only about 2 mi. to Union Falls.

SHOSHONE LAKE AREA

Note: For information on canoeing Shoshone Lake see page 238.

Shoshone Lake Trail
(Kepler Cascades to Dogshead Trailhead)

Kepler Cascades to:

Lone Star Geyser	2.5 mi.
Grants Pass	6.0 mi.
Junction with Bechler Trail	6.4 mi.

Junction with North Shore Trail	8.3 mi.
Shoshone Geyser Basin	8.5 mi.
Moose Creek	15.5 mi.
Lewis Channel Outlet	18.0 mi.
Dogshead Trailhead	22.5 mi.

From Kepler Cascades the trail follows the Firehole River to Lone Star Geyser, then climbs over Grants Pass. (For information on the first 6 mi. of this trip, see the descriptions for Lone Star Geyser trail on page 113 and the Kepler Cascades to Three River Junction Trail on page 115.) About 0.5 mi. beyond Grants Pass you will find an ice-cold spring bubbling up on the left side of the trail. The trail then crosses a nice open meadow and follows Shoshone Creek down to the geyser basin. Slides have caused some sections of this trail to be rerouted high above the creek.

Shoshone Geyser Basin is full of thermal activity, and is a fascinating place to explore. However, the area is so very fragile. Please walk lightly here. Also, there are no boardwalks, so be careful. A backcountry traveler tragically died here in 1988 after falling into a hot spring.

According to Scott Bryan, author of *The Geysers of Yellowstone,* which is *the* source of information on the park's geyser basins, Shoshone Geyser Basin ranks as one of the world's most important basins with over 70 geysers. One of the most prominent is Minute Man Geyser, which frequently erupts from a large 12 ft. by 5 ft. cone. When active, Union Geyser is one of the park's largest, noisily erupting to a height of over 100 feet. Unfortunately, Union has been dormant since the mid-1970s.

The west shore of Shoshone Lake is a wonderful place to relax, soak in the solitude, and observe waterfowl along the meadows and lakeshore. From here the trail climbs 400 feet over a forested ridge before dropping into scenic Moose Creek Meadows. Notice the fine view to the southwest of the Pitch-stone Plateau. As you near the outlet area notice how the 1988 fires spotted about, sparing clumps of trees and burning others. The crossing of the Lewis River Channel can be a problem in June (along with sections of deep snow), but by midsummer it is about knee deep. From this point you have about 5 mi. of forested trail to the Dogshead trailhead on South Entrance Road.

DeLacy Creek Trail
(DeLacy Trailhead to Lewis River)

DeLacy Trailhead to:

Shoshone Lake	3.5 mi.
Lewis River at Outlet	7.5 mi.
Dogshead Trailhead	12.0 mi.

The DeLacy Creek Trail begins from Old Faithful–West Thumb Road and is located about 8 mi. east from Old Faithful. The trail provides the shortest access to Shoshone Lake, and is also quite scenic through the meadows where the creek enters the lake. Look for moose here along with various shorebirds. Beyond DeLacy Creek the trail enters the forested edge of the long northeast shore of Shoshone Lake. There are some nice views out on the lake and some occasional fine gravel beaches, where centuries of strong southwest winds have pulverized the rocky shore. As you near the Lewis Channel you will enter a burned area from 1988. At the outlet is a ranger station. From here you are 4.5 mi. from the Dogshead trailhead on South Entrance Road.

Shoshone Lake North Shore Trail (7.0 mi.)

This relatively new forested trail connects DeLacy Creek Trail with the Shoshone Geyser Basin, thus permitting a loop hike. There are some nice views of the lake along the trail, which is relatively level. About 3.5 mi. east from the geyser basin you may spot a spur trail leading down to the lake. Here you will find a cabin where the Shoshone Lake backcountry ranger is often stationed during patrols on the lake.

Dogshead Trail to Shoshone Lake (4.5 mi.)

This trail provides the closest access to Shoshone Lake from South Entrance Road. Most of the route traverses a lodgepole forest that burned during 1988.

Lewis Channel Trail to Shoshone Lake (7.0 mi.)

Although longer, this is the more scenic approach to Shoshone Lake from South Entrance Road. The trail stays right along the shore of Lewis Lake and the edge of Lewis Channel, so you are exposed to much of the same fine scenery paddlers enjoy on their canoe trips into Shoshone Lake. Note that the burn of 1988 here was mixed; the fires burned with varying intensity, consuming the canopies of some trees, scorching others, and only burning the forest floor in other spots. The Lewis Channel and Dogshead trails provide one of the few loop hikes available in the park where you end up at the same spot you began.

OLD FAITHFUL AREA

Upper Geyser Basin–Biscuit Basin Loop (5.0 mi. roundtrip)

Yellowstone holds about 70 percent of the world's geysers and most are concentrated in the Upper Geyser Basin. Be sure to obtain a detailed map and guide to the basin (nominal charge) from the Old Faithful Visitor Center, where you can also find prediction times posted for all the major predictable geysers in the area. Old Faithful is still the star of the show since it is a large geyser that erupts frequently and can easily be predicted.

The best place to view Old Faithful is from Plume Geyser on Geyser Hill, where you leave behind the congestion and noise. From the visitor center follow the walkway around the east side of Old Faithful Geyser to the footbridge that crosses the Firehole River. From the bridge this sparkling river, which mountain man Jim Bridger claimed "runs downhill so fast it gets hot on the bottom," looks like a normal mountain river. However, each day several hundred thousand gallons of hot water and tons of mineral matter flow into it, transforming the Firehole into one of the world's most unique waterways. From the bridge continue past the Observation Point trailhead (see page 115) to a fork in the trail. Take the left fork and proceed to Plume Geyser, which erupts about every 30 to 45 minutes. Have a seat here on the boardwalk and enjoy the next eruption of Old Faithful, which from here is spectacular. If you time the duration of the eruption you can easily predict the next one to within 10 minutes (usually, of course). A two-minute duration will result in a 54- to 58-minute interval; a four-minute duration will cause an interval of 85 to 92 minutes.

Proceed to Lion Geyser and turn left toward Grand Geyser, which is the world's largest active geyser. If Grand is predictable during your visit try to arrange the time to see this glorious fountain geyser. From Grand the boardwalk passes Beauty Pool, crosses the river again, passes Giant Geyser (usually inactive), and joins the paved trail at Grotto Geyser, with its interesting geyserite formations. Turn right and proceed past Riverside Geyser, which erupts about every seven hours, to the colorful Morning Glory Pool.

Few people continue past this pool along the dirt trail. The solitude will be an added delight as you pass by Artemesia Geyser, with its large pool and extensive terraces, and Gem Pool, a very large, deep blue spring. Beyond Gem Pool the trail turns to the left toward Biscuit Basin. Changes in the runoff from nearby Mirror Pool resulted in a new footbridge being built here in 1989. Cross the road and enter the Biscuit Basin boardwalk. After passing Sapphire Pool, which erupted to 150 feet after the 1959 earthquake (blasting away the biscuitlike mineral formations from which the basin got its name), take the right loop in the boardwalk. Avoco Spring and Shell Geyser are other interesting features to view.

Refer to your Upper Geyser Basin map and guide and take the trail back along the southwest side of Biscuit Basin. Biscuit Basin is the "top" of your loop trip unless you plan to extend your hike by continuing on to Mystic Falls (see p. 107 for information on this trail). The trail back leads through a meadow to a footbridge across the Firehole River. The trail crosses the road and enters a lodgepole pine forest that burned in 1988. Notice the barren "thermal burns" where the ground is too warm for vegetation to exist; the bison and elk droppings you see in them date back to winter.

You will pass through a meadow that contains Cyclops Spring, then pass through a nonburned section of woods to the Daisy Geyser area. Daisy is usually quite active, erupting about every 85 to 115 minutes. (Of course, geysers are constantly changing, so be sure to check on current geyser activity at the visitor center.) From Daisy the trail loops around to Punch Bowl Spring. You may want to walk 0.2 mi. past Punch Bowl to see Black Sand Pool, a large and deep blue spring so named for the black obsidian sand around the area. From Punch Bowl the trail leads back down to the paved trail near Grotto and leads back the last mile to the visitor center. You will pass the huge cone of Castle Geyser, which is one of the park's oldest geysers. The buildup of geyserite (siliceous sinter) occurs at the slow rate of only about one inch per 100 years, thus Castle probably started forming about 10,000 to 12,000 years ago following the last glacial period in the area. Castle erupts about every 11 hours and exhibits a very noisy and powerful water and steam phase lasting 45 to 50 minutes. On the way in you may want to walk inside the lobby of the magnificent Old Faithful Inn, one of the world's largest and most unique log buildings, built in the winter of 1903–1904.

Mystic Falls Loop Trail   (3.2 mi.)

The trail starts from Biscuit Basin, 2 mi. north of Old Faithful. A footbridge crosses the Firehole River, beyond which board-walks traverse the basin. There are numerous interesting thermal features here, including Sapphire Pool, which erupted to over 150 feet following the big earthquake of August 1959. The eruptions blew away the biscuitlike formations from which the basin got its name. On the west side of the basin the trail enters the forest and follows the Little Firehole River 0.7 mi. all the way to the falls. The Summit Lake Trail junction is passed at the 0.6-mi. mark. The wildflowers along the way, especially Indian paintbrush, are superb. The switchbacks pass several cascades to a nice overlook of the 70-ft. drop at the top of the falls. From this point continue up the trail (rather than turning around) to the junction of the Little Firehole Meadows Trail. Then turn right and proceed to a scenic overlook situated on the edge of the Madison Plateau. From this viewpoint about 500 ft. above Biscuit Basin it is possible to see eruptions of most of the major geysers in the Upper Basin, including Old Faithful. From here the trail follows a series of switchbacks to descend from the plateau to rejoin the trail you came in on at a point 0.3 mi. from the basin.

Fairy Falls–Imperial Geyser Trail (3.4 mi.)

Fairy Falls and Imperial Geyser can be reached by starting either 1 mi. south of the Firehole River bridge on Fountain Flat Drive or at the old steel bridge 1 mi. south of the Midway Geyser Basin parking lot on Old Faithful–Madison Road. This entire area burned extensively during 1988, but the revegetation on the forest floor is quite colorful and interesting. From the old steel bridge the trail passes below the edge of Madison Plateau with Midway Geyser Basin in view to the north. Numerous thermal features are found along the first mile. Look for Canada geese in the meadow just off to your right. Prior to the fires of 1988 about the only way to obtain a good view of Grand Prismatic Spring (the park's largest) was to rent a helicopter. Now you can scramble up the burned ridge above you to gain a breathtaking panorama of this huge and colorful spring. After 1 mi. the trail turns to the west and enters the burned forest. Fairy Falls at a height of 200 ft. is a splendid and graceful waterfall. Views of the falls are much easier to obtain now that the spruce and fir forest canopy has burned away. The pool at the base of the falls was reduced recently when the logjam dam broke loose.

After leaving the falls the trail reaches a junction in a meadow. The right fork leads through Fairy Creek Meadows back to Fountain Flat Drive near Goose Lake (this trail is the other alternative for reaching this area). The left fork leads to Imperial Geyser. The steam you see rising from across the meadow is from Spray Geyser, which erupts continuously. Although the trail does not lead there you can either walk over to it directly or follow the runoff channel from Imperial Geyser. Unfortunately, as of this writing, Imperial Geyser has become dormant, but the pool is still quite colorful. If you scramble up the ridge behind Imperial Geyser you will find a lilypad pond and some fine views of North and South Twin Buttes, Midway Geyser Basin, and Fairy Falls.

Summit Lake Trail
(Biscuit Basin to Summit Lake)   (7.5 mi.)

Start from Biscuit Basin, located on Madison–Old Faithful Road, 2 mi. from Old Faithful. There is a parking lot provided here, and a footbridge across the Firehole River leads to the trailhead, located on the far side of Biscuit Basin. The Summit Lake Trail follows the Mystic Falls Trail for a short distance, then forks off to the left. The next 0.3 mi. takes you through a low-lying meadow and across the Little Firehole River. The trail then begins a long, steady climb of 7 mi. to Summit Lake. From this point, the trip is not recommended. The trail climbs about 1,300 ft. through dry and uninteresting lodgepole forest to Summit Lake. There is no drinking water along the way.

Summit Lake is appropriately named, as it is located just to the east of the Continental Divide at 8,553 ft. For the most part, the trail follows an intermittent stream that serves as the outlet to Summit Lake, but by mid-July it is completely dry except for occasional stagnant pools.

After you have climbed to about 8,200 ft. and are halfway to the lake, you will notice obsidian along the trail. Obsidian is a natual black volcanic glass, which was formed by a volcanic flow of rhyolite that cooled so quickly it did not crystallize. The glass substance contains very sharp edges, which can cut you if not handled carefully. Indians made knives, arrowheads, and spears out of it.

Summit Lake is quite large, surrounded mostly by lodgepole forest, with a small meadow on the south end. From here it is 8.4 mi. to the western park boundary and the West Boundary Trail used for border patrol. (This hike runs through dry and uninteresting country across Madison Plateau and is not recommended.) For those who complete the strenuous trip to Summit Lake, it is worthwhile to continue about 1 mi. past the lake to a second, shallower lake on the south side of the trail that contains numerous hot springs. Just beyond this, on the north side of the trail, is another lake. The water temperature here varies from cool to warm in different areas.

Fairy Creek Trail
(Biscuit Basin to Fairy Creek)   **(13.0 mi.)**

The trailhead is located at Biscuit Basin, 2 mi. north from Old Faithful on Grand Loop Road. There is a loop parking lot on the west side of the road here. A footbridge crosses the Firehole River, beyond which boardwalks traverse the Biscuit Basin area. One boardwalk leads by Sapphire Pool (a blue-green pool that at one time used to erupt to over 100 ft.) to the actual trailhead on the west side of the basin. From here, trails lead to Mystic Falls and Summit Lake, in addition to Fairy Creek.

Within the first 1.5 mi. the trail climbs to a wonderful overlook situated at about 8,200 ft., then descends about 350 ft. to the Little Firehole River, and at 5 mi. enters Little Firehole Meadows. This is an ideal grazing spot for wild animals, especially bison and elk. There are brown and rainbow trout here in the Little Firehole River, but this far upstream you may have trouble hooking one of appreciable size.

Three unnamed forks come together in Little Firehole Meadows to form the headwaters of the Little Firehole River. The trail climbs gently out of Little Firehole Meadows and continues through lodgepole pine that burned in 1988 to the headwaters of Fairy Creek at the 8.5-mi. mark. At 9 mi. you will reach the edge of Madison Plateau, from which Fairy Falls plunges only 1 mi. away to the east. Twin Buttes at 7,923 ft. and 7,865 ft. (south and north, respectively) are directly ahead. The trail descends from the plateau and passes below south Twin Butte. The Twin Buttes are actually hills of glacial drift that were cemented by siliceous sinter resulting from preglacial geyser and hot spring action. There are several active fumaroles on both hills. The earthquake of 1959 initiated apparent massive slumping that created several large steaming fissures as much as 15 ft. deep on both hills. Some of these fissures are now active fumaroles. There are several ponds located at the base of Twin Buttes.

Below south Twin Butte the trail passes by Imperial Geyser (see *Fairy Falls–Imperial Geyser Trail*). From here it is 3.1 mi. to the Firehole River bridge.

Fern Cascades Loop Trail (3.0 mi.)

The east leg of the loop trail can be reached by following the Lone Star Geyser Trail from Old Faithful Ranger Station to the Fern Cascades Trail junction, or you can take the western loop, beginning from the Old Faithful government trailer court. From the ranger station you walk 0.7 mi. before a trail forks off to the right leading to Fern Cascades 1.5 mi. away. If you take the entire loop trail, the distance is about 3 mi. This is a nice ski trail, but I don't highly recommend it. The 1988 fire completely burned over this trail.

Mallard Lake Trail
(Old Faithful to Mallard Lake) (3.5 mi.)

The trailhead for this hike is located on the first Old Faithful Lodge cabin road coming in from the right as you drive into the lodge area. The trail actually begins 330 yds. down the cabin road.

This trip takes you over rolling hills through a lodgepole pine forest to Mallard Lake. During the months of June, July, and early August it provides an excellent area for viewing wildflowers. At 0.2 mi. the Firehole River is crossed on a footbridge. At 0.4 mi. you will notice a small thermal area that contains a mudpot to the left of the trail, a large hot pool, and other, smaller features. Because of the thin crust here, be careful in approaching the area. The largest concentration of Douglas fir along the way is noted at the 1-mi. mark.

At the 2.2-mi. mark the trail enters a narrow canyon high on the left side, but gradually drops to meet the canyon floor. The scenery becomes spectacular through this gorge, especially when (at 2.6 mi.) you pass through a narrow defile with large boulders scattered on both sides. High up on the left is a cliff face showing twisted ancient lava flows, and from the right, on top of an exposed cliff, it is possible to view distant parts of Upper Geyser Basin. Old Faithful can be seen erupting from here. (This observation point is 0.25 mi. from the trail and can be reached from 100 yds. farther uptrail.)

Mallard Lake does not become visible until you are almost upon it. A steep timbered ridge slopes away from the southeast shore of the lake, providing a good spot from which to take photos. Cutthroat trout once thrived, but now the lake seems to be barren. There is usually a variety of birdlife on the lake's waters. Near the lake is the junction with Mallard Creek Trail, which is mostly used as a ski trail in winter. This trail leads 3.5 mi. through lodgepole pine forest extensively burned in 1988 to Old Faithful–Madison Road. The trail then parallels the road for about 2 mi. before entering the Upper Geyser Basin near Morning Glory Pool. During summer most hikers take the 7-mi. roundtrip hike to Mallard Lake. However, during winter the Mallard Lake–Mallard Creek Loop provides a fine 11.5-mi. ski trip.

Sentinel Creek and Meadows Trail (3.0 mi.)

The trail begins at the Firehole River bridge on Fountain Flats Drive, 1.3 mi. from the main highway. Sentinel Meadows is a wild and beautiful little valley, measuring about 2 mi. by 0.25 mi. at its widest point. The meadows generally are too wet for travel until late July. The large sinter mound in the center of the meadows is Steep Cone; a small but active hot spring perched on top continues to build the cone. Notice the island of trees just south of Steep Cone; a closer look reveals that this area is an "island" of sinter where thermal water once flowed. The hardy lodgepole pine and succulent, desertlike plants have taken hold now on this dry surface. The trail continues west to some beautiful hot springs called the Queens Laundry. The old log-frame structure nearby was constructed in 1880 to be a bath house, but was never actually finished. The decaying log structure is considered to be the oldest in the park. Considering the scalding water in the Queens Laundry springs, it is a mystery as to just where tourists would have bathed. Thermal bathing is illegal today. The trail ends at the base of a 200-ft. rocky ridge on the north side of the meadows. A spectacular view of the entire meadows may be enjoyed from the top.

Lone Star Geyser Trail (2.5 mi.)

The trailhead for this trip is located near Kepler Cascades, a 2.7-mi. drive southeast from Old Faithful overpass (toward West Thumb) on Grand Loop Road. (There is a small parking lot where you may leave your car.) The Kepler Cascades are a series of small falls on the Firehole River totaling about 125 ft. amid canyon walls. A boardwalk leading to an overlook provides a fine view. The trail to Lone Star Geyser and points beyond begins about 100 yds. up the road from Kepler Cascades. You can also reach Lone Star Geyser by beginning from Old Faithful Ranger Station, but it is approximately 1 mi. longer, and the trail closely parallels Grand Loop Road part of the way. For the first 2.5 mi. from Kepler Cascades to Lone Star Geyser you will actually be following the old Lone Star Geyser spur road, which was restricted in 1972 to a hiking and bicycle trail.

As you follow the old spur road along the river, you will pass by the mouth of Spring Creek at 1.6 mi. Watch for wild-flowers here, especially harebell and Indian paintbrush. At the 2-mi. mark you will pass by a meadow through which the Fire-hole winds. This is a good spot to look for elk, particularly in early morning and late afternoon. Near this spot, to the right of the trail up on a hill, is a clearing containing numerous small trees where a fire burned in the late 1960s. The area provides a nice preview of what much of Yellowstone's forest will look like around 2010, as the result of the fires of 1988.

Lone Star Geyser is a geyserite cone 10 to 12 ft. high. Eruptions occur every three hours or so, lasting for about 25 minutes. Minor eruptions begin one hour before the main eruption.

It is important to keep on the established trail in this area, as there are a number of potentially dangerous thermal features. If Lone Star Geyser is the primary objective of your hike, you may want to make a loop trip back, following the 3.8-mi.-long trail to Old Faithful Ranger Station. Incidentally, Lone Star erupts to 30 or 40 ft.

Divide Lookout Trail (1.7 mi.)

The trail begins at the parking area on the south side of Grand Loop Road, 6.7 mi. southeast of the Old Faithful overpass. It crosses Spring Creek and enters a dense forest, with lodgepole pine predominating and alpine fir common. At 0.3 mi. you will pass to the right of an area containing very rich undergrowth, due to abundant moisture in a small, marshy lakebed. Look for wildflowers here. The trail continues through a mature forest. At 1.3 mi., Shoshone Lake becomes visible on the left, but there are no unobstructed distant views available since the lookout tower was dismantled and removed in 1991. Follow the Upper Geyser Basin trail across the Firehole River (see p. 105) to our trail, which climbs 200 feet to a viewpoint of Old Faithful. From here the trail leads west to Solitary Geyser, which erupts to a height of 6 ft., then rejoins the UGB trail near Lion Geyser.

Bechler River Trail
(Kepler Cascades to Three River Junction)

A complete trip across the Bechler country from Kepler Cascades to Bechler Ranger Station is an excellent way to see the area, but trail connections are something of a problem. For this reason, the trail description begins at Kepler Cascades and ends at Three River Junction. The mileage table does contain distances beyond Three River for those who wish to make the complete trip.

Kepler Cascades to:

Lone Star Geyser	2.5 mi.
Grants Pass	6.0 mi.
Shoshone Lake Trail Junction	6.4 mi.
Littles Fork	11.0 mi.
Three River Junction	15.5 mi.

Colonnade Falls	20.0 mi.
Bechler River Footbridge	23.5 mi.
Bechler Ranger Station	29.0 mi.

Kepler Cascades is 2.7 mi. east from Old Faithful. The first 2.5 mi. follows the Firehole River to Lone Star Geyser (see p. 113).

Continuing south from Lone Star Geyser, the trail passes through dense lodgepole for 0.5 mi. before meeting the bridge crossing the Firehole. The Firehole was named by early trappers who found a burnt-over forested valley, or "hole," through which the water coursed. The warm waters provide excellent dry-fly fishing, weeks ahead of other park streams. The angler will find early hatches of insects all along the Upper Firehole.

After crossing the Firehole, the trail heads into heavy timber, touching on the river only once more at the 4-mi. mark (from Kepler Cascades, 1 mi. from the bridge). There are several more hot springs in this area. Just upstream the river meanders through a large meadow carpeted with harebell and fringed gentian during July.

The trail now begins to climb steadily toward Grants Pass through extremely dry timbered land consisting almost exclusively of lodgepole pine. At Grants Pass you will have traveled 6 mi. from the trailhead at Kepler Cascades. The pass itself is quite inconspicuous, marked only by an old sign on a tree. Look for a nice spring along the trail a few hundred yards from the pass. The trail descends 0.4 mi. to the edge of an open area and the junction with Shoshone Lake Trail, which forks off to the left (southeast). From here it is 2 mi. to Shoshone Geyser Basin, and 3 mi. to Shoshone Lake (see *Shoshone Lake Trail*).

For the next 4 mi. the route continues once again through heavy timber, crossing the Continental Divide three times before reaching Littles Fork, at which point you will have traveled 11 mi. from Kepler Cascades. When you finally emerge from the forest at Littles Fork, Douglas Knob appears directly in front of you a little less than 1 mi. away. (Trischman Knob looms 2 mi. in the distance to the northwest, but you cannot see it unless you walk up Littles Fork a short way. These natural features were named after two early park rangers who had reputations as extremely rugged mountain men.)

In 1963 a USAF B–47 crashed about 1 mi. west of Douglas Knob. Since the plane "pancaked" into the forest there is little evidence of a crash around the site. The aircraft did not disintegrate and is relatively intact. The trees surrounding the plane were not sheared off. *If you are experienced in traveling cross-country with a map and compass* the plane is relatively easy to find. If you look at your topo map you will notice that Littles Fork makes a sharp bend (similar to a backward "c") at the southernmost point in the meadow just west of Douglas Knob. If you begin at the bottom of this bend in Littles Fork (near the Douglas Knob sign) and follow a compass bearing of 254°, you should find the plane, which is located 1.1 mi. from the trail. Following your compass, it should take about 1 hour to walk to the plane from the trail.

Despite the fact that the plane crashed about 30 years ago, is over 16 mi. from the nearest road, is over 1 mi. from the nearest trail, and the plane cannot be seen until you are practically right on top of it, the National Park Service has proposed airlifting this airplane out of the park. Many people, including the author, feel that this plane is now part of Yellowstone's human history and should be left alone.

The Firehole River rises from two springs below Trischman Knob, then flows into Madison Lake. The lake was visited by Professor F. H. Bradley of the U.S. Geological Survey, and was appropriately named Madison Lake by Bradley, since he realized that it was the ultimate lake source for the Madison River. The Firehole flows from Madison Lake to Madison Junction, at which point the Firehole and Gibbon rivers unite to form the Madison River. (At Three Forks in Montana, the Madison, Gallatin, and Jefferson rivers unite to form the mighty Missouri River.)

Twister Falls, which consists of a series of small falls and cascades between perpendicular canyon walls, is reached at the 13-mi. mark. Another 0.5 mi. brings you to the edge of a canyon where you can see Gregg Fork below and, 0.3 mi. to the north, Tempe Cascade of Littles Fork, which joins Gregg Fork at this point.

The trail continues along Gregg Fork until Ferris Fork and Ragged Falls come into view on the south side of the trail (15 mi.). Here you cross Ferris Fork and once again emerge from heavy timber to enter the Three River Junction area. Here the Ferris, Phillips, and Gregg forks unite to form the Bechler River (see p. 90).

Thorofare Region

The Thorofare can appropriately be termed Yellowstone's premier wilderness region. The Snake and Upper Yellowstone rivers are among the chief streams; Heart and Yellowstone lakes are the major bodies of water; extensive meadows abound—particularly in the southeast corner; the craggy peaks of the Absarokas to the east are most impressive. The region is the summer home for a great many elk. Members of both the Jackson Hole and the Northern Yellowstone herds summer in the Snake River and Upper Yellowstone areas.

The number of backpackers who travel deep into Thorofare is small. Much of the travel is by horseback. The size of this area forces special considerations on backpackers planning extended visits. A week or more is required if you wish to travel deep into the southeast corner of the park, so plan accordingly when assessing miles-per-day, weight of pack (types of food, etc.), and comfortable gear (boots, etc.). In the southeast corner you will be over 30 mi. from the nearest road.

Most of the Thorofare is impassable in early summer due to high waters, so you should plan your trip for no earlier than July 15 for best results. The Indian Summer is a particularly good time to visit because the many meadows are tinted a beautiful gold, the high peaks are often frosted with white, and the elk are in rut. The region also encompasses Yellowstone Lake, which offers a wilderness paradise for canoeists venturing into the lake's Southeast, South, and Flat Mountain arms. (Note that the fishing season in the lake opens several weeks earlier than that for many streams of the Upper Yellowstone drainage. Current fishing regulations may be obtained from any ranger station or visitor center.)

The Promontory and Yellowstone Lake

There are several possible routes for touring the Thorofare. You can make a number of wide loops of the region or you can travel straight through, crossing over the park boundary into the Teton Wilderness. One of the most beautiful trips in Yellowstone, and the best in Thorofare, begins from the Eagle Creek trailhead in Shoshone National Forest on Cody–East Entrance Road, 7 mi. from the East Entrance, and goes up Eagle Creek, through Eagle Creek Meadows, and over Eagle Pass into Yellowstone Park. You then descend the Howell Fork of Mountain Creek to Mountain Creek itself, and down Mountain Creek to the Upper Yellowstone River. From here you enter the "true Thorofare," ascend Lynx Creek on the South Boundary Trail over Two Ocean Plateau to Mariposa Lake, and proceed down to the Snake River. The South Boundary Trail then takes you over Big Game Ridge to Harebell Creek, up to Heart Lake, and out at South Entrance Road. This trip covers about 85 mi., requires perhaps two weeks, and offers some of the grandest scenery to be found anywhere.

THOROFARE REGION TRAILS

Thorofare Trail	34.0 mi.
Mountain Creek Trail (Eagle Pass Trail)	10.0 mi.
South Boundary Trail	39.0 mi.
Snake River Trail	18.0 mi.
Heart Lake Trail	17.4 mi.
Trail Creek Trail	29.7 mi.
Two Ocean Plateau Trail (Passage Creek Trail)	12.0 mi.
Riddle Lake Trail	2.5 mi.
Mt. Sheridan Trail	3.0 mi.

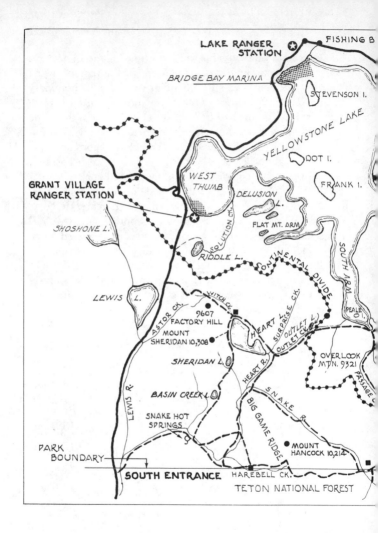

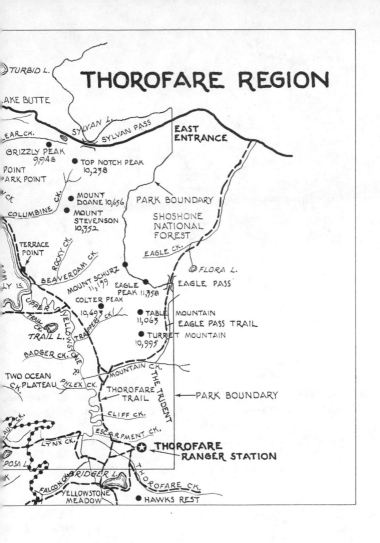

THOROFARE REGION

TURBID L.

LAKE BUTTE

SYLVAN L.

SYLVAN PASS

CLEAR CK.

EAST ENTRANCE

GRIZZLY PEAK 9,948

TOP NOTCH PEAK 10,238

POINT

PARK POINT

CK.

COLUMBINE CK.

MOUNT DOANE 10,656

PARK BOUNDARY

MOUNT STEVENSON 10,352

SHOSHONE NATIONAL FOREST

TERRACE POINT

ROCKY CK.

EAGLE CK.

FLORA L.

BEAVERDAM CK.

MOUNT SCHURZ 11,139

EAGLE PEAK 11,358

EAGLE PASS

COLTER PEAK 10,693

TRAPPERS CK.

TABLE MOUNTAIN 11,063

EAGLE PASS TRAIL

LY IS.

UPPER

CK.

TRAIL

YELLOWSTONE

TRAIL L.

TRAPPERS CK.

TURRET MOUNTAIN 10,995

BADGER CK.

YELLOWSTONE R.

MOUNTAIN CK.

TWO OCEAN CK. PLATEAU

PHLOX CK.

THE TRIDENT

THOROFARE TRAIL

PARK BOUNDARY

CLIFF CK.

ESCARPMENT CK.

CK.

LYNX CK.

★ **THOROFARE RANGER STATION**

POSA L.

BRIDGER L.

FALCON CK.

THOROFARE CK.

YELLOWSTONE MEADOW

HAWKS REST

Thorofare Trail

Thorofare Trailhead to:

Cub Creek	1.5 mi.
Clear Creek	3.0 mi.
Park Point Cabin	6.5 mi.
Columbine Creek	9.0 mi.
Terrace Point	15.0 mi.
Beaverdam Creek	18.0 mi.
Trail Creek Trail Junction	20.5 mi.
Trappers Creek	23.0 mi.
Turret Mountain Meadow	23.5 mi.
Eagle Pass Trail Junction	25.0 mi.
Cliff Creek	30.0 mi.
Escarpment Creek	31.5 mi.
Thorofare Ranger Station	32.0 mi.
Bridger Lake	34.0 mi.

Lake Butte trailhead (also called Ten-Mile Post), on the south side of East Entrance Road, 10 mi. east of Fishing Bridge, is the starting point for Thorofare Trail. From East Entrance Road, the trail descends steeply into a fine grove of spruce and fir. Cub Creek is crossed at 1.5 mi. Then the trail crosses Clear Creek at 3 mi.; here a spur trail leads to Elk Point Bay, 0.5 mi. west. Unless you take this trail or walk through the trees down to the shore, you will not see Yellowstone Lake until you reach Park Point. Unfortunately, the Thorofare Trail along Yellowstone Lake's Southeast Arm provides only occasional views of the lake. It was apparently designed for horse travel down to Thorofare and not for scenic value.

As you approach the Park Point patrol cabin area from the north, you come first to a meadow that is a popular spot for elk and mule deer. The trail continues across this meadow, but the right fork leads over about 0.5 mi. to the cabin area on the shore with superb views of the lake. From Park Point you can witness a spectacular sunset over Yellowstone Lake. Frank Island lies directly west, with Dot Island just northwest of Frank, Promontory looming directly to the south, Flat Mountain to the southeast, the upper half of Mt. Sheridan also to the southeast, and portions of the Absaroka Range to the south. Immediately south of the cabin is a lagoon in which cutthroat trout are frequently trapped by a sand dam. Meadow Creek empties into the lake a few hundred yds. to the south of the cabin. The mouth of the creek here is actually a wide slough, and in June and early July you can see cutthroat trout spawning.

For the next 2 mi. beyond Park Point, the trail skirts along the lake's edge—though high above it—and the views themselves are worth the hike. Promontory rises directly across from you, and the entire shape of the Southeast Arm unfolds before you to the south. The huge meadow region at the southern tip of the arm (the mouth of the Upper Yellowstone River) is faintly visible.

Shortly before crossing Columbine Creek you will once again come to the lake's shore, at which point Mt. Doane (10,656 ft.) with its snowcap is partially visible to the west. Columbine Creek is crossed at the 9-mi. mark. (Note that the water here is not very good for drinking.) The trail continues to below Brimstone Basin through stands of lodgepole pine with almost no undergrowth. If the wind is right you will notice the sulphur odor from the basin.

At the 15-mi. mark Terrace Point is reached. If you walk

over to the lake's edge you will be rewarded with some excellent views. It is in this vicinity that the geological evidence was found that proves that Yellowstone Lake was once 160 ft. higher than it is today. A mile beyond Terrace Point the trail swings into the open. The delta region of the mouth of the Upper Yellowstone River is laid out before you, with the Molly Islands clearly visible to the southwest and Colter Peak (10,683 ft.) dominating the skyline to the southeast. The view of the mouth of the Upper Yellowstone, surrounded by extensive meadows, with numerous birds soaring overhead, is particularly enjoyable.

Colter Peak is named for John Colter, the first white man to visit Yellowstone's wonders, in 1807. Colter probably entered what is now Yellowstone Park by following Thorofare Creek to the Upper Yellowstone River. From here, he may have crossed the Continental Divide at Two Ocean Pass south of the present park boundary, or ascended Lynx Creek, which would have taken him by Mariposa Lake on his way to the south fork of the Snake River. On September 7, 1870, Lt. Gustavus C. Doane and Nathaniel P. Langford sketched the first known authentic map of Yellowstone Lake.

At the 17-mi. mark the mouth of Beaverdam Creek is reached. This is the cutoff point beyond which motorboats are not allowed. The crossing of Beaverdam Creek (by ford) is another mile beyond the mouth of the stream. From here Mt. Schurz is partially visible to the east. At 11,139 ft. it is the second highest peak in the park. Colter Peak is again in view to the southeast.

When walking in the high willow brush, or anywhere in the Thorofare area for that matter, be sure to make a certain amount of noise, as it is a fact that grizzlies often use this trail. Chances are you will see some tracks along the trail—particularly between the Beaverdam Creek area and Thorofare Ranger Station. Grizzly tracks may be distinguished from those of a black bear by the indentations of the claws on the front paws. A grizzly's claws may extend up to 6 in., but a black's claws are curved and do not extend beyond the front paws. The distance between the holes, or "dots," made by the claws and the front paws will key you to the bear's species (see page 24).

After leaving the willow brush beyond Beaverdam Creek, the trail re-enters lodgepole pine. Portions of this area burned in 1988. As you near the 20-mi. mark, a short loop trail leads down to the river. (The patrol cabin was heavily damaged by grizzly bears and has been relocated.) Be sure to follow this trail down to the Upper Yellowstone River (0.2 mi. away) as the wild beauty of this area is indeed special. Look for elk and moose in the meadows here. The trail leading down to the river is actually the Trail Creek Trail, which ends at Cabin Creek "cabin," where it joins the Thorofare Trail.

About 1 mi. south of Cabin Creek the trail passes through dense spruce and fir. At the 23-mi. mark Trappers Creek is crossed; 0.5 mi. south of the creek you will enter Turret Mountain Meadow, where there is a fine view of extremely rugged Turret Mountain (10,995 ft.) to the east and Two Ocean Plateau to the west. Turret Mountain consists of volcanic conglomerate. When a climb by the Sierra Club was attempted in 1926, an overhanging cliff of very brittle material only 100 ft. from the summit prevented hikers from reaching the top. At 25 mi. you will come to the Mountain Creek Trail junction (Eagle Pass Trail), located among lodgepole pine. Eagle Pass is 10 mi. to the northeast. Another mile brings you to the crossing of Mountain Creek, where Turret Mountain is once again in view to the northeast. During early summer, grizzlies are often seen in this area feeding on spawning Yellowstone cutthroat trout. Just beyond the creek is the other Mountain Creek Trail junction (lower cutoff trail), which also leads to Eagle Pass.

As the trail continues southward it begins to enter more

meadows, and the scenery is truly spectacular—you are now entering the "real" Thorofare. In two places the Upper Yellowstone River winds right next to the trail to offer a view of one of America's wildest and most beautiful streams. Two Ocean Plateau looms as a backdrop to the west. The second meeting of river and trail (farthest south) at the 29-mi. mark requires a stop. The views include the Upper Yellowstone winding through the meadow, the massive Two Ocean Plateau rising to 10,115 ft. just across the river to the west, and the sharp cliffs of the northern Trident immediately above you to the east. Looking back across the river to the southwest you can easily distinguish where Lynx Creek and the South Boundary Trail are located.

The northern fork of Cliff Creek is crossed at the 30-mi. mark, and 0.5 mi. beyond the trail enters another meadow affording more fine views. As you leave the meadow from this point and re-enter the forest, a cold spring is located just to the west of the trail. Immediately before the trail junction at 31.5 mi. you will cross Escarpment Creek. The southern Trident (10,631 ft.) lies to the east. The streambed is not permanent but takes on a new course almost every summer following the big floods, of which evidence can easily be noted here. From the trail junction across the stream a trail leads 0.5 mi. to Thorofare Ranger Station, located beneath the southern Trident. A ranger is normally stationed here throughout the summer.

From the ranger station two trails lead to Bridger Lake, 2 mi. away, just across the park boundary in the Teton Wilderness. (For travel in this particular area around Bridger Lake it is strongly suggested that you order a 15-min. topo map of Two Ocean Pass, Wyoming, which you can get from USGS, Distribution Section, Denver, Colorado 80225. A Wyoming fishing license is required for any fishing you may do south of the park boundary.) The westernmost trail is probably the most scenic route, leading to the west corner of Bridger Lake. The fording of Thorofare Creek is no easy matter, as it is quite wide and deep most of the summer; the name should be Thorofare *River*. From Thorofare Creek to Bridger Lake, you walk through an extensive meadow that provides fine views of Two Ocean Plateau to the west and Hawk's Rest to the south. The trail then crosses the park boundary, leads through a stand of lodgepole, and comes out in a corner of the famous 7-mi.-long Yellowstone Meadow.

Although the general vicinity of Bridger Lake is not technically included within the park's boundaries, it certainly is a part of the park for several reasons. The Upper Yellowstone River rises only a few miles south of Bridger Lake, then flows through Yellowstone Meadow into the park. About 7 air miles southwest of Bridger Lake is famous Two Ocean Pass, where the first cutthroat trout apparently crossed over and started the unique population in Yellowstone Lake. Also at Two Ocean Pass, Two Ocean Creek makes its separation right on the Continental Divide, forking into Pacific Creek to the west and Atlantic Creek to the east. The area is rich in historical associations. Fur trappers used to trap along the Upper Yellowstone in the early 1800s. John Colter passed through here in 1807, and in 1830 the legendary Jim Bridger camped for a time at the lake that is now named in his honor and also discovered Two Ocean Pass. Other fur trappers who visited this area in the 1830s were Milton Sublette, Joe Meek, Thomas Fitzpatrick, and Jedediah Smith. Their rather "easy" survival in the Yellowstone wilderness lends support to the old fur trappers' slogan: "A fur trapper is tough, or he is dead." You may want to climb Hawk's Rest, which provides a spectacular view of Bridger Lake, the Upper Yellowstone River, and Yellowstone Meadow.

Mountain Creek Trail
(Eagle Pass Trail) - (10.0 mi.)

The starting point is at Thorofare Trail Junction. This trail follows Mountain Creek (incorrectly shown as Monument Creek on some maps) for a short distance, then takes Howell Fork up to near Eagle Pass (10 mi.). Much of the Howell Creek drainage burned in 1988.

The climb up to the pass is almost 2,000 ft. Turret Mountain, Table Mountain, and Eagle Peak (all about 11,000 ft.) provide constant mountain scenery to the west, but also block out any possible views of Yellowstone Lake as you approach the pass. Eagle Pass (9,628 ft.) runs to the east of Eagle Peak, which at 11,358 ft. is the highest peak in Yellowstone. Some of the most beautiful views of the Absaroka Range are visible as you cross over Eagle Pass and enter Shoshone National Forest. The Forest Service Eagle Creek Trail then joins and continues 18 mi. to exit at Cody Highway, 7 mi. east of the East Entrance. Although not currently maintained, an old outfitter trail follows Mountain Creek (the Eagle Pass Trail follows Howell Creek) across the boundary and up to a 10,900-ft. pass (a distance of about 8 mi.), which provides access to the USFS trail that descends Fishhawk Creek. The distance is 20 mi. from the pass out to Cody Road, where the trail terminates 10 mi. east of the East Entrance. The scenery is spectacular along this route, but since the trail is not maintained from Howell Fork up to the pass, you may expect downed timber and rock slides.

South Boundary Trail

South Boundary Trail
(from South Entrance) to:

Snake Hot Springs	5.0 mi.
Heart Lake Trail Junction	6.0 mi.

Snake River Trail Junction	10.0 mi.
Harebell Cabin	12.5 mi.
Big Game Ridge	19.0 mi.
Fox Creek Cabin	24.0 mi.
Two Ocean Plateau Trail Junction	27.0 mi.
Mariposa Lake	28.0 mi.
Lynx Creek	31.0 mi.
Yellowstone River Ford	36.0 mi.
Thorofare Creek	37.0 mi.
Thorofare Ranger Station	39.0 mi.

This trail begins at the park's South Entrance. Most backpackers making extended trips into the Thorofare country from South Entrance Road begin at the Heart Lake Trail; however, if the Snake River route is your objective, you can begin at the South Entrance. Most of the summer the Snake River is too deep to ford safely at the South Entrance; in this case, you can begin at the Snake River Bridge, located near Flagg Ranch (3 mi. south of the South Entrance gate). From here you follow the river along its eastern bank until you join the South Boundary Trail. (This adds about 3 mi.)

After crossing the river, the trail leads across a large meadow into a lodgepole forest. Around the 3.5-mi. mark you come to a bridge that extends through a dense growth of willows (you may see moose). There are occasional open areas along the way that contain many species of wildflowers. As you approach the 5-mi. mark and the Snake Hot Springs group, the scenery becomes very good. On first entering the meadow from the west you will come to a bridge that crosses a hot-flowing stream tinted a deep blue-green. The stream's source is located only a few yds. away at a large hot spring. From the spring the blue-green stream flows beneath a large rock outcropping, then under the footbridge, and on into the Snake River.

At 6 mi. Heart Lake Trail Junction is reached. At this point you enter a burned area that continues for the most part all the way up and over Big Game Ridge. The revegetation is proceeding well in the moist valley areas. In steeper terrain where spruce and fir prevailed, the process of regrowth takes longer. Note that without shade the climb up Big Game Ridge can be quite arduous on a warm day. An early start will help.

The cutoff trail appears at the 9-mi. mark at the head of a large meadow through which the Snake River flows. Another mile brings you to the junction of the Snake River Trail; at this point the Snake River courses to the northeast, leaving the South Boundary Trail. The South Boundary Trail crosses Harebell Creek a short distance beyond the junction. From the stream crossing, the trail climbs to Harebell patrol cabin, where a spur trail from the Snake River joins South Boundary Trail. From the cabin a climb of 2,400 ft. begins to the top of Big Game Ridge, 7 mi. away at over 10,000 ft. For the first 3 mi. the trail continues along Harebell Creek. Look for a regrowth of ferns and mosses, berries, mushrooms, and many wildflowers, particularly harebell, Indian paintbrush, aster, and monkshood.

From the top of Big Game Ridge on a clear day the Absarokas to the east, the Tetons and Wind River ranges to the south, and the park's Gallatin Range to the northwest are all visible. Mt. Hancock, situated roughly in the middle of Big Game Ridge, lies directly to the north. (This peak, 10,214 ft., was climbed in 1871 by Captain J.W. Barlow, who named it after General W.S. Hancock, Commander of the Military Department.) It is a rare day when several elk are not spotted somewhere on Big Game Ridge. Much of the trail over the ridge skirts south of the park boundary into Teton National Forest, but there are adequate trail marker signs. Big Game Ridge is subject to quite severe weather conditions, particularly in September and October.

When you complete your descent from Big Game Ridge, the Snake River and valley at the confluence of Fox Creek open before you. Snake River Trail joins the South Boundary Trail at the river. Fox Creek patrol cabin is located on South Boundary trail east of the river. An unnamed stream flows behind the cabin; this is often mistaken for Fox Creek, which joins the Snake River right on the park boundary, near the South Boundary–Snake River Trail Junction. From Fox Creek cabin there is a USFS trail leading southward to Fox Park patrol cabin. You may want to take time to walk down this, as it is only 0.5 mi. to Fox Park, a large and beautiful meadow through which the Snake River meanders, and where Plateau Creek flows into the Snake. From Fox Creek cabin the trail crosses a meadow, then enters lodgepole. The Two Ocean Plateau Trail junction is reached at the 27-mi. mark (3 mi. east of Fox Creek cabin). From here, the trail climbs 500 ft. in 1 mi. to Mariposa Lake, at about 9,100 ft. The lake sits in a small depression, with meadows tinted purple in late summer by thousands of monkshood sloping away on the east, south, and west sides. The northern shore is mostly wooded, and there are a few patches of timber surrounding the lake, which appears quite shallow. At such a high elevation (the Continental Divide is only about 1 mi. away to the east), it is surprising that it supports a small population of cutthroat trout.

The trail continues to climb to the Continental Divide, where you enter a large meadow for the start of the beautiful descent down Lynx Creek. From the divide there is a wonderful view of the Absaroka Range to the east. Shortly beyond the divide, the headwaters of Lynx Creek appear. The trail and creek then enter a burned spruce and fir forest, and begin their descent of 1,500 ft. to the Yellowstone River. There you are deep in the wilderness, over 30 mi. from the road in any direction. As you follow Lynx Creek down to the Yellowstone River, you will cross Lynx Creek several times. Occasional views of the 10,000-ft. ridge of Two Ocean Plateau to the south appear along the way down. When you reach the Upper Yellowstone River at Yellowstone Meadow, you will be on the threshold of some of Yellowstone's wildest and most beautiful backcountry scenery. The trail parallels the Upper Yellowstone River for a short distance, offering spectacular views of the Trident and Turret mountains to the east. The sheer Two Ocean Plateau directly west of the river is interrupted only by a green slope halfway up the cliff. To the south, Hawk's Rest can be seen east of the river. The three arms of the Trident are in full view to the east. The ford is not too bad since it is upstream from where Thorofare Creek empties into the Yellowstone. The South Boundary Trail ends at Thorofare Creek where it joins the Thorofare Trail. Bridger Lake is 1 mi. to the south from this junction.

Snake River Trail   (18.0 mi.)

The Snake River Trail starts 10 mi. east of South Entrance. The Snake River Trail from the junction of Harebell Creek to the junction of Fox Creek is not highly recommended for hiking. Essentially a horse trail, it contains many needless ups and downs, and crosses the river back and forth over a dozen times. While much of the scenery along the river is indeed beautiful, the views are constantly limited by sloping ridges on both sides of the trail. The 1988 fires burned a 6-mi. stretch of this area between Barlow Peak and Mt. Hancock.

The South Boundary Trail over Big Game Ridge and the Trail Creek Trail from Heart Lake are certainly more desirable routes for traversing the Thorofare area. Highlights of the Snake River Trail include several narrow rock gorges through which the Snake gushes, and the vicinity surrounding the confluence of the Heart and Snake rivers, where there are several hot springs, a sizable meadow, and an impressive view of Mt. Sheridan.

Heart Lake Trail

Heart Lake Trailhead to:

Heart Lake Cabin	7.5 mi.
Rustic Geyser	8.0 mi.
Mt. Sheridan Trail	8.2 mi.
Sheridan Lake	11.0 mi.
Basin Creek	12.0 mi.
Basin Creek Lake	13.0 mi.
Snake River	17.0 mi.
South Boundary Trail	17.4 mi.
South Entrance	23.5 mi.
Flagg Ranch Bridge	26.5 mi.

The trailhead is just north of Lewis Lake on the east side of South Entrance Road, 7.4 mi. south of West Thumb. For the first 5 mi. the trail traverses gently rolling terrain through lodgepole pine. You then reach an overlook from which Witch Creek, the Heart Lake Geyser Basin, and Heart Lake can be seen. Factory Hill (9,607 ft.) dominates the view to the south. (The mountain was named for its apparent resemblance, noted as early as 1829, on a frosty morning, to an early American factory town.) Factory Hill is the northern terminus to the Red

Mountain Range, which occupies much of the land between Lewis and Heart lakes, with Mt. Sheridan (10,308 ft.) dominating. (The Red Mountain Range derives its name from the prevailing color of the volcanic rocks; when exposed to sun, the porphyry becomes a dark red.) Most of the range is completely timbered to the summit. In 1926 the Sierra Club held its Yellowstone outing in this area, and several climbs were made of peaks here and in the Absarokas along the eastern boundary. The trail descends to Witch Creek (named for the many thermal features along its course) and through a large meadow. The last 3 mi. to the lake pass through a burn area from the 1988 fires.

A number of hot springs spill into the stream, raising the creek's temperature to 80°F. As a result, there are no trout except close to where the creek enters the lake.

Heart Lake patrol cabin is on the northwestern shore of the lake near the trail. There is usually a ranger here during the summer months who should be able to give you up-to-date information on trail conditions. Heart Lake contains cutthroat and lake trout. The lake trout (or mackinaw) grow quite big here but are difficult to catch. (The largest one ever caught in Yellowstone weighed 43 lbs., and was caught several years ago at Heart Lake.) The big fish live in very deep water during the summer months, but come into the shallow areas in October and November to spawn.

Along the western shore (at the 8-mi. mark) is Rustic Geyser, which ceased erupting in 1985. In 1872, Dr. A.C. Peale of the Hayden Expedition found Rustic Geyser "bordered by logs which are coated with a crystalline, semi-translucent deposit of geyserite. These logs were evidently placed around the geyser by either Indians or Whitemen a number of years ago, as the coating is thick and the logs firmly attached to the surrounding deposit." Unfortunately, in the fall of 1990 vandals caused irreparable damage to the delicate features by throwing objects into the vents and breaking off some sinter deposits.

The junction of the Mt. Sheridan Trail is met just south of Rustic Geyser at 8.2 mi. The hike up the mountain consists of a 3,000-foot climb in 3 mi. The Tetons lie to the south, the Pitchstone Plateau to the west, and Heart Lake, Lewis Lake, Shoshone Lake, and Yellowstone Lake can be seen. (Mt. Sheridan was named by Captain Barlow of the 1871 expedition after General Philip H. Sheridan, a distinguished soldier who often visited the park and worked for its interest.) It was near Mt. Sheridan that Truman Everts, a member of the Washburn Party, was lost for 37 days in September 1870. Everts' diet consisted almost solely of "Everts" thistle. However, not everything in the woods is edible. The extremely poisonous water hemlock is quite common in the Heart Lake vicinity. A hiker died here in 1985 after consuming some, mistaking it for cow parsnip. Although some members of the Parsnip plant family are edible, I recommend against it because similar-appearing species are deadly.

As you continue along the western shore of Heart Lake below the east face of Mt. Sheridan, you will notice some distinctive avalanche chutes where tons of snow have roared down on the lake in past winters. During the winter of 1968, an avalanche of tremendous proportions swept away hundreds of tall trees here, depositing many in the lake.

Continuing beyond Heart Lake the trail passes Sheridan Lake in open country at the 11-mi. mark. Much of the trail passes through open country, which burned in 1988, for the next 5 mi. Basin Creek is crossed at 12 mi. At 12.5 mi., the Basin Creek Cutoff Trail leading to the Snake River Trail (2 mi. away) is joined. Basin Creek Lake appears at 13 mi. At Basin Creek Lake the trail re-enters timber for a short distance, then emerges into a sizable meadow through which Red Creek runs. The Snake

River, with its wide gravel streambed, is reached at 17 mi., where a ford is required. You join the South Boundary Trail at 17.4 mi. From here it is 6.1 mi. to the South Entrance or 9.1 mi. to the Flagg Ranch Bridge.

Trail Creek Trail

Heart Lake Trailhead on South Entrance Road to:

Heart Lake Cabin	7.5 mi.
Beaver Creek	9.2 mi.
Heart River Cutoff Trail	12.0 mi.
Outlet Creek Meadow	13.0 mi.
Outlet Lake	15.0 mi.
Grouse Creek Crossing	17.5 mi.
Passage Creek Cutoff	20.5 mi.
Trail Creek Cabin	24.5 mi.
Yellowstone River	29.2 mi.
Thorofare Trail	29.7 mi.

You can reach Heart Lake patrol cabin via Heart Lake Trail from South Entrance Road. The Trail Creek Trail starts here and provides 22.2 mi. of truly gentle wilderness. It is very level for most of the way, with flowering meadows (ideal habitat for moose and elk), deltas, and sloughs.

From Heart Lake cabin the trail skirts the sandy beach along the north shore of the lake, enters a lodgepole forest, then emerges into the first of many fine meadows. Beaver Creek is crossed in this meadow at the 9.2-mi. mark.

At 12 mi. the Heart River Cutoff Trail provides access to the Snake River Trail 3 mi. south. Just beyond the trail junction is the confluence of Surprise and Outlet creeks, which unite to form a fork of the Heart River (the other fork is the outlet for Heart Lake). For the next 6 mi. you see evidence of the great fire season of 1988. In a forested bowl at the head of a meadow at the 15-mi. mark lies Outlet Lake, the source for Outlet Creek. Prior to the Ice Age, this very meadow may well have been the outlet for Yellowstone Lake, emptying it into the Pacific Ocean. Eventually, the channel from Yellowstone Lake to Heart River dammed at the Continental Divide. Yellowstone Lake now drains into the Atlantic.

From Outlet Lake you leave a body of water that eventually flows into the Pacific and climb only 200 ft. in 0.5 mi. over the Continental Divide to Grouse Creek, which eventually flows into the Atlantic. This is one of the easiest divide crossings among the park's trails. Grouse Creek courses through another meadow toward the South Arm of Yellowstone Lake. To the north sits Channel Mountain and to the south Overlook Mountain—both of which comprise portions of Chicken Ridge. At the 17.5-mi. mark the trail crosses Grouse Creek and bends away from the meadow and stream.

During early summer cutthroat trout spawn in the streams of this area; the activity attracts a variety of wildlife, including the grizzly bear. The southern shore of the South Arm sees its share of grizzlies all summer, and if you look along the sandy beaches here, chances are you will spot grizzly tracks. Across the bottom of the arm to the east lies Peale Island (see *Canoeing on Yellowstone Lake*).

Just short of 20.5 mi., the cutoff trail to the Two Ocean Plateau Trail is joined at the southernmost slough of the South Arm. This remote slough is actually a miniature arm of Yellowstone Lake itself, an area that contains moose, elk, and a variety of birdlife. Chipmunk Creek, another active trout-spawning stream, is crossed in a further meadow (21.8 mi.).

At 22.7 mi., you reach the junction of the Two Ocean Plateau Trail in a marshy meadow; here there is a shallow lake that usually sports a number of ducks and occasionally trumpeter swans.

Trail Creek patrol cabin (notice numerous claw marks made by grizzlies) and the Southeast Arm appear at 24.5 mi. From here the trail skirts the shore of the lake for about 1 mi., then enters a large meadow at the mouth of Trail Creek. Although this area burned extensively several years prior to 1988, notice the revegetation. During late July the lupine and fireweed display here is spectacular. Some maps show a trail leading over to nearby Trail Lake; however, none was present in 1990.

The Upper Yellowstone River ford is reached at the 29.2 mi. mark. There are dropoffs in this area, so be careful to seek out a wide, shallow crossing. The southernmost ford upstream is often an easier crossing, but conditions change. Expect to find the river thigh deep even as late as September. Cabin Creek and the Thorofare Trail are reached at the 29.7-mi. mark.

Two Ocean Plateau Trail

Trailhead from Trail Creek Trail Junction to:

Continental Divide	9.0 mi.
Plateau Creek	11.6 mi.
South Boundary Trail	12.0 mi.

Two Ocean Plateau Trail is seldom traveled. It disappears from sight in several places where large open areas are crossed. If you are interested in forest fire ecology this trail is for you. Much of Two Ocean Plateau burned in 1988, but this is nothing new here. Even during the total fire suppression years prior to 1972 large fires burned here.

Start at Trail Creek Trail, 1.8 mi. west of the patrol cabin. As the trail nears the confluence of Chipmunk and Passage creeks, you will emerge into a large burned-over area known as the Chipmunk Burn. The fire occurred in 1941 and burned 11,000 acres of spruce, fir, and lodgepole forest. By the 1980s the area was beautifully revegetated, providing ample evidence of nature's power of regeneration. The cycle began anew in 1988 for much of this area.

After crossing the Chipmunk Burn, the trail begins a steady climb up to the Continental Divide, reached around the 9-mi. mark. After a steep climb up to the divide at over 9,200 ft., the trail actually follows the Continental Divide for about 1 mi. Once on top, subalpine conditions prevail. Keep a close watch for the trail marker poles at this point, and look for large herds of elk in this area.

At 11.6 mi. you will cross Plateau Creek. Approximately 1.2 mi. upstream from here is Plateau Falls (75 ft.), which is rarely visited. The junction of the South Boundary Trail is reached after the 12-mi. mark. Mariposa Lake is now only 1 mi. away to the east (see *South Boundary Trail*).

Riddle Lake Trail   (2.5 mi.)

Start from South Entrance Road, 4.3 mi. south of Grant. The trail proceeds through forest and meadow to Riddle Lake, which is the source for Solution Creek. There are large meadows to the west and south of the lake, where bird activity is abundant. Fine views of Mt. Sheridan and the Red Mountains provide a nice backdrop from the north shore. This area is good habitat for moose and grizzly, and because of the latter the trail is often closed during June.

During the 1870s it was believed that there was a lake in this area that contained major drainages to both oceans. Once the actual location of the Continental Divide was determined, the "riddle" was solved, and the stream draining the lake was the "solution." Indeed, the Continental Divide is only 1 mi. away to the south and east, and is crossed just beyond the trailhead, though you would never know it from the level terrain.

Riddle Lake was a great cutthroat fishery as recently as the 1970s, but heavy consumptive fishing pressure ruined it. As of 1990 the lake is closed to fishing. This sad story provides evidence as to why catch-and-release regulations now apply on most park waters.

Mt. Sheridan Trail (3.0 mi.)

The Mount Sheridan trail begins 5 mi. south of the Heart Lake patrol cabin (see p. 135). From Heart Lake the trail climbs 2,858 feet to the summit of Mount Sheridan, where a ranger is stationed in the fire lookout during the summer fire season. The mosaic pattern of the 1988 fires can be observed in the forest below. The magnificent views include the majestic Tetons, Absarokas, Pitchstone Plateau, and Heart, Yellowstone, Lewis, and Shoshone lakes. The hike makes a great side trip while camping in the Heart Lake vicinity. The 22-mile roundtrip hike is not recommended for a day trip unless you get a very early start and are in excellent physical condition. Remember, you do not want to be walking in grizzly country after dark (see p. 25).

Central Plateau Region

This region includes most of Hayden Valley, which is home to many elk that come here in the summer. Moose are commonly sighted, particularly close to Canyon–Lake Road. Herds of bison are a common sight throughout the valley. These tough beasts also spend the winter here, near a number of hot springs in the area. Furthermore, Hayden Valley is prime grizzly bear country. For this reason you should remain very alert while hiking, being careful not to surprise a bear along the trail. The grizzly ranks as one of the most magnificent animals in the world, and it is indeed unfortunate that its domain has now been reduced to Yellowstone and Glacier national parks and a few surrounding areas. Estimates of the grizzly population in Yellowstone range from 200 to 275. This amounts to only one bear per 14 sq. mi. throughout the park, but before you rule out the possibility of encountering one, you should realize that the grizzly often gathers in high numbers in suitable habitats—such as Hayden Valley and Pelican Valley; also, grizzlies often range about, covering an extensive area in a short time. Park officials occasionally restrict the use of some trails when grizzlies appear to be unusually active. You will be informed of any such restrictions when you request a backcountry use permit.

The Hayden Valley is also rich in history. It was through this region in 1877 that General Howard of the U.S. Army pursued the Nez Perce Indians led by Chief Joseph. Although Chief Joseph was not a war-provoking chief, several renegades broke away from his tribe and bolted through the Hayden Valley, terrorizing a group of tourists visiting the park. George Cowan,

Mary Lake

the leader of the touring party from Radarsburg, Montana, was shot near Mary Mountain on Nez Perce Creek. His wife rushed to his aid but was dragged away by Indians, and another shot at close range struck Cowan in the forehead. He was left to die. The Indians finally released Mrs. Cowan and the rest of the party near Mud Volcano, from where they made it safely to Bozeman. Cowan began a slow crawl back to the party's Lower Geyser Basin camp 9 mi. away. A passing Indian spotted his movement and shot him in the side. Cowan managed to play dead until darkness and then, amazingly, continued back to camp. On August 28, four days later, he was found at the camp by two of General Howard's scouts, and his slow but dogged recovery began.

For most hikers traveling through the Central Plateau region the goal is Mary Lake, which lies roughly in the center of the wilderness region.

CENTRAL PLATEAU REGION TRAILS

Mary Mountain Trail	11.0 mi.
Cygnet Lakes Trail	4.5 mi.
Nez Perce Trail	10.0 mi.
Elephant Back Mountain Loop Trail	3.5 mi.
Artist Paintpots Trail	0.5 mi.

Mary Mountain Trail

Trailhead on Canyon–Lake Road to:

Violet Creek	5.0 mi.
Highland Hot Springs	9.0 mi.
Mary Lake	11.0 mi.

CENTRAL PLATEAU REGION

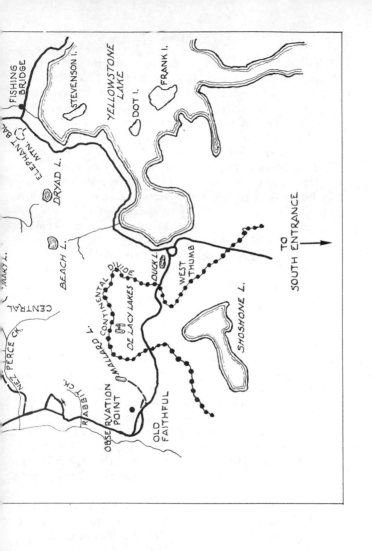

The trailhead is located opposite a pullout on Canyon–Lake Road about 5 mi. south of Canyon Junction. This open valley is home for many animals, including the grizzly. Because this is prime grizzly habitat no overnight camping is permitted in Hayden Valley and the number of dayhikers is limited. Check at Canyon Ranger Station before departing. Most of the trail traverses open country (binoculars are a must). Large bison herds occasionally disperse across this end of the valley, making travel down the trail next to impossible. A detour is often needed or you may have to turn around. Do not walk through a herd of bison.

Extensive bison activity can also be seen in the marks made on trees in the forested islands in the valley. In fact, a topo map is necessary since trail marker poles are usually knocked down by bison. The trail stays on the north side of Alum Creek until it crosses a small fork of the creek near Highland Hot Springs. Several other hot springs are located along the way, especially near Violet Creek, which drains a thermal area.

According to Jim Bridger, the Yellowstone contained a stream (Alum Creek) that when forded by elk caused their hooves to shrink to the size of those of an antelope. The shrinking properties of Alum Creek have yet to be proven, but in some sections it is not very palatable, as Jim must have discovered.

As you cross Violet Creek at the 5.0-mi. mark and begin to move away from Alum Creek, you approach a forest to the west that provides excellent wildlife, including the grizzly bear. Most animals prefer this "edge effect" where forest and open land meet. As you enter the forest and leave the large grassland and sagebrush of Hayden Valley behind, Mary Lake is only about 3 mi. away to the west.

Lest you think that the trail crew got carried away here with its saws, realize that portions of the first 1.5 mi. of trail here were used as a fireline to stop advancing fires in 1988.

At about the 9-mi. mark, you will cross a fork of Alum Creek, which winds through an open forest meadow to Highland Hot Springs. Notice the number of large animal tracks leading to and from Mary Lake. The trail continues around the north end of the lake past the patrol cabin. The National Park Service patrol cabin, of course, is for official use only and is locked at all times. There is a tree immediately behind the patrol cabin that contains some very obvious and large claw marks — probably made by a grizzly.

Mary Lake has no permanent inlet or outlet, and there are no fish populations here. There is usually some form of birdlife, with duck the most common.

Cygnet Lakes Trail (4.5 mi.)

Start from the south side of Norris–Canyon Road, 5 mi. west of Canyon Junction. The trail winds through a lodgepole forest, much of which burned in 1988, to Cygnet Lakes and meadow. Here a large meadow contains a series of five lakes named after the young of the trumpeter swan. The trumpeter once seemed hopelessly headed for extinction. In 1930, only 21 trumpeters were counted in the park. However, due to protection of its habitat both in and out of the park, the bird has made a strong comeback. Unfortunately, for reasons that are not yet clear, the trumpeter's numbers are in decline again today. Note that the trail has not been maintained beyond Cygnet Lakes for many years.

Nez Perce Trail

Trailhead on Old Faithful–Madison Road to:

Magpie Creek	5.0 mi.
Cowan Creek	6.8 mi.
Mary Lake	10.0 mi.

This trail begins on the east side of Madison–Old Faithful Road, 6 mi. south of Madison. It follows Nez Perce Creek through forest and meadow most of the way to Mary Lake. (This is the same route that General Howard used in 1877 to pursue the Nez Perce Indians.) At the 6.8-mi. mark, in a fine meadow through which the Nez Perce runs, it crosses a stream known as Cowan Creek. Cowan is named for George Cowan, as it was near here that he was first shot down.

The meadows in this area provide excellent habitat for grazing animals, and bison are often spotted. Nez Perce Creek contains brown and rainbow trout. (Mary Lake itself does not contain any fish.)

Elephant Back Mountain Loop Trail (3.5 mi.)

The trailhead is located about 1 mi. south of Fishing Bridge Junction on the road to the Lake area. The primary lure of this hike is the outstanding view of Yellowstone Lake. A vertical climb of 750 ft. through a lodgepole forest brings you to the prized overlook of the lake and the spectacular Absaroka Range.

Artist Paintpots Trail (0.5 mi.)

The trailhead is on the east side of Norris–Madison Road, 4.2 mi. from Norris. This short walk is best early in the day before many people arrive. The trail leads through a lodgepole forest to an interesting thermal area at the base of Paintpot Hill, which burned during 1988. There are numerous pools of varying colors. The trail loops up to a small hill where a nice thick mudpot is located.

Gallatin Region

The Gallatin Region provides excellent opportunities for high mountain hiking, as the Gallatin Range, with its 19 peaks stretching from south to north, is the featured attraction. The range is actually only about 20 mi. in length. Electric Peak (nearly 11,000 ft.) marks the northernmost point (and the highest) and Mt. Holmes (10,336 ft.) the southernmost. The mountains are part of an uplifted block of stratified shales, limestones, and sandstones dipping slightly northward. The forces of erosion slowly carved this raised block to form the present peaks and cirques. Since the rock layers dip northward, the younger and higher beds are found in Electric Peak, and the older layers are exposed on Mt. Holmes.

The major streams of this region include the Gallatin and Gardner rivers, located, respectively, to the west and east of the Gallatin Range, and the Madison River, located in the southwest corner of the region. The Gardner River and Gardners Hole (not to be confused with the town of Gardiner) were named for Johnson Gardner, a fur trapper for the American Fur Company in 1832.

In the extreme northwest corner of the park is an area containing rugged peaks dominated by Bighorn Peak, a petrified forest, and a number of beautiful high mountain lakes.

GALLATIN REGION TRAILS

Bighorn Peak Trail (Black Butte Creek to High Lake)	17.0 mi.
Sportsman Lake Trail	26.5 mi.

Electric Peak

High Lake Spur Trail	3.0 mi.
Fawn Pass Trail	21.5 mi.
Fan Creek Trail	8.0 mi.
Bighorn Pass Trail	20.5 mi.
Daly Creek–Skyrim Trail	10.0, 21.0 mi.
Bacon Rind Creek Trail	2.5 mi.
Mt. Holmes Trail	10.3 mi.
Trilobite Lakes Trail	3.0 mi.
Grizzly Lake Trail	2.0 mi.
Gneiss Creek Trail	14.0 mi.
Monument Geyser Basin Trail	1.0 mi.
Purple Mountain Lookout Trail	3.3 mi.
Harlequin Lake Trail	0.5 mi.
Beaver Ponds Loop Trail	5.0 mi.
Sepulcher Mountain Loop Trail	10.0 mi.
Howard Eaton Trail (Golden Gate to Mammoth)	3.0 mi.

Bighorn Peak Trail

Black Butte Creek to:

Bighorn Peak	6.0 mi.
Shelf Lake	9.0 mi.
Crescent Lake	12.0 mi.
High Lake	17.0 mi.

The starting point is U.S. 191 at Black Butte Creek crossing, 2.4 mi. inside the north boundary. Black Butte Creek lies to

GALLATIN REGION

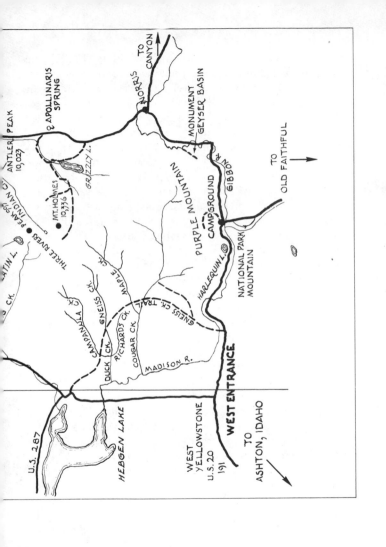

the northwest of very conspicuous Black Butte. The hike up to the top of Bighorn Peak must rank as one of the most strenuous in the park, as you gain over 3,000 ft. in only 6 mi.—the last 4.5 mi. climbing 2,330 ft. Once the Skyrim Trail is joined, though, your efforts will be rewarded with some very rugged mountain scenery. At about the 3-mi. mark during the steep climb you will enter the Gallatin Petrified Forest. This is interesting, but does not compare with the standing petrified forest on Specimen Ridge (see *Specimen Ridge Trail*). When above timberline the trail may become difficult to follow—watch closely for rockpiles and orange markers. When atop the large, grassy west shoulder of Bighorn Peak, you will have reached an elevation of 9,909 ft.; the Skyrim Trail is joined here. To the north it follows the park boundary for 8 mi. (see p. 164); to the east it continues 3 mi. to Shelf Lake. The actual summit of Bighorn Peak is reached via a very narrow trail with steep dropoffs on both sides. Follow the trail carefully—one hiker fell to his death here in 1969. The summit seems much higher than 9,930 ft. The view is magnificent in all directions, particularly of the snowcapped Spanish Peaks to the northwest. You should find a summit register tube planted by the National Park Service in the rockpile atop the peak.

As you follow the ridge along the park boundary to Shelf Lake, note the scraggly whitebark pine that grow at these high elevations. There are also fine views of the Gallatin Range along the way. About halfway from Bighorn Peak to Shelf Lake, Crescent Lake can be spotted in the distance to the southeast, sitting at the foot of a cirque. To the northeast is prominent Sheep Mountain (10,095 ft.), with its conspicuous relaying equipment perched on top. Watch for bighorn sheep while on the Skyrim Trail.

At the 8.7-mi. mark the trail drops down from the ridge to Shelf Lake, located at nearly 9,200 ft. If you continue on the ridge above Shelf Lake, the trail will take you to the summit of Sheep Mountain. From the lake you may want to take the time to climb the grassy ridge to the north, which has a fine view of Ramshorn Peak to the northwest (10,289 ft.) and also a very beautiful bird's-eye view of Shelf Lake itself. From the top of this ridge the rather poorly marked Skyrim Trail continues to the summit of Sheep Mountain, where it terminates.

If you climb Sheep Mountain you will be rewarded with one of the finest views in the park (provided you don't mind standing underneath a microreflector the size of a drive-in movie screen!). From its 10,095-ft. summit, the 360° view includes the Yellowstone River and Paradise Valley to the northeast, Pilot and Index peaks to the west, and the Tetons to the south. From Shelf Lake the trail descends 1,400 ft. in 2 mi. to North Fork Specimen Creek at the 11-mi. mark, then climbs 850 ft. in 1 mi. to Crescent Lake, located in an impressive cirque. The lake was stocked with trout years ago, but it is now barren. From Crescent Lake the trail bends to the northeast toward the park boundary (near "9669" on your topo), then drops to the southeast to High Lake. About 2 mi. northeast of Crescent Lake you will pass another impressive cirque, but the lake has filled in due to natural succession (your topo depicts the lake). When you near the park boundary (0.5 mi. southeast of "9669") you will be standing above a great cirque that contains a small unnamed lake; your elevation at this point is 9,360 ft.—fine mountain views surround you. From here the trail descends 580 ft. to High Lake, situated in a large meadow and fed by several springs (see p. 159).

Sportsman Lake Trail

Sportsman Lake Trailhead
(from U.S. 191) to:

North Fork Specimen Creek	2.0 mi.
High Lake Spur Trail	6.5 mi.

Sportsman Lake	11.0 mi.
Electric Peak Saddle	14.0 mi.
Lower Gardner River Crossing	21.8 mi.
Cache Lake (via spur)	23.5 mi.
Snow Pass	25.0 mi.
Mammoth Road	26.5 mi.

From the west, the trail begins from Specimen Creek on U.S. 191, 5 mi. inside the north boundary. From the east, it begins at Mammoth–Norris Road, 2.5 mi. south of Mammoth. From the U.S. 191 trailhead you soon pass below a large rock slope; look and listen for pika and marmot. There are also aspen here. The combination of a lush forest, rushing stream, large meadows, and mountain views provides delightful scenery for the first 2 mi. Watch for soaring hawks overhead. Sportsman Lake appears at the 11-mi. mark. A large meadow runs all around the south end of the lake, and to the northwest a steep ridge rises some 1,200 ft. A few miles away to the east is Electric Peak. A large boulder on the eastern shore, known as Yahoo Rock, provides a fine overview of the lake. This area burned in 1988; in fact the backcountry cabin here was the only one lost to the fires.

Sportsman Lake Trail continues to the south up and over the saddle to the southwest of Electric Peak. It is a long, hard climb (2,100 ft.) to the top of this saddle. About three-fourths of the way up is a splendid view of Sportsman Lake. Notice the weatherbeaten, scraggly growths of lodgepole and whitebark pine as you near timberline. Above timberline you may see bighorn sheep. From the top of the saddle, at over 9,800 ft., continue to follow the ridge to the northeast if you wish to climb to the summit of Electric Peak. The view from this highest Gallatin peak is superb. There is a register box on the summit.

Electric Peak was named in 1872 by Henry Gannet of the Hayden party, who wrote of his July 26, 1872, climb of the peak: "A thunder-shower was approaching as we neared the summit of the mountain. I was above the others of the party, and, when about fifty feet below the summit, the electric current began to pass through my body. At first I felt nothing, but heard a crackling noise, similar to a rapid discharge of sparks from a friction machine. Immediately after, I began to feel a tingling, or prickling sensation in my head and the ends of my fingers, which as well as the noise, increased rapidly, until, when I reached the top, the noise, which had not changed its character, was deafening, and my hair stood completely on end." Should your hair ever stand completely on end, let that be a warning that lightning may be about to strike.

As you begin your descent of the ridge, watch for animals — especially elk — grazing along the high, grassy slopes to the south. The Gardner River is crossed at the 21.8-mi. mark. The Cache Lake spur trail is reached 1 mi. beyond the Gardner River; it is only 0.75 mi. up to the lake. From the east end of Cache Lake, there is a magnificent view of Electric Peak. There are no fish in Cache Lake, but it is ideal for duck and other waterbirds, and you may even spot a pair of trumpeter swans here.

From the Cache Lake spur trail Sportsman Lake Trail continues down the headwaters of Glen Creek, crossing Snow Pass between Clagett Butte and Terrace Mountain at the 25-mi. mark. The old stage coach road from Mammoth used to cross this 7,450-ft. pass before the present Kingman Pass (Golden Gate) Road was built. Only 1.5 mi. east of Snow Pass is Mammoth–Norris Road.

High Lake Spur Trail (3.0 mi.)

Start at Sportsman Lake Trail, 6.5 mi. from U.S. 191. From there it is a climb of about 750 ft. to High Lake, which sits at

8,774 ft., only 0.1 mi. inside the park boundary. High Lake, surrounded by meadows, is fed by several springs and a small tributary that tumbles into the lake via a pretty, flower-laden grotto on the north shore. From the meadow above the grotto are fine views of the Gallatins. Cutthroat trout thrive here. A trail also leads to Crescent Lake from here (see p. 157).

Fawn Pass Trail

Fawn Pass Trailhead to:

Gardner River	4.5 mi.
Fawn Creek	5.0 mi.
Fawn Lake	5.5 mi.
Patrol Cabin	11.0 mi.
Fawn Pass	12.0 mi.
Cutoff Trail	16.0 mi.
U.S. 191	21.5 mi.

From the west, the trail begins from U.S. 191, 3 mi. north of Divide Lake. From the east, the trail begins from Mammoth–Norris Road 2.5 mi. south of Mammoth. Snow Pass, which contains the old road used by stagecoaches before the present Kingman Pass (Golden Gate) Road was built, is crossed at 1.5 mi. From Glen Creek at the 2-mi. mark you cross Gardners Hole to the Gardner River, where you may spot elk, especially in early summer. Only 0.5 mi. beyond the Gardner River is Fawn Creek; both streams contain brook trout. As you enter the forest from Gardners Hole you pass a meadow and pond. The trail then begins a gradual climb to Fawn Pass, following Fawn Creek most of the way to the top. About the 8-mi. mark you will be opposite a cirque to the south called the Pocket. A small lake is located there.

As you continue to gain elevation on Fawn Pass Trail, you begin to pass through more open areas that afford splendid views of the surrounding country. Gray Peak (10,292 ft.) is prominent to the north; its high, grassy, southern slopes are the summer home for a number of animals, particularly elk.

Fawn Pass provides an ideal habitat for the grizzly bear, and at times there is a rather large concentration of bears in the area. There have been a few bear encounters along Fawn Pass and Bighorn Pass trails. The National Park Service may restrict use of the trails to parties of four or more. Bear incidents among large parties are very rare—they usually involve only one or two hikers.

A grizzly usually detects human presence with his incredibly sensitive nose. If the wind is in your face, he may have to rely on his hearing to detect you. A grizzly's hearing is thought to be about equal to that of humans, so if the wind is in your face and howling through the timber, a good loud pair of bear bells will prove to be most effective.

Evidence of bear activity can be seen at the Fawn Pass patrol cabin (the 11-mi. mark). The cabin is located to the south of the trail across Fawn Creek, and claw marks all around indicate that bears have tried to enter. You may also notice bear diggings and droppings along the way.

Atop the pass (9,100 ft.) is a small lake, which is the source for Fawn Creek. As you continue west from Fawn Pass the trail remains at a high elevation, affording fine views of the large meadows to the southwest. Along this stretch you will encounter dense patches of timber. Evidence of the 1988 fires is seen to the north. At about the 14-mi. mark (8,200 ft.) there is a superb view to the southeast of Three Rivers Peak. The steep cirque above Gallatin Lake (the lake cannot be seen from here) usually contains snow throughout the summer. The forest below consists chiefly of spruce and fir.

At 16 mi. the Bighorn Pass Cutoff Trail permits a loop hike back on the Bighorn Pass Trail if desired. From this point, the trail continues through mostly open country. Many signs of bear are often noticeable along this stretch. At about the 18.5-mi. mark, several cold springs on both sides of the trail provide good drinking water. Fan Creek is reached at 19.5 mi. During 1974 a fire burned several hundred acres here. By 1990 the area looked like a Christmas tree farm. In order to reach U.S. 191 a crossing of the Gallatin River is required. A footbridge was present in 1990. The vegetation surrounding the river consists of dense willow brush, which is a good habitat for moose.

Fan Creek Trail   (8.0 mi.)

Fan Creek Trail connects Sportsman Lake Trail with Fawn Pass Trail, thus permitting an extensive loop trip utilizing these two trails. The trailhead begins from Fawn Pass Trail only 1.5 mi. from U.S. 191. The trail proceeds upstream along Fan Creek through some nice meadows where grizzly sign is often observed. This area along with Fawn Pass and Bighorn Pass trails often contains travel restrictions as part of a bear management area; check at a ranger station before departing. Note that a ford of Fan Creek, which is quite deep until the snow melt subsides in early to mid-July, is required about 4 mi. along the trail.

Bighorn Pass Trail

Bighorn Pass Trail from
Indian Creek Campground to:

Indian Creek	2.0 mi.
Panther Creek	3.0 mi.

Bighorn Pass	8.5 mi.
Cutoff Trail	15.0 mi.
U.S. 191	20.5 mi.

From the west, the trail begins at U.S. 191, 1 mi. north of Divide Lake. From the east, it begins at Indian Creek Campground on Mammoth–Norris Road, 8.5 mi. from Mammoth. From Indian Creek Campground the trail crosses the southern tip of Gardners Hole and reaches Panther Creek at 3 mi. Johnson Gardner trapped beaver in this area as early as 1832. Another trapper, Osborne Russell, visited Gardners Hole in 1839, according to his journals.

Panther Creek, which contains small brook and rainbow trout, is followed for most of the way to Bighorn Pass. The climb from Gardners Hole to Bighorn Pass is 1,820 ft. As you begin the steep hike for the last 2 mi. up to Bighorn Pass, you will come on fine views of Bannock Peak to the north and Antler Peak to the south. (Bannock Peak and Indian Creek were named in honor of the tribe of Indians who inhabited the area to the southwest of the park.) The Bannock Trail passed near the Bighorn Pass Trail, following the valley of Indian Creek into Gardners Hole.

The valley below Bighorn Pass Trail to the south contains several fishless lakes. When above timberline around the pass, watch for bighorn sheep. Grizzlies are also common in this area, as at Fawn Pass. Atop Bighorn Pass (9,110 ft.) there are fine views to the east and west. One mi. south of Bighorn Pass (no trail) at 8,834 ft. is Gallatin Lake. Three Rivers Peak rises 1,122 ft. almost straight up from the lake. (The peak derives its name from the three streams—Gallatin River, Indian Creek, and Grayling Creek—that rise from its slopes.) From Bighorn Pass the trail descends sharply through a burn area to the Gallatin River at the 10.3-mi. mark. The Gallatin River watershed contains brown and rainbow trout; both species were artificially introduced and have greatly displaced the native species of cutthroat and grayling. At 15.0 mi. is the cutoff trail that joins the Fawn Pass and Bighorn Pass trails, and permits a loop hike if desired. From this point, the trail continues 5.5 mi. to U.S. 191, passing through more meadows along the way. Much of this region burned in 1988. The trail exits 1 mi. north of Divide Lake.

Daly Creek–Skyrim Trail (from U.S. 191)

U.S. 191 to:

Park Boundary and Skyrim Trail	5.0 mi.
Bighorn Peak	10.0 mi.
Shelf Lake	13.0 mi.
Crescent Lake	16.0 mi.
High Lake	21.0 mi.

The Daly Creek and Skyrim trails are seldom traveled. The trailhead is located 1 mi. inside the north boundary on U.S. 191. The trail passes through a nice valley through which Daly Creek meanders. The scenery consists of stands of aspen, impressive mountain views, and fine meadows as you hike up the valley.

The old elk corral near the trailhead was used by the National Park Service during the 1960s to capture elk in an attempt to regulate their population. Present park policy is to let nature take its course and not tamper with animal populations (see p. 189). The Skyrim Trail is reached on the park boundary at 5 mi. The Skyrim Trail from here to Bighorn Peak is essentially a game trail; it is poorly marked and maintained and has *very steep* ups and downs. When hiking in the northwest corner of the park, 15-minute quads of Crown Butte and Miner are highly recommended.

Most of the Skyrim Trail is above 9,200 ft., so the views along the way are spectacular. On the way to Bighorn Peak you will enjoy views of the Buffalo Horn Lakes, the Yellowstone River, Tom Miner Basin, petrified stumps, Crown Butte, and the Spanish Peaks. The 9,909-ft. west shoulder of Bighorn Peak is reached via a steep climb at the 10-mi. mark. If you are continuing on to Shelf Lake, High Lake, etc., see pp. 153–7.

Bacon Rind Creek Trail   (2.5 mi.)

The trailhead is located on U.S. 191, 3.2 mi. north of Divide Lake. The first 2.5 mi. along the creek are most enjoyable (look for moose). Beyond the park boundary there are trails that continue into the high country of the Lee Metcalf Wilderness Area in the Gallatin National Forest.

Mt. Holmes Trail

Mt. Holmes Trailhead to:

Winter Creek	1.0 mi.
Grizzly Lake Trail Junction	2.5 mi.
Trilobite Lake Trail Junction	5.5 mi.
Summit of Mt. Holmes	10.3 mi.

The trailhead is on the west side of Mammoth–Norris Road (0.3 mi. south of Apollinaris Springs). The climb of 3,000 ft. to the summit is strenuous, but once on top you will have magnificent views of the surrounding country. Almost all of this trail passes through forest burned in 1988. At the 2.7-mi. mark you reach the Grizzly Lake Trail, which leads 1.5 mi. south to the lake. Continuing on the right fork, you reach a meadow at the 5.5-mi. mark. From here the trail really begins to climb sharply, gaining about 2,500 ft. in the last 4 mi. to the summit. Timberline is reached at the saddle between White Peaks and Mt. Holmes. Below you to the northwest is the source of Indian Creek.

Mt. Holmes (10,336 ft.) was named in 1878 for W.F. Holmes, a geologist with the U.S. Geological Survey. The views from the summit on a clear day take in most of the park's prominent features. A fire lookout is stationed here for most of the summer.

Trilobite Lake Trail (3.0 mi.)

This marked but poorly maintained trail begins from behind the Winter Creek patrol cabin (located at the western end of Winter Creek Meadow at 5.5 mi. along the Mt. Holmes Trail — see p. 165). Be sure to have your topo handy in case you lose the trail. This hike offers some of the most spectacular mountain scenery in the park. After passing through forest and flower-laden and boulder-strewn meadows, the trail ends at Lower Trilobite Lake, situated in a forested setting between Dome Mountain and Trilobite Point. Although there is no trail, Upper Trilobite Lake is reached easily by following its drainage, which flows between the two lakes. The scenic alpine setting here is breathtaking. It is feasible to reach the summit of Mt. Holmes from here by climbing up the saddle west of the lake and then continuing up the steep north slope of Holmes.

Incidentally, a trilobite is a small prehistoric sea creature. When on top of the Gallatins, look for fossilized sea shells and trilobites, which lend evidence to the fact that a vast sea once covered this region.

Warning: This is grizzly country; there should be a minimum of four members in your party.

Grizzly Lake Trail

Grizzly Lake Trailhead to:

Grizzly Lake	2.0 mi.
Junction with Mt. Holmes Trail	3.5 mi.
Mt. Holmes Trailhead	6.0 mi.

This trail passes through an extensive burn area and begins from the wide loop in the road about 1 mi. south of Beaver Lake. The trail then crosses a marshy area that sometimes contains moose. The lake lies deep in a narrow valley. When you first see it, you will be about 350 ft. above, and will command a splendid view — especially after the fires opened up the forest — with Mt. Holmes as an impressive backdrop. The trail descends to the north end of the lake.

Gneiss Creek Trail

Gneiss Creek Trailhead to:

Cougar Creek	4.0 mi.
Maple Creek	7.0 mi.
Gneiss Creek	9.0 mi.
Campanula Creek	12.0 mi.
Trailhead on U.S. 191	14.0 mi.

The trailhead is on the north side of West Entrance Road at 7-Mile Bridge, 7 mi. from the entrance station. The trail parallels the Madison River for about a mile, then turns north through burned lodgepole and Douglas fir for a short distance before entering a large and beautiful open valley. Notice the many seedlings coming back. There are some nice stands of aspen along the way, and the views of the Gallatin and Madison ranges are superb. Look above and you may spot a red-tailed hawk soaring above the valley in search of prey. This is also grizzly country, so make noise and be alert. You may spot some bison grazing here.

A trail junction is reached at 1.5 mi.; the right fork bends to the northeast before ending at Cougar Creek in 2.5 mi. (in a meadow), and our trail bends to the northwest, eventually crossing lower Cougar Creek at the 4- mi. mark. Although subject to change, there usually is a designated campsite along the way at Cougar Creek, Maple Creek, and Gneiss Creek. Fishing is generally good in the streams of the Madison Valley, though mostly for smaller sizes.

A short overnight trip into the Madison Valley is a wonderful and easy introduction to the wild Yellowstone backcountry.

Monument Geyser Basin Trail   (1.0 mi.)

The starting point for this trail is on the west side of Norris–Madison Road, 5 mi. south of Norris (at the bridge). The trail follows the Madison River upstream for 0.5 mi., then climbs 700 ft. in the next 0.5 mi. This thermal region was discovered by Park Superintendent P.W. Norris in 1878. Monument Geyser usually has a small spray of water erupting from its 8-ft. cylindrical cone. Several other smaller cones grouped nearby are now dormant. A boiling sulphur caldron and some steam vents are also located in this group.

To the north of Monument Geyser Basin on the base of the ridge is the Sylvan Springs group, which can easily be viewed across Gibbon Meadows from the road. It contains steam vents, mudpots, and a large mud caldron formed as a result of the 1959 earthquake. You can reach this area by walking along the southern edge of Gibbon Meadows (avoiding the wet, marshy meadow itself), but the thermal regions here contain thin crusts in some areas, so be extremely cautious.

Purple Mountain Trail (3.3 mi.)

Begin from the north side of Madison–Norris Road, 0.7 mi. from Madison Junction. A climb of 1,600 ft. through the forest brings you to the summit. Along the way you will get a good view of the mosaic pattern of the 1988 fires.

At 1.8 mi. and for the remainder of the hike to the summit, the Terrace Spring area, the steam from Fountain Paint Pots area and Midway Geyser Basin (to the right of Fountain Paint Pots) can all be seen. As you approach the summit at the 3.3-mi. mark, the views of the entire Madison area—including Madison Canyon, National Park Mountain, and the junction of the Gibbon and Firehole rivers—become more spectacular. It was at this junction, below what is now known as National Park Mountain, that members of the 1870 Washburn Expedition sat around a campfire on the evening of September 19, 1870, and discussed the marvels they had just discovered.

On a clear day you will be able to see parts of the Beartooth Range, the Absaroka Range, Mt. Washburn, and the Teton Range. Take binoculars on this trip.

Harlequin Lake Trail (0.5 mi.)

The trail begins 1.7 mi. from Madison Junction on the north side of West Entrance Road. This short path winds through dense lodgepole that burned in 1988 to the lake (actually just a lilypad pond). Purple Mountain (8,433 ft.) rises to the northeast. No fish live in this small body of water, but there are usually ducks, and occasionally trumpeter swans. A beaver lodge is located on the north end of the lake. Notice the many lodgepole seedlings that have taken hold following the 1988 fires.

Beaver Ponds Loop Trail (5.0 mi.)

Start from the old Mammoth-to-Gardiner dirt road. The total distance for this trail is 5 mi., as it loops back to the Mammoth area, exiting behind the U.S. magistrate's building (just north of Liberty Cap). The scenery consists of a series of lakes set amid a forest of Douglas fir. This trail is best early or late in the hiking season. Among the Douglas fir are fields of wildflowers of all colors during June. Mule deer are common in this area; you may also spot some antelope in the open sagebrush country below you to the east. A series of dams, constructed by beavers along the stream, has resulted in several lakes at different levels. The beavers are seldom seen during the day. They do most of their work in the evening, beginning shortly before sundown.

Sepulcher Mountain Loop Trail (10.0 mi.)

Start from behind the federal magistrate's house (0.1 mi. north of Liberty Cap). The trail climbs over 3,200 ft., making for a very strenuous trip, although from the summit (9,652 ft.) there are fine views of Electric Peak, Gardners Hole, and the Mammoth area. The peak was apparently named for a tomblike rock (complete with prominent foot- and headstone) on the northwest slope, which can be seen from the North Entrance. On the lower slopes is a large, light-colored deposit of travertine, and hot springs that are currently active.

Sepulcher Mountain is included in an interesting geological structure, which consists of a downthrown block of the earth's crust. Some of the youngest known marine deposits in the park

region are found here, as well as evidence of the earliest volcanic activity associated with the withdrawal of an ancient sea
that once covered this region. From the summit you may choose
to descend the mountain the same way, or complete the loop
by descending to Snow Pass and exiting on Mammoth–Norris
Road, 2.5 mi. north of Mammoth. The distance is about the
same either way.

Howard Eaton Trail
(Golden Gate to Mammoth)   (3.0 mi.)

One of the most delightful short hikes available in the park is
this portion of the old Howard Eaton Trail between Golden
Gate and Mammoth. Howard Eaton was a famous horseman
and early Yellowstone guide. The trail bearing his name at one
time covered about 150 miles and basically paralleled the present
Grand Loop road system so most sections of the trail today are
abandoned and no longer maintained.

Begin this trail at the Glen Creek trailhead across from where
Bunsen Peak Loop Road begins. The trail quickly forks to the
right away from Glen Creek and climbs up to an impressive
overlook of the Golden Gate, Bunsen Peak, Swan Lake Flats,
and the Gallatin Range. Then the trail descends into a fascinating jumble of huge travertine boulders called The Hoodoos,
which have broken away from Terrace Mountain over the centuries. This area is good habitat for yellow-bellied marmots,
also called rockchucks or whistlepigs. You begin a descent of
over 1,000 feet and consequently will witness an incredible
diversity of plant life. I know of no other short trail in the park
that offers such a variety of plants. The 1988 fire burned this
area, so many of the large Douglas fir are gone. In late summer
black bears are often found in this area feeding on buffalo berries. As you near the upper terrace area you will pass several

colorful hot springs. In 1991 one of the most beautiful and active terrace formations was the Narrow Gauge, hidden from those driving Upper Terrace Road, but in full view from the trail. You can exit here or continue down to Clematis Gulch behind Liberty Cap. It is also possible to loop back up to Golden Gate by taking Snow Pass Trail around Terrace Mountain and joining Glen Creek Trail.

Washburn Region

There are few trails in this wilderness region that burned extensively in 1988. Three major streams—Blacktail Deer, Lava, and Tower creeks—originate at the foot of the Washburn Range and flow north to the Yellowstone River. The Washburn Range is actually the upper portion of a much more extensive mountain range, which was covered by lava flows millions of years ago.

The trails described in this section exist only along the perimeters of the Washburn region. Special permission must be obtained for those experienced hikers who wish to traverse the region without the benefit of trails.

WASHBURN REGION TRAILS

Cascade Lake Picnic Area to Beaver Lake	18.0 mi.
Grebe Lake Trail	3.0 mi.
Ice Lake Trail	0.25 mi.
Cascade Lake Trail	2.5 mi.
Observation Peak Trail	3.0 mi.
Osprey Falls Trail	2.0 mi.
Bunsen Peak Trail	5.0 mi.
Wraith Falls Trail	0.3 mi.
Lost Falls Trail	0.5 mi.
Lost Lake Trail	0.5 mi.
Tower Creek Trail	5.0 mi.

Cascade Lake *(Photo by Tom Caples)*

Cascade Lake Picnic Area to Beaver Lake

Cascade Lake Picnic Area to:

Cascade Lake	2.5 mi.
Observation Peak (via spur trail)	5.5 mi.
Grebe Lake	5.0 mi.
Wolf Lake	7.0 mi.
Ice Lake	10.5 mi.
Solfatara Creek	15.0 mi.
Mammoth–Norris Road	18.0 mi.

Start from the trailhead at the picnic area, 1.25 mi. north of Canyon Junction on the Canyon–Tower Road. However, this hike may be varied considerably by joining the trail at other locations, taking either the Cascade Lake, Grebe Lake, or Ice Lake trails. The trail passes through forest, meadow, and marshland to Cascade and Grebe lakes. In early summer there are occasionally a few grizzlies in this area, but they generally move on as the summer progresses. Separate trails lead into both Cascade and Grebe lakes. A spur trail leads to the top of Observation Peak (9,397 ft.). This trail, which is 3 mi. long, begins just east of Cascade Lake and climbs 1,400 ft. to the top. The view of Grebe Lake, the heavily forested Solfatara Plateau, and the Canyon area is magnificent. (see p. 180.)

Wolf Lake is almost surrounded by meadows and is an excellent area for moose and elk. There are arctic grayling and rainbow trout in the lake. (Grayling are quite rare in Yellowstone and found mainly in Ice, Wolf, and Grebe lakes; catch-and-release regulation is in effect—none may be kept.) From Wolf Lake to Ice Lake the trail continues through dense lodgepole, sections of which burned in 1988, crossing the Gibbon

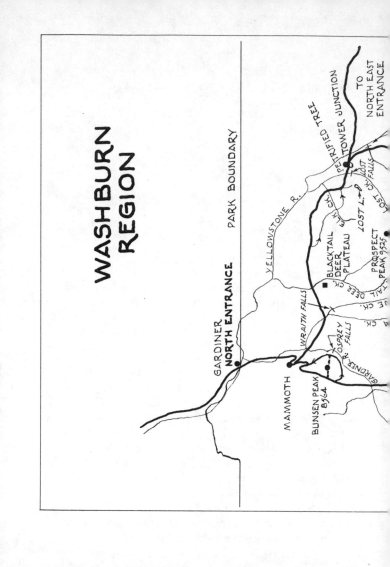

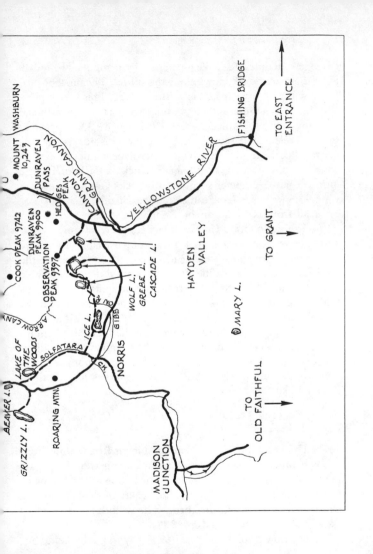

River several times. Ice Lake is completely surrounded by lodge-pole; there are no meadows along the shores. The most beautiful view is at sunrise from the western shore. This lake reportedly holds a population of grayling; the park's last artificial stocking of fish took place here in 1961, when 10,000 grayling fry were released. However, the fishing here is poor — perhaps because Ice Lake does not have a permanent inlet or outlet. There are almost always a number of duck on the lake, but the more elegant trumpeter swan usually picks Grebe Lake for a summer home. (Ice Lake can also be reached by a short 0.25-mi. trail from Norris–Canyon Road.)

At 15 mi. Solfatara Creek is reached. Norris Campground and Ranger Station are only 1 mi. downstream. Extensive meadows appear near the headwaters of the creek at the 14.5-mi. mark. Lake of the Woods lies amid dense lodgepole about .2 mi. northeast of the trail. Reports in the late 1880s told of fish here, but currently there are none. Just southeast of Lake of the Woods is a solfataric area and a large hot spring — Amphitheater Springs — which is the source for Lemonade Creek. Indians used the substantial amounts of vermillion in the springs area for paint. The trail follows Lemonade Creek down to Mammoth–Norris Road and emerges just south of Beaver Lake.

Grebe Lake Trail (3.0 mi.)

Grebe Lake parking area on Canyon–Norris Road, 3 mi. from Canyon Junction, is the starting point for this trail. This particular day hike is rather popular — partly due to the fishing at Grebe Lake, but also because of the beauty of the lake and vicinity. The entire 3 mi. runs through dense lodgepole pine forest, most of which burned in 1988.

At one time a road led most of the way to Grebe Lake, but

it is now closed to all vehicles. At the 2-mi. mark be sure to take the trail that forks left; do not continue down the road. After 3 mi. of lodgepole, Grebe Lake is a welcome sight as you emerge from the forest. On the east, north, and west shores are meadows, in which you can usually see wildlife during early morning and late afternoon. The lake is at an elevation of 8,020 ft. and is the source of the Gibbon River, which flows from its western end.

A pair of trumpeter swan often spends most of the summer here. Grebe Lake is also one of the last strongholds of the arctic grayling in Yellowstone Park. Competition from such artificially introduced species as the rainbow and brown trout has limited their distribution to Grebe, Wolf, and Ice lakes, and portions of the Gibbon River connecting these. The arctic grayling does not compete well with other species, and in an attempt to preserve this beautiful fish, as well as other species, all fishing at Grebe Lake is catch-and-release.

At one time a small fish hatchery was located on the eastern end of the lake where a small stream enters it. Here, in early June during spawning season, thousands of grayling race back and forth. (The grayling is easily distinguished from other trout by its small mouth and large, beautifully colored dorsal fin.)

In the Grebe Lake area you should be extra alert for signs of grizzly bear. In recent years sightings have grown to be rather common, especially during spring and early summer. A clean and odor-free camp is a must. Note that mosquitoes are extremely thick in the Grebe and Cascade lakes areas during June and July, so carry insect repellent.

Ice Lake Trail   **(0.25 mi.)**

Ice Lake can be reached via a 5-minute walk from the trailhead located 3.5 mi. east of Norris on Canyon–Norris Road. See the Cascade Lake–Beaver Lake trail description (p. 178) for information on the Ice Lake area.

Cascade Lake Trail   (2.5 mi.)

The preferred route begins from the Cascade Lake Picnic Area 1.4 mi. north of Canyon Junction on Canyon–Tower Road. There are beautiful flower-laden meadows along the way with numerous spring-fed brooks. The summit of Observation Peak can be seen in the distance. After about 1 mi. you join the Cascade Creek Trail, which leads in from just west of Canyon Junction on Canyon–Norris Road. This trail has fewer open meadows and some horse traffic, so plan to go in from Cascade Lake Picnic Area. Cascade Lake and the surrounding areas are good moose country. In early summer there are occasionally a few grizzlies, but they generally move on as summer progresses.

Observation Peak Trail   (3.0 mi.)

This trail begins from the northeast corner of Cascade Lake. The preferred route to Cascade Lake is the 2.5-mi. trail from Cascade Lake Picnic Area. Much of Observation Peak burned during 1988; however the revegetation is coming along nicely and the flower display in the burned area is spectacular, particularly the lupine and arnica. On the way up you get a fine view of Cascade Lake before going around behind the mountain. After a while Grebe Lake will come into view below. From the top you will have a view that rivals that from Mt. Washburn (and without the crowds). To the west are the Gallatins; to the south are Mt. Sheridan, the Tetons, Hayden Valley, Yellowstone Lake, and Grebe and Wolf lakes; to the north are Cook, Folsom, and Prospect peaks and the rugged drainages of Tower and Carnelian creeks; the view to the east is somewhat obscured by trees. The mosaic pattern of the 1988 fires can be easily observed from here.

Osprey Falls Trail (2.0 mi.)

Start from the trailhead off Bunsen Peak Loop Road, a 6-mi., one-way dirt road beginning from Mammoth–Norris Road (east side) 0.2 mi. south of Rustic Falls and the Golden Gate (5 mi. from Mammoth). The road is narrow and mostly downhill. It is closed at dark and also when conditions are unsafe. The trailhead, which should be marked, is on the right side of the road, about 3 mi. along. This trip is often overlooked, but offers some of the most spectacular scenery available in the park for such a short distance. The trail follows a series of switchbacks to the bottom of the very impressive 800-ft.-deep Sheepeater Canyon, through which the Gardner River flows. The Sheepeater Canyon, with Osprey Falls at its head, ranks second only to the Grand Canyon of Yellowstone as the park's most impressive canyon. As you begin your descent, Sheepeater Cliffs across the gorge will come into full view. These cliffs were named by P.W. Norris for the Sheepeater Indians, a small band of poor and crudely equipped people who occupied this area of the park. Bighorn sheep are occasionally spotted along the cliff's rims. The canyon has been carved into the durable volcanic rock through countless ages, mostly by stream and glacial erosion. At the bottom the trail parallels the raging Gardner River. Osprey Falls (150 ft.) is hidden from view until the last possible moment due to a rise in the trail; the magnificent cataract bursts into view on crossing this small hill. It is impossible to climb up to the brink without extreme danger. The only other feasible view of Osprey Falls (but from a mile off) is obtained from Bunsen Peak Loop Road. Note that much of this area burned in 1988. Try this hike in early summer, when the falls are at full volume.

Bunsen Peak Trail (5.0 mi.)

Start from Bunsen Peak Loop Road, 0.2 mi. south of Rustic Falls and the Golden Gate (5 mi. from Mammoth). The summit of Bunsen Peak is 1,345 higher than the road. There is a small TV tower on top. Bunsen Peak was named for the eminent physicist and chemist Robert W. Bunsen, who invented the Bunsen burner, and who was first to thoroughly investigate the phenomenon of geysers. From the summit there is a magnificent view of Gardners Hole, including Swan Lake Flat, the Mammoth area, and Electric Peak. In 1872, E.S. Topping and D. Woodruff discovered Norris Geyser Basin from this summit, as they spotted large columns of steam rising far to the south. The 1988 fires burned over much of this area.

Wraith Falls Trail (0.3 mi.)

The south side of Mammoth–Tower Road, 5 mi. from Mammoth, is the starting point for this walk. It begins in a meadow, but enters a forest consisting of lodgepole, spruce, and fir near the foot of the falls. Wraith Falls is actually a cascade about 80 ft. high. The scenery is delightful, with Lupine Creek rushing over boulders amid rich forest undergrowth. Evidence of the 1988 fires can be seen here, especially above the falls.

Lost Falls Trail (0.5 mi.)

This short walk begins directly behind Roosevelt Lodge. From Roosevelt Lodge, follow Lost Creek upstream to the foot of the falls in a steep timber-covered canyon. Lost Falls plunges 40 ft. over the canyon's edge. Lost Lake lies about 0.5 mi. west of the falls.

Lost Lake Trail (0.5 mi.)

This short delightful trail begins from the Petrified Tree parking lot. A short spur road leads to the Petrified Tree from the Tower–Mammoth Road, 1.4 mi. north of Tower Junction. The petrified tree is actually an ancient redwood. There used to be two other petrified stumps here but they were carried off piece by piece, hence the need for the fence enclosure.

The trail follows a small stream through a little valley that is carpeted with wildflowers during June. Douglas fir and aspen line the valley. Look for moose. Lost Lake is situated in a very scenic setting, perfect for a short hike and picnic lunch.

Tower Creek Trail (5.0 mi.)

The trail winds along Tower Creek, which rushes over boulders and through gorges, and collects in pools and riffles. The lush mixed forest is superb, with spruce and fir common. This hike is a favorite for the fishing enthusiast. The junction of Tower and Carnelian creeks is reached at the 5-mi. mark. The 1988 fires burned the upper stretches along this trail.

Cutoff Mountain *(Photo by Tom Caples)*

North of Yellowstone River Region

This wilderness region is the smallest of the seven backcountry areas included in this book. However, it borders the Beartooth–Absaroka Wilderness Area to the north, so the continuous wilderness is quite extensive. Elevations range from 5,500 ft. along the Yellowstone River to more than 9,200 ft. on the Buffalo Plateau along the northern boundary and 10,638 ft. atop Cutoff Peak in the northeastern section. The mountain scenery in the northeast is extremely rugged, comparable to that of Glacier National Park in northern Montana.

Although there are a number of connecting trails, three extensive backcountry trips are available in this region. One begins from Hellroaring Creek and follows the Yellowstone River to Blacktail Deer Creek or Gardiner. The second takes the Buffalo Plateau Trail, which begins from near Hellroaring Creek, loops into the Beartooth–Absaroka Wilderness Area, and ends at Slough Creek. The third possibility is to hike up Slough Creek, take Elk Tongue Creek Trail over Bliss Pass, then Pebble Creek Trail downstream to Pebble Creek Campground or upstream to near the Northeast Entrance — both on Northeast Entrance Road.

NORTH OF YELLOWSTONE RIVER REGION TRAILS

Yellowstone River Trail
(Hellroaring Creek to Gardiner)   19.0 mi.

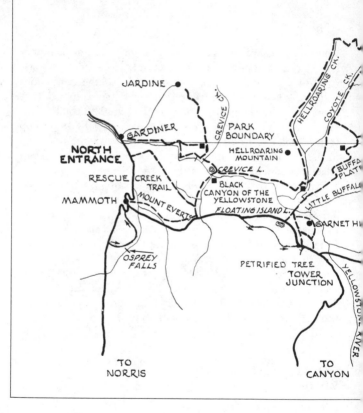

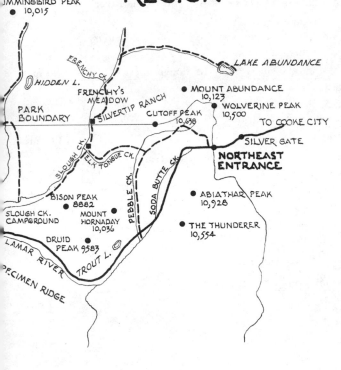

NORTH OF
YELLOWSTONE RIVER
REGION

HUMMINGBIRD PEAK
● 10,015

FRENCHY CK.

LAKE ABUNDANCE

HIDDEN L.

FRENCHY'S MEADOW

SILVERTIP RANCH

● MOUNT ABUNDANCE
10,123

WOLVERINE PEAK
10,500

PARK BOUNDARY

CUTOFF PEAK
10,638

TO COOKE CITY

SILVER GATE

SLOUGH CK.

ELK TONGUE CK.

NORTHEAST ENTRANCE

PEBBLE CK.

SODA BUTTE CK.

● ABIATHAR PEAK
10,928

BISON PEAK
8882

SLOUGH CK. CAMPGROUND

MOUNT HORNADAY
10,036

● THE THUNDERER
10,554

DRUID PEAK 9583

LAMAR RIVER

TROUT L.

SPECIMEN RIDGE

Rescue Creek Trail (Mammoth–Tower Road to Gardner River)	8.0 mi.
Lava Creek Trail	6.0 mi.
Lower Blacktail Trail (Mammoth–Tower Road to Yellowstone River)	4.0 mi.
Hellroaring Creek Trail (Mammoth–Tower Road to Northern Boundary)	7.0 mi.
Buffalo Plateau Trail (Mammoth–Tower Road to Slough Creek)	21.0 mi.
Slough Creek Trail (Slough Creek Campground to Northern Boundary)	11.0 mi.
Pebble Creek Trail	13.0 mi.
Bliss Pass Trail via Slough Creek Trail and Pebble Creek Trail	20.5, 19.5 mi.
Trout Lake Trail	0.5 mi.

Yellowstone River Trail
(Hellroaring Creek to Gardiner)

Hellroaring Trailhead to:

Yellowstone River Bridge	1.0 mi.
Hellroaring Creek Bridge	2.0 mi.
Cottonwood Creek	6.0 mi.
Blacktail Bridge	10.0 mi.
Crevice Lake	10.5 mi.
Knowles Falls	12.0 mi.
Gardiner, Montana	19.0 mi.

The trail begins at the Hellroaring Creek trailhead (see p. 193). A suspension bridge gets you across the mighty Yellowstone River, then a footbridge crosses Hellroaring Creek. You are now heading down the Yellowstone River Trail. This hike is a hot one most of the summer due to the low elevation, but it is the ideal trip in spring, early summer, and late fall, when most of the higher trails are snowed in. In early spring look for bighorn sheep, elk, deer, and antelope. In late autumn, when the first heavy snows begin to fall, deer and elk begin their migration down from atop the plateau to the Yellowstone River in search of food.

From Hellroaring Creek the trail leads through open sage-brush dotted with several glacial ponds and into the depths of Black Canyon, so named for the shaded canyon walls rising high above the river. Crevice Lake at the 10.5 mi. mark has no inlet or outlet and sits in a deeply depressed bowl. There are no fish. The trail passes high above the lake on its northeast side, with a fine view of Black Canyon in the background.

As you hike from Crevice Lake to Knowles Falls you may notice some antlers, bones, and skulls—chiefly elk, but also perhaps a few deer and bighorn. Many more used to be seen here but poachers removed many antlers. Many poachers are caught and receive stiff fines. Hundreds of elk winter in this area each year, and sometimes there is simply not enough food for all. Only the fittest survive. This natural process of winterkill helps control the animal populations and ensures a strong breed for reproduction. Severe winter conditions that stretch well into spring may result in a winterkill as high as 10 percent of Yellowstone's elk herds.

To some, 1,000 dead elk seems like an unfortunate waste; however, it is important to realize that in a large, natural ecosystem nothing is wasted. Most carcasses are picked clean by meat-eaters and scavengers within a matter of days, with the rest decomposing, thus recycling nutrients back to the soil. Even the antlers are utilized by gnawing animals such as chipmunks and ground squirrels (another good reason for the park rule: take nothing but pictures; leave nothing but footprints). Death in the Yellowstone ecosystem is neither good nor bad; it just is. What seems "bad" for the elk is "good" for the coyote, cougar, bear, eagle, and raven, and vice versa.

At the 12-mi. mark you reach Knowles Falls, where the Yellowstone River takes a roaring 15-ft. plunge. The last 3 mi. into Gardiner are through a dry, desertlike area. (Some hikers prefer to exit the canyon back at Blacktail Bridge and climb 1,000 ft. in 4.5 mi. along Blacktail Deer Creek.)

Fencelike columnar basalt formations are common through the canyon. Note the layered lava flows on the ridge above Blacktail Bridge. Campsites are usually located near Cottonwood Creek (beautiful area, easy river access) and Little Cottonwood Creek (spectacular vista of river and canyon, but no realistic river access). Take a canteen on this hike. Look for a spring just west of Little Cottonwood Creek.

Rescue Creek Trail
(Mammoth–Tower Road to Gardner River)   (8.0 mi.)

The trailhead is on the north side of Mammoth–Tower Road, 7 mi. from Mammoth, west of Blacktail Deer Creek. This trail chiefly traverses open sagebrush and is interesting during spring and fall as the wildlife-viewing opportunities are good, especially for antelope. However, during the summer the trip is hot and dry. There are several ponds along the way whose origins trace back to large glacial lakes formed by retreating glaciers. There are usually various waterbirds on the lakes.

Truman Everts was supposedly found at Rescue Creek on October 16, 1870, after 37 days of wandering in Yellowstone's wilderness. Actually, Everts was found about 2 mi. up the eastern fork of Blacktail Deer Creek (south of Mammoth–Tower Road). He was in critical condition, but eventually recovered to live to the age of 85.

At 5 mi. Rattlesnake Butte appears to the north. (There are no poisonous snakes in Yellowstone, with the exception of the lower elevations in this area, where an occasional rattler is found. (In the early 1980s dinosaur bones were discovered near here.) The trail crosses the Gardner River (bridge provided) and joins the road 0.7 mi. from the North Entrance. Less than 1 mi. south of this point is MacMinn Bench, on the lower slopes of Everts Mountain. From October to June, this area contains fascinating wildlife. During early morning and late afternoon you may expect to see herds of bighorn sheep, antelope, deer, and elk grazing on the slopes, with an occasional coyote checking the edges of the herds for a weak specimen. Access to the slopes of the bench is gained easily from the Gardner River footbridge.

Lava Creek Trail (6.0 mi.)

Lava Creek Trailhead to:

Mouth of Lava Creek	1.0 mi.
Undine Falls	3.0 mi.
Lava Creek Picnic Area	3.5 mi.
Junction with Blacktail Creek Trail	6.0 mi.

To get to the trailhead turn down the service road located across from Mammoth Campground and proceed past the Mammoth School and take the dirt road to the river. The trail begins at a footbridge crossing the Gardner River in a beautiful setting. The marsh area along the river here is a good place to view a variety of bird activity. The trail goes up the east side of the river with signs of beaver activity along the way. At about the 1-mi. point you will see the mouth of Lava Creek as it enters the Gardner River. The trail continues another 2 mi. through steep-walled Lava Creek Canyon until you reach terraced Undine Falls. The upper falls are 60 ft. high and the lower falls are 50 ft. high. (Male hikers should be on the lookout for undines here! Folklore has it that undines are female water spirits who live around waterfalls and can capture the souls of mortal men by marrying them and bearing their children.) From the falls the trail continues upstream 3 mi. more to the junction with the Blacktail Trail. Some hikers just turn around here; others cross Lava Creek and proceed over to Mammoth–Tower Road at the Lava Creek Picnic Area.

Lower Blacktail Trail
(Mammoth–Tower Road to Yellowstone River)   **(4.0 mi.)**

This hike is quite popular as it provides access to a beautiful area in Black Canyon. Start out from the same trailhead as Rescue Creek Trail. The trail passes through open sagebrush and descends over 1,000 ft. to the river, which makes for a rough return trip on a hot summer day. Soils here are glacial till, deep and well drained; as a result, there is little surface moisture. The trail does pass close to a small falls along Blacktail Deer Creek at the 2.5-mi. mark, which makes for a delightful rest break. On the way down to the river you may spot deer, antelope, and even an occasional bighorn sheep. During May and June, elk often calve in this area while traveling from their low-lying winter range to the high plateau country. Blacktail Bridge affords access across the Yellowstone River and to such attractions as Knowles Falls, Crevice Lake, and Black Canyon.

Hellroaring Creek Trail
(Mammoth–Tower Road to Northern Boundary   (7.0 mi.)

Hellroaring Creek Trailhead to:

Yellowstone River Suspension Bridge	1.0 mi.
Junction with Buffalo Plateau Trail	1.5 mi.
Junction with Yellowstone River Trail	2.0 mi.
Hellroaring Creek Bridge	3.5 mi.
Northern Boundary	7.0 mi.

The trail begins on the north side of Mammoth–Tower Road, 3.3 mi. from Tower and just north of Floating Island Lake. The trail descends some 750 ft. in 1 mi. to the Yellowstone River, passing Garnet Hill on the east. (Garnet Hill is composed of ancient granitic gneiss over a billion years old.) A suspension bridge crosses the Yellowstone River at a point where it rushes through a deep gorge. After passing the Buffalo Plateau Trail Junction in open sagebrush, you will see ponds of glacial origin where there are almost always some ducks.

At the 3-mi. mark you reach Hellroaring Creek, with a patrol cabin across the stream. (Gold prospectors along the Yellowstone River in 1867 described this creek as a "real hell roarer," and the name stuck.) A footbridge across Hellroaring Creek is provided. (There is also a stockbridge 0.5 mi. upstream from the cabin.) Do not attempt any fords here in early summer. A hiker and a fisherman died in this vicinity in the early 1980s. The creek contains a population of cutthroat trout; however, high waters often persist through mid-July.

The prominent cone-shaped mountain to the northwest is Hellroaring Mountain, one of the park's few granite peaks not covered by volcanic lava flows of the Tertiary period. From the Hellroaring Creek patrol cabin area you have several choices: follow the creek up into the Absaroka Primitive Area; do the same by following Coyote Creek Trail; or angle up the ridge in a northeasterly direction to the Buffalo Plateau Trail, which is the only feasible hike if you plan to loop back down in the park. If you continue north along Hellroaring Creek across the park boundary, lakes, waterfalls, mountains, forest, and meadows await you in the Absaroka Primitive Area of Gallatin National Forest. (A Montana state fishing license is required if you plan to do any fishing.)

Buffalo Plateau Trail
(Mammoth–Tower Road to Slough Creek)

Buffalo Plateau Trailhead to:

Yellowstone River	1.0 mi.
Patrol Cabin	9.0 mi.
Park Boundary	9.5 mi.
Buffalo Fork Creek	13.0 mi.
Hidden Lake	16.0 mi.
Slough Creek	19.0 mi.
Slough Creek Campground	21.0 mi.

A complete hike of the Buffalo Plateau Trail ranks as one of the finest available in the park; the scenery is wild and quite varied. Set out from the same trailhead as Hellroaring Creek Trail. The Buffalo Plateau Trail begins 0.4 mi. north of the suspension bridge over the Yellowstone River. However, a good plan is to camp on Hellroaring Creek and then join the Buffalo

Plateau Trail by angling up the open slopes in a northeasterly direction. Otherwise it is a long, hard climb of 3,000 ft. up to the plateau, and unless you get a very early start, you may not make it to Buffalo Fork Creek in the Absaroka Primitive Area, which is by far the best available camping spot. If you do decide on this plan, be certain to cross over Coyote Creek Trail to Buffalo Plateau Trail and not go up Coyote Creek by mistake.

A trip on the Buffalo Plateau requires a 15-min. topo map of Mt. Wallace, Montana, since the trail crosses over the park boundary. If camping on Hellroaring Creek, be sure to take a good look at the summit of Hellroaring Mountain high *above* you, for when you reach the top of the plateau, it will be far *below* you. The trail climbs steadily through open sagebrush to the top, providing wide vistas of the surrounding country-side. Herds of antelope are common.

The prominent skyline of the Gallatin Range lies to the west and the Washburn Range to the south. Peaks are easily identified by referring to your topo map, especially Electric Peak, Mt. Holmes, and Mt. Washburn. As you climb higher you begin to enter patches of forest, with Douglas fir predominating. The trail becomes difficult to follow over open areas, so look closely for the orange trail markers. When you reach the Buffalo patrol cabin, you will have climbed to near the 9,000-ft. mark. (The cabin is usually occupied during the fall hunting season to ensure against hunters crossing over the boundary.)

The next mi. beyond the cabin passes through superb subalpine scenery, with the rugged Beartooth Range to the north. When the boundary is crossed, you will note a steep rise to your left that contains a trail—*do not take this;* rather, continue due north until you reach the USFS Buffalo Plateau Trail, which extends west–east and is well marked all the way to Buffalo Fork

Creek. In the early 1900s, this trail was maintained by poachers, but it is now official, though some signs still refer to it as "Poacher's Trail." Much of this area burned in 1988.

When you have descended nearly 2,000 ft. from the plateau down to Buffalo Fork Creek, you emerge into a meadow that is a fine place to camp. The creek provides excellent fishing for small but tasty rainbow trout. Hummingbird Peak (over 10,000 ft.) provides a beautiful background. If you decide to spend an extra day here, you may want to explore the trail to the north, up Buffalo Fork Creek for about 3 mi., where you enter another extensive meadow. About 0.5 mi. east of the trail (across the creek) is Hidden Lake, which, as its name suggests, lies hidden between a small hill and the side of a mountain. The lake covers about 10 acres and is quite deep, with talus slopes extending to the water at the southeast end. Remember, a Montana fishing license is required for waters north of the park.

Buffalo Plateau Trail crosses Buffalo Fork Creek, where fires burned in 1988, then follows the meadow around to its southeast end (away from the creek), where it continues mostly through timber and high on the ridge above Buffalo Creek before emerging into a large, open area containing groves of aspen. (Many of the trees show scar rings caused by the continuous rubbing of elk antlers on the bark.) From the edge of the plateau in this open country you can see Slough Creek Valley below and craggy Cutoff Peak (10,638 ft.) to the northeast. If you have binoculars, scan the valley below you for wildlife—especially moose, elk, and the occasional coyote. You must ford Slough Creek, which can be treacherous in early summer during high water, and this particular ford is not recommended until the water level goes down in mid-July. The trail then joins an old wagon road leading to Slough Creek Campground, 2 mi. away.

**Slough Creek Trail
(Slough Creek Campground to
Northern Boundary)** (11.0 mi.)

*Slough Creek Trail from
Slough Creek Campground to:*

Slough Creek Meadows	2.0 mi.
Plateau Creek	5.0 mi.
Elk Tongue Creek Trail Junction	8.0 mi.
Northern Boundary	11.0 mi.

Beautiful scenery, with views of rugged peaks, and fine aspen groves await those who travel up Slough Creek. The starting point is Slough Creek Campground, reached by a dirt road from Tower–Northeast Entrance Road. After 2 mi. the trail breaks into Slough Creek Valley. Watch here for moose, elk, and deer. Cutoff Peak dominates the view at the head of the valley. In 1867 a gold prospector, when asked by a traveling party about this stream, described it as "but a slough." However, when the party reached the creek they encountered a rushing torrent and lost a fully loaded pack horse while crossing it. Generally speaking, the fishing for Slough Creek's cutthroat trout improves as you work your way upstream. All fishing here is catch-and-release.

Above the confluence of Slough and Elk Tongue creeks, at the 8-mi. mark, you will begin to see evidence from the 1988 fires, including mud slides. From here Elk Tongue Creek Trail begins its climb of 2,600 ft. up to Bliss Pass. If you continue upstream along Slough Creek, you come upon Silvertip Ranch, just north of the park boundary. During the early 1900s, Frenchy Duret, a man of French-Canadian descent lived here.

He maintained a small herd of cattle that he often illegally allowed to graze inside the park. Duret was also a noted poacher of park game, but although rangers tried to catch him in the act, he always managed to elude them. Rumor had it that he harbored a particular hatred for grizzlies, since his pet dogs had been killed by one. One summer's morning in 1922 Duret discovered a huge grizzly caught in one of his steel bear traps. He returned to his cabin, retrieved his rifle, and proceeded to shoot the bear. Apparently he did not strike a vital spot, for the bear lunged forward and broke free from the trap, falling on Duret and wounding him severely. The grizzly then left the scene. Duret, upon regaining consciousness, began a slow crawl back to his cabin, 0.75 mi. away. He made it to the edge of his property, then died under his own fence. Frenchy Duret was buried near his cabin. His gravestone, near the Silvertip Ranch, reads "Joseph Duret, Born in France 1858, Died 1922."

The bear, whose bloody trail led down Slough Creek, was never found. Newspaper clippings and a 1922 letter from Horace Albright—then the park's superintendent—that discuss the fruitless search for the grizzly, are posted in the lobby of Silvertip Ranch. According to Albright, it left behind the largest set of tracks he had ever seen in Yellowstone. Presumably, offspring of this bear inhabit Yellowstone Park today. Frenchy's Meadow is 3.0 mi. north of Silvertip Ranch.

Pebble Creek Trail

Pebble Creek Trailhead to:

Upper Pebble Creek Meadows	2.5 mi.
Bliss Pass Trail Junction	5.5 mi.
Pebble Creek Campground	13.0 mi.

The trailhead is located at Warm Creek Picnic Area, 1.2 mi. from the Northeast Entrance. The first 5.5 mi. of this trail to the Bliss Pass Trail contain some of the best mountain scenery in the park. The trail climbs over 1,000 ft. to a saddle before descending into lovely Upper Pebble Creek Meadows, surrounded by rugged peaks. Wildflower displays throughout these meadows are impressive during July.

Below the Bliss Pass Trail Junction the trail stays along Pebble Creek in a mostly forested setting. Several fords are required, which could present a problem prior to July.

Bliss Pass Trail via Slough Creek Trail

Slough Creek Trailhead at Slough Creek Campground to:

Bliss Pass Trail Junction	8.0 mi.
Bliss Pass	12.0 mi.
Junction with Pebble Creek Trail	14.0 mi.
Pebble Creek Campground via Pebble Creek Trail North	20.5 mi.
Warm Creek Picnic Area near Northeast Entrance via Pebble Creek Trail South	19.5 mi.

The trail starts out near the confluence of Slough and Elk Tongue creeks on the old wagon road 8 mi. from Slough Creek Campground. However, if you wish to start at the other end of the hike, you may begin on Pebble Creek Trail at Pebble Creek Campground, 9.5 mi. from the Northeast Entrance, or the trailhead 1.2 mi. inside the Northeast Entrance. It is a hard 4 mi. up Elk Tongue Creek to Bliss Pass, as you climb over 2,600 ft., mostly through timber. When you near Bliss Pass, you will pass a small pond on your right (southeast); at this point be sure to climb the small ridge to your left (northwest) for a fine view of Slough Creek Valley, which you cannot see from the pass itself. The Bliss Pass vicinity is good habitat for bear, so make noise and be alert. At the actual summit of the pass there is a good view of the rugged peaks to the northeast. The large meadow to the northeast contains the north Pebble Creek Trail, which exits near the Northeast Entrance. From Bliss Pass down to Pebble Creek and out to the road, the trail passes through spectacular mountain scenery that is among the best Yellowstone has to offer.

The trail drops practically straight down to Pebble Creek on a series of switchbacks. At Pebble Creek you reach one of the most beautiful campsites in Yellowstone Park, yet it is seldom used. Here you come to a stream with cutthroat trout. Evidence of the 1988 fires is in view here. If you continue south on Pebble Creek Trail, you will pass under Baronette Peak (10,404 ft.) to the east and Mt. Hornaday (10,036 ft.) to the west before reaching Pebble Creek Campground 7.5 mi. away. The more scenic trip, and also the shorter trip to the road, is made by continuing up Pebble Creek Trail, which bends around to the east and exits near the Northeast Entrance. The trail passes through spruce and fir for 2 mi. before entering the large meadow that is visible from Bliss Pass. The fishing is still good this far upstream, although mostly for smaller sizes. The trail leaves Pebble Creek and makes a short climb up to the saddle in the ridge, then begins a descent of about 1,000 ft. to Northeast Entrance Road. The views of Abiathar Park (10,928 ft.) across the way and of the valley through which Soda Butte Creek courses are spectacular. The trail reaches the road at the Warm Creek Picnic Area 1.2 mi. from the Northeast Entrance. For a wonderful short trip that provides spectacular scenery, the

1.5-mi. hike from here over the saddle down to Pebble Creek cannot be topped.

Trout Lake Trail (0.5 mi.)

This is a very good short trip, whether you plan to fish or not. Start from Tower–Northeast Entrance Road, 12.7 mi. from the Northeast Entrance (about 1.8 mi. south of Pebble Creek Campground). It climbs sharply over a small ridge that for most of the way is carpeted with wildflowers. At the top of the hill you reach a huge Douglas fir. From here you have good views of The Thunderer (10,554 ft.) to the east and Mt. Hornaday (10,036 ft.) to the north. Trout Lake is surrounded by meadows to the west and north. You may notice an artificial spillway at the lake's outlet; it was constructed in conjunction with the fish hatchery once operated here. The lake is quite deep and contains mostly whopper-sized rainbow trout, which are not easy to catch. Nearby Buck and Shrimp lakes contain few, if any, fish. Fishing at Trout Lake is catch-and-release only. In 1989 a nice footbridge was constructed across the spillway.

Fern Lake

Mirror Plateau Region

The Mirror Plateau Wilderness Area is very large and contains some of the wildest and most interesting backcountry scenery to be found in Yellowstone. There are extensive thermal areas, fossil forests, a portion of the Grand Canyon of Yellowstone, rugged mountain scenery, fine meadows and valleys, and abundant wildlife.

Although most access to this large wilderness region is via the Lamar River and Pelican trails, there are some spectacular and seldom traveled mountain trails entering the park via the North Absaroka Wilderness in Shoshone National Forest. Three such trails are Republic, Crandall, and Sunlight (see p. 222).

During early summer many of the trails in this region are impassable due to high water conditions. For this reason it is best to plan your longer trips for no earlier than mid-July.

MIRROR PLATEAU REGION TRAILS

Lamar River Trail (and Side Trips from Cold Creek Junction)	17.5, 23.5, 24.0 mi.
Miller Creek Trail (and Side Trips from Upper Miller Creek	8.5 mi.
The Thunderer Cutoff Trail	7.5 mi.
Cache Creek Trail	21.6 mi.
Pelican Creek–Astringent Creek Loop Trail	35.0 mi.
Wapiti Lake Trail	14.5 mi.
Specimen Ridge Trail	17.5 mi.

MIRROR PLATEAU REGION

CRANDALL CK.
CANOE L.
COOKE CITY
SILVER GATE
NORTHEAST ENTRANCE
AMPHITHEATER MTN. 10,847
REPUBLIC PASS
CACHE MTN. 9596
THE NEEDLE 9907
SOUTH CACHE CK.
BARRONETTE PEAK 10,404
ABIATHER PEAK 10,928
AMPHITHEATER CK.
PEBBLE CK.
THE THUNDERER 10,554
MOUNT NORRIS 9936
CACHE CK.
OPAL CK.
DRUID PEAK 9583
SODA BUTTE CK.
LAMAR RANGER STATION
RIDGE
SLOUGH CK.
CRYSTAL CK.
SPECIMEN CK.
QUARTZ CK.
AGATE CK.
DEEP CK.
YELLOWSTONE R.
BROAD
TOWER JUNCTION
TOWER CK. FALLS
TOWER FALLS
MOUNT WASHBURN 10,243
WASHBURN HOT SPRINGS

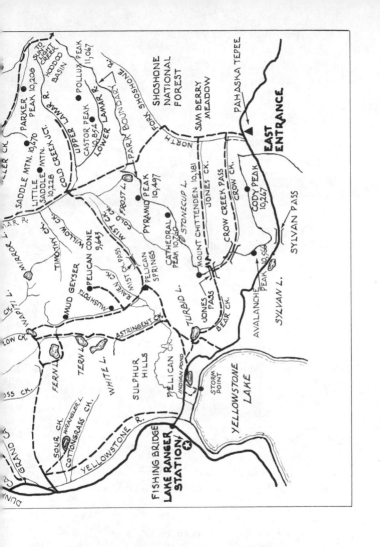

Yellowstone River Overlook Trail	2.0 mi.
Tower Falls Trail	0.5 mi.
Avalanche Peak Hike	2.0 mi.
Storm Point Trail	2.0 mi.
Turbid Lake Trail	3.0 mi.
Hoodoo Basin Trail (Sunlight Creek at Sulphur Camp to Hoodoo Basin)	18.0 mi.
Canyon to Lake Trail	14.5 mi.

Lamar River Trail
(and Side Trips from Cold Creek Junction)

Lamar River Trail from Soda Butte Trailhead to:

Cache Creek	3.3 mi.
Calfee Creek	7.5 mi.
Miller Creek Trail	8.5 mi.
Cold Creek Junction	17.5 mi.
Upper Lamar Cabin	23.5 mi.
*Upper Miller Cabin	16.5 mi.
*Parker Peak	21.5 mi.
*Hoodoo Basin	24.0 mi.

The trailhead is on Tower Junction–Northeast Entrance Road, 15 mi. east of Tower Junction (4.3 mi. east of the Lamar Ranger Station), which provides access to a small bridge across Soda

---

*Distances if you turn up Miller Creek Trail.

Butte Creek. There are two other trailheads located between Lamar Ranger Station and the Soda Butte trailhead for horse parties. The first 3.5 mi. traverse a large meadow in the Lamar Valley and lead down to Cache Creek. Along the way there are several stands of aspen. Aspen in Yellowstone has been on a steady decline. This is believed to be the result of winter over-grazing by elk, and also the lack of forest fires, which, as in the case of the lodgepole pine, play an instrumental role in the reproduction of the species. The 1988 fires helped the aspen spread but elk seem to be consuming it. The reintroduction of wolves would most likely help bring nature into a better balance (see p. 68).

At the 3.3-mi. mark you come to a trail junction where Cache Creek Trail forks to the east. From this junction, Lamar River Trail descends sharply to Cache Creek. Cache Creek derives its name from a prospecting party in 1863 that was surprised by Indians while camped on the creek. All their stock was lost or stolen except for a few mules, and as a result the party was forced to "cache" much of their gear at this location and pick it up later. Unfortunately for the backpacker there is no bridge across the icy waters of the creek. This crossing is not recommended before mid-July, due to very high water.

The trail from Cache Creek to Cold Creek Junction contains very little change of scenery, as it follows the Lamar River through mostly wooded country. Small open areas along the way contain numerous buffalo droppings, indicating the passage of these animals through here in spring and early summer. You may spot an occasional bull at any time during the summer and early fall. At the 7.5-mi. mark you cross Calfee Creek, and just beyond the creek about 0.3 mi. is a patrol cabin. At 8.5 mi. there is a trail junction. Here Miller Creek Trail forks to the east, leading to some very wild, seldom visited country. Lamar River Trail crosses Miller Creek and continues along the

Lamar River, mostly through unchanging scenery. Just before reaching Willow Creek you will enter an extensive burn area from 1988 that extends to Cold Creek Junction and to the Upper Lamar area.

As you approach the meadows leading to Cold Creek Junction, mountains come into view. The Absaroka Range appears to the southeast. The Cold Creek patrol cabin lies 0.5 mi. short of Cold Creek Junction, on the west side of the Lamar River. Cold Creek Junction makes an ideal spot in which to set up base camp and plan a stay of several days. From here Lamar River Trail continues 6 mi. more to the Upper Lamar River patrol cabin, where it terminates; Frost Lake Trail climbs 6 mi. up to the park boundary; and the Mist Creek Trail leads over Mist Creek Pass to Pelican Springs and Pelican Valley. Little Saddle Mountain near Cold Creek Junction offers a very rewarding climb. (Any travel away from established trails should be by experienced hikers, and permission must be obtained.)

The trail up to the Upper Lamar River patrol cabin follows the Lamar River on the north side and remains low in the valley, with prominent peaks rising on both sides. Saddle Mountain (10,670 ft.) lies to the north of Upper Lamar River Trail, and may be climbed without too much difficulty by zigzagging up the slopes following open areas to the top. If you do not travel up Upper Lamar River Trail, Little Saddle Mountain (10,228 ft.) can be climbed, beginning from your camp at Cold Creek Junction. Both peaks offer almost the same view, which is magnificent. The climb up Little Saddle Mountain is easier than it used to be since the 1988 fires opened much of the forest here.

From the top of Little Saddle Mountain you command a spectacular 360° view. To the west across the Lamar River is Pelican Cone (9,648 ft.), with its fire lookout visible on top. Beyond Pelican Cone is a bird's-eye view of Yellowstone Lake.

Portions of the Pelican Valley are also visible. To the north-west lies Lamar Valley, where you began your hike. Rugged peaks reminiscent of Glacier National Park rise sharply to elevations of over 11,000 ft., Castor and Pollux to the southeast being the most prominent. Buffalo normally spend the summer in the high country, and you may spot a herd from the summit.

Frost Lake Trail is another splendid side trip available from Cold Creek Junction. The trail's name is rather misleading, as it does not actually lead to Frost Lake, but passes within 1 mi. of it. Getting to the lake requires crossing USFS land that is not shown on the USGS topo map of Yellowstone. If Frost Lake is your main objective, it is wise to have a USGS 15-minute map of Pelican Cone to aid in locating the lake. Frost Lake is situated in a fine subalpine setting, but there are no mountain views from the lake's shores.

Before entering the forest and beginning the steep climb up to the park boundary, Frost Lake Trail provides a good view of Little Saddle Mountain from the Lamar River. Near the park boundary you will approach about 9,600 ft. and will command spectacular views of Castor Peak, Pollux Peak, and Notch Mountain. Close to the park boundary, a sign pointing to the west says, "Frost Lake: 1 mile;" since there is no trail, it may be difficult to find without a map depicting USFS land. There is a small lake at the park boundary all summer. Due to heavy horse use, Frost Lake Trail is often in poor hiking condition. Hikers have been known to refer to horses as "1,500-pound cookie cutters."

From Cold Creek Junction it is 11 mi. to Pelican Springs, following Mist Creek Pass Trail. The hike is through dense forest, much of which burned in 1988, all the way except for one meadow through which Mist Creek runs. Cold Creek and Mist Creek both contain populations of small cutthroat. From Pelican Springs it is 7 mi. out to the trailhead on Fishing Bridge–East Entrance Road. (See *Pelican Creek–Astringent Creek Trail.*)

Miller Creek Trail
(and Side Trips from Upper Miller Creek)   (8.5 mi.)

Start from the point on Lamar River Trail that is 8.5 mi. south of Soda Butte Creek Bridge and 1 mi. south of Calfee Creek patrol cabin. This trail leads up into a wild portion of the rugged northern Absarokas, seldom visited. Miller Creek, which contains some cutthroat, was named in 1880 by Park Superintendent Norris for Adam "Horn" Miller, the discoverer of Soda Butte, as a result of Miller's narrow escape from Indians in 1870 when he descended this stream. Canoe Lake Trail, 1 mi. west of the patrol cabin, climbs sharply up the ridge and leads to Canoe Lake and the park boundary 4 mi. away. The lake, at 9,200 ft., is very narrow and contains no fish. Timber Creek Trail (USFS) leads from the park boundary to Sunlight Basin Road about 19 mi. away.

After you reach the Miller Creek patrol cabin at the 8.5-mi. mark there is a trail that continues up the creek to Bootjack Gap (9,180 ft.) on the park boundary, 4 mi. from the cabin. This is quite steep and rocky. A spectacular mountain trail leads to the Hoodoo Basin area 7 mi. away. From the cabin, Hoodoo Trail climbs over 2,000 ft. to just north of Parker Peak (10,203 ft.). It was north of Parker Peak that Superintendent Norris discovered, in 1880, the remains of a strategic Indian camp perched high on the grassy pass, with views of all possible approaches for miles around. The camp, which contained 40 decaying lodges, apparently was used by Indians during the summer. Norris concluded that the remains of white men's blankets, bedding, china, and male and female clothing were evidence of Indian raids.

Hoodoo Basin was named for the "goblins" or "hoodoos" that "inhabit" the area (the result of the many eroded rock pinnacles in grotesque forms). From the basin, the trail crosses the park boundary and follows the Absaroka Range a few miles before descending into the old Sunlight mining region (about 10 mi. from the boundary). From here a dirt jeep road leads to the Sunlight Ranger Station (USFS). A 15-min. USGS topo map of Sunlight Peak is needed for travel in this area (see p. 222).

The Thunderer Cutoff Trail (7.5 mi.)

Start from the trailhead 1 mi. northeast of Pebble Creek Campground on Tower–Northeast Entrance Road. The trail begins from near the confluence of Soda Butte and Amphitheater creeks. Abiathar Peak and Amphitheater Mountain—both over 10,800 ft.—are prominent to the northeast. The trail climbs almost 2,000 ft. over a series of sharp switchbacks to the north ridge of The Thunderer, so named for its apparent focus for thunderstorms. The Thunderer, at 10,558 ft., contains talus slopes and a number of impressive cliff bands at the north end. Be careful to stay on the trail here. A hiker fell to his death near here in 1985. From the top of the saddle you will view about 70 sq. mi. of forest that burned in 1988. To the southeast you will see The Needle, a pinnacle that dominates the valley of Lower Cache Creek. The impressive "needle's eye" arch extends about 35 ft. above the rock ridge: a cross-country bushwhacking hike of about 3 mi. from Cache Creek Trail is necessary to reach it. The trail descends sharply to Cache Creek 0.3 mi. south of Cache Creek patrol cabin.

Cache Creek Trail (16.6 mi.)

Cache Creek Trailhead to:

Junction with Thunderer Cutoff Trail	11.0 mi.
Republic Pass	16.6 mi.
Cooke City	21.6 mi.

The Cache Creek environs certainly changed in 1988 as just about the entire length of the trail from the Lamar River up to Republic Pass burned. The area is revegetating, but the process requires time, especially on the steep slopes.

Lamar River Trail 3.3 mi. south of Soda Butte Creek Bridge is the starting point for this trail. It stays high above the north bank of Cache Creek until the 2-mi. mark, at which point Death Gulch is visible on the south side of the creek. The hydrogen sulphide gas from the vents in this gloomy gulch has caused the death of many animals over the years, from bears and coyotes to numerous smaller mammals. In certain wind conditions the gulch can be extremely dangerous, and hikers are warned against entering this area.

With Mt. Norris to the west and The Needle to the east, the trail continues upstream along Cache Creek, reaching the patrol cabin at the 11.3-mi. mark. Republic Pass is reached on the park boundary at about 10,000 ft. The rugged mountain scenery from here is spectacular. The Republic Creek Trail (USFS) leads down the east side past an old mining site to Cooke City. There is also another trail (not shown on most maps); it continues up the middle fork of Cache Creek (just north of Cache Mountain—marked, but not maintained) and crosses Crandall Pass at 9,920 ft. on the boundary, providing access to North Fork Crandall Creek Trail (USFS). Jack Crandall was a prospector killed by Indians along Crandall Creek on July 1, 1870. His unmarked grave is located in the North Fork Crandall Creek area.

Pelican Creek–Astringent Creek Loop Trail

The trailhead is at the end of a short dirt road located on the north side of Fishing Bridge–East Entrance Road, 3.3 mi. from Fishing Bridge (across from Indian Pond).

Pelican Creek Trail to:
(Note: Distances are listed as one way from Pelican Creek trailhead, assuming a loop hike taken counterclockwise going north up Pelican Creek to Wapiti Lake, and then south down Astringent Creek.)

Pelican Valley	2.0 mi.
Pelican Springs	7.0 mi.
Raven Creek	8.0 mi.
Pelican Cone Trail	8.7 mi.
Mudkettles/Mushpots	11.0 mi.
"Hot Springs" Mudpot	14.0 mi.
Fern Lake Cutoff Trail	15.0 mi.
Wapiti Lake	19.0 mi.
Fern Lake	23.0 mi.
Tern Lake	23.5 mi.
White Lake	25.5 mi.
Pelican Creek Crossing	31.5 mi.
Trailhead (out)	35.0 mi.

Pelican Creek Trail: It is about 2 mi. before you emerge into spacious Pelican Valley. The area is ideal grizzly habitat and travel is often restricted. Check at a ranger station before departing. You will probably spot several bear droppings and diggings along the way. Make noise and remain alert as you traverse the valley. Coyotes searching for small game are occasionally sighted throughout the valley. At the 3-mi. point you reach Pelican Creek and a junction with the old fire road used to provide access to forest-fire areas. Pelican Creek moves along rather slowly. The water is not very cold and therefore makes poor drinking water. There are good populations of cutthroat in this stream, however. If you are making the loop hike, continue along the trail near the south side of the creek and do not cross at the bridge. As you walk through Pelican Valley, you see the Sulphur Hills in the distance (northwest) and Pelican Cone Lookout (9,648 ft.) to the northeast. At the 4.5-mi. mark (1.5 mi. beyond the old road trail junction), you come to an unnamed stream. A small waterfall is located here. Pelican Springs patrol cabin lies at the valley's far end (7 mi.). Directly across from the cabin (southeast) is a small spring.

As you continue your loop hike, Raven Creek is crossed 1 mi. past Pelican Springs. (There are cutthroat trout here.) Another 0.7 mi. brings you to the junction of the trail leading to Pelican Cone Lookout. The climb up Pelican Cone (4.5 mi.) is about 1,600 ft. It affords a fine view of Yellowstone Lake to the southwest and Saddle Mountain to the east. At Pelican Creek you will come to the terminus of the old fire road. You have now traveled 9 mi. From this point on up Pelican Creek the trail is overgrown in many places, as this area receives little travel. The orange trail markers will help guide you up the valley. At the 11-mi. mark you will come to a thermal area that consists of the Mudkettles to the west and the Mushpots to the east. The Mudkettles are the more interesting, consisting mainly of a series of deep mudpots. Remember to be very careful when near such thermal areas — stay off ground that appears to be unstable. Another 3 mi. (14 mi. from the trailhead) brings you to one of the most interesting thermal areas in the Mirror Plateau. Located about 75 yds. to the east of the trail, "Hot Springs" is actually a very large mud geyser in a state of constant mild eruption, with occasional bursts of up to 30 ft. (Near the headwaters of Pelican Creek, one of the park's most notorious poachers, a man by

the name of Howell, was captured while skinning several buffalo he had just slaughtered.)

About 1 mi. past the mud geyser the trail forks to the left down
to Pelican Creek and a meadow. Here you will find a trail junction. To the north is Fern Lake patrol cabin (*not* located on Fern
Lake) 0.5 mi. away. Wapiti Lake is 4 mi. to the north. You have
now reached the "top" of your loop hike, unless you decide to
continue to either of these destinations. Broad Creek and Astringent–Broad Creek Trail are only 0.7 mi. away. Throughout your
trip to Pelican Creek you will have noticed a small but prominent ridge to the west that separates Pelican Creek from Broad
and Astringent creeks. You are now about to cross it.

When you reach Broad Creek, you will actually be at the
Broad Creek–Astringent Creek trailhead, and signs are posted
there to that effect. Just to the north of the trail junction, Fern
Lake Trail leads across the creek to the lake. There are populations of small rainbow trout farther downstream, but here
the fishing is very slow. Fern Lake lies deep in the forest at an
elevation of 8,245 ft., with a wooded slope rising from the north
shore. Fires burned here in 1988. At the east end of the lake
where the trail emerges from the forest several hot springs are
near the shore. There are no fish. The trail climbs up again from
the lake, passes through an old burned area, then re-enters a
forest. As you continue away from the lake (southwest), you
will pass through a meadow extending north to south, and 1.5
mi. from the east end of Fern Lake you will come to the Ponuntpa
Springs group. There is a fine meadow here, but the springs
are mostly inactive and dried up.

Astringent Creek Trail: Astringent Creek Trail, from Broad
Creek near Fern Lake down to Pelican Creek, offers wild and
beautiful scenery. At 1.2 mi. you come to Tern Lake, which

teems with various forms of birdlife—duck, goose, and quite probably trumpeter swan. The lake is very shallow, with marshy areas all around. (There are few, if any, fish in Fern, Tern, or White lakes.) Beyond the lake to the west is a ridge that has been burned over by a forest fire. The trail continues to follow Broad Creek through mostly open country. At 2.5 mi., White Lake will be only partially visible to the west of the trail. The main body of the lake is about 0.5 mi. from the trail. White Lake is very similar to Tern Lake in that it is in open marshy surroundings and an ideal habitat for a great variety of birdlife. White Lake is the source for Broad Creek. In 1984 a young woman was tragically killed by a grizzly bear in this vicinity. She apparently did nothing to invite or provoke the attack, though she was camping alone in prime grizzly habitat. Despite intense efforts, the bear was never trapped or located.

The next creek you see at the 3-mi. mark will be Astringent Creek. From the moment you come to Astringent Creek until you enter Pelican Valley, you may enjoy a spectacular display of wildflowers, especially during late July and early- to mid-August, when the trail follows Astringent Creek through meadows literally painted with flowers: western yarrow (white), harebell (blue), fringed gentian (purple), Indian paintbrush (pink and red), arnica (yellow), larkspur (blue), lupine (blue and purple), and wild geranium (pink to lavender).

As you approach Pelican Valley the rounded shape of Lake Butte at 8,348 ft. appears directly to the south, and Mt. Chittenden (10,181 ft.) overlooks the valley to the southeast. On re-entering Pelican Valley, scan the hillsides for animals—you may spot a coyote searching for rodents. When you cross the old fire road bridge across Pelican Creek you will have come 8 mi. from the Astringent Creek trailhead at Broad Creek. It is another 3 mi. across Pelican Valley to the trailhead on Fishing Bridge–East Entrance Road (across from Indian Pond).

Wapiti Lake Trail (14.5 mi.)

Start from Artist Point, reached via the spur road on the south rim of the canyon or from the parking lot at the bridge across the Yellowstone River (on the Artist Point spur road). After leaving the Grand Canyon of Yellowstone, Wapiti Lake Trail enters dense lodgepole forest that continues all the way to the lake. For this reason it is not highly recommended. If the Fern Lake area is your objective, you should take the more scenic Pelican Creek or Astringent Creek trails beginning from Pelican Valley. Some people prefer to leave Wapiti Lake Trail and explore many of the thermal areas of the Mirror Plateau (these are not reached by trail). With compass and topo map, experienced hikers who have permission may leave Wapiti Lake Trail at Moss Creek and make a loop, exploring Whistler Geyser and Josephs Coat Springs, Coffee Pot Hot Springs, Rainbow Springs, and the Hot Springs Basin group before rejoining Wapiti Lake Trail.

The Cook–Folsom–Peterson Expedition of 1869 passed through here while exploring the Yellowstone region. These three men received very little recognition for their findings, as publishers refused to incorporate all their material for fear of being accused of exaggeration. However, the following year the Washburn party made their historic journey, and their reports were received with more respect. Wapiti Lake—small and in dense woods—is the source for Shallow Creek.

Specimen Ridge Trail (17.5 mi.)

Specimen Ridge Trailhead to:

Grand Canyon of Yellowstone	1.0 mi.
Junction with Agate Creek Trail	3.0 mi.
Summit of Amethyst Mountain	12.0 mi.

Lamar River Ford	16.0 mi.
Lamar Trailhead	17.5 mi.

The starting point is east of the Yellowstone River bridge on Northeast Entrance Road, 2.5 mi. from Tower Junction. If the petrified trees rather than a cross-country hike are your primary objective, it is recommended that you take the ranger-conducted hike or ask a Tower area ranger for the exact locations of the best petrified-tree specimens, since there are no trails. If this is not possible, use binoculars to pick out some exposed stumps as your destination from the road. The enclosed topo map reveals the location of some excellent specimens.

Yellowstone contains the most extensive and remarkable petrified forest in the world. The trees here extend over 40 sq. mi., a larger area than any other known fossil forest. Most specimens are still standing upright, unlike those in California and Egypt, or in Arizona, whose noted Petrified Forest National Park consists of scattered, petrified driftwood. Finally, in addition to the petrified tree trunks, thousands of fossilized imprints of twigs, leaves, seeds, needles, and cones have been found in the volcanic rocks of this region.

The "frozen" tree trunks you see standing upright are the ancient remains of a deciduous forest that existed 55 million years ago at an elevation of only 2,000 ft. There are oaks, maples, sycamores, dogwoods, hickories, walnuts, and chestnuts—similar to what you would find in the Great Smoky Mountains of east Tennessee, for example, today. When volcanic activity began in the area, lava flows completely engulfed the forest; the buried trees absorbed silica from the ash and mud, and as a result were preserved. Scientists have discovered 27 layers of petrified trees in this area. After one volcanic eruption, thousands of years would pass before the soil and conditions allowed another forest to take hold and grow. Then another volcanic eruption would once again cover the forest, and the process would start again. The very hard and colorful trees of the top layers have withstood the processes of erosion, and as a result now stand exposed up to 15 ft. in some places on the slopes. With binoculars it is possible to spot such trees from Northeast Entrance Road near the Lamar River bridge. The most striking examples of layering are found on the north side of Specimen Ridge above the Lamar River Valley.

Naturalist-conducted hikes are given during the months of July and August and usually last all day. The roundtrip distance is about 3.5 mi. with a steep elevation gain of 1,150 ft. (For information, inquire at any of the park's visitor centers.) *Visitors are reminded that it is against the law to collect specimens, and violators risk severe penalties.*

The name "Specimen Ridge" seems appropriate when you consider the names of the streams that drain this region — Quartz, Agate, Crystal, Jasper, Amethyst, and Chalcedony creeks. In late summer, however, streams are hard to find (with the exception of Agate Creek). (Note: A 4-mi. spur trail at the 3-mi. mark provides access to the Yellowstone River at Quartz and Agate creeks.) If you are traveling Specimen Ridge at this time of year you may need to take water with you, particularly if you plan to stay on top in open, rather dry country. During early summer you may spot a number of grizzlies in these open areas, so be alert. Amethyst Mountain is the trail's high point (9,614 ft.) at the 12-mi. mark. From here the trail begins a steady descent to the Lamar River, which you must ford to gain access to Lamar River Trail. This leads across open country to the Soda Butte Creek Bridge and Northeast Entrance Road.

Yellowstone River Overlook Trail (2.0 mi.)

This trail begins from the Yellowstone River Picnic Area, 1.5 mi. from Tower Junction on Northeast Entrance Road. It winds up a grassy slope that contains a few patches of Douglas fir. Soon the trail reaches and follows the rim of the spectacular Grand Canyon of the Yellowstone River. As you approach The Narrows you will be standing over 700 ft. above the river. Below you to the southeast near the small island in the river is the historic Bannock Ford. From 1840 to the late 1870s Indians crossed the great river here heading for their summer hunting grounds. Historians also believe that John Colter, the first white man to enter the Yellowstone country in 1807, crossed the Yellowstone River at this point. This trail joins Specimen Ridge Trail (see p. 218), but the simplest and shortest way back is the way you came.

Tower Falls Trail (0.5 mi.)

The trail starts from the Tower Falls overlook. Tower Falls is one of Yellowstone's most popular attractions. Many have witnessed its 132-ft. plunge, but few take the trail to the base. From there the falls looks completely different and very impressive. On a sunny morning, a rainbow frames the foot of the falls. Minarets, or "towers," extend above the brink for which the cataract was named by members of the 1870 Washburn party. Everyone used to wonder when the large boulder perched on the brink would fall. Early pictures taken in 1872 showed it at the same spot. The boulder finally fell in 1986 before an audience of no one. It is believed that John Colter crossed the Yellowstone River in 1807 where Tower Creek empties into it.

Avalanche Peak Hike (2.0 mi.)

Start from the first parking area west of Eleanor Lake on Fishing Bridge–East Entrance Road (about 1.3 mi. west of Sylvan

Pass). Although there is no maintained trail, a well-worn path winds its way up to the summit and offers some magnificent scenery. A Sierra Club work crew improved the trail's drainage system in 1988. Naturalist-conducted trips are occasionally made here during late summer; inquire at any visitor center for information. From the road you climb about 2,000 ft. in 2 mi. to the summit at 10,566 ft., passing through flower-laden alpine meadows along the way. Yellowstone Lake dominates the view from the summit, with distant mountain ranges visible on clear days.

This hike is best after mid-July when the snowfields have subsided and flowers are blooming in the meadows. Once above timberline it will be necessary to ascend steep scree slopes to reach the summit.

Storm Point Trail (2.0 mi.)

The trailhead is located at the Indian Pond parking area about 3 mi. east of Lake Junction. The point is aptly named as the shore of Yellowstone Lake here receives the brunt of the powerful southwest winds. Thousands of hikers have traveled this trail but only recently a perfect teepee ring was discovered near here, causing one to pause and ponder just how many secrets the Yellowstone country still holds. This area is fine habitat for moose and waterfowl. Grizzlies like the trail too and they receive first priority, so check at the Fishing Bridge Visitor Center before departing.

Turbid Lake Trail (3.0 mi.)

The trail begins from the Pelican Creek trailhead, 3 mi. east of Fishing Bridge across from Indian Pond. This is actually an old dirt road that leads through forest and a couple of large meadows to a thermally active lake. The name is appropriate as thermal features under the 143-acre lake cause the water to appear turbid and foamy. This region contains a variety of wild-life activity; look for bison and elk or their signs. This is also prime grizzly country; in fact a man was mauled by one here in 1986, so remain alert. Check at Fishing Bridge Visitor Center or Lake Ranger Station for trail restrictions before departing. The open hillside on the north end of the lake provides a nice spot to sit amid the flowers and enjoy the view of the basin below. From Turbid Lake it is possible to continue on the old road another 3 mi. around Lake Butte to East Entrance Road.

Hoodoo Basin Trail
(Sunlight Creek at Sulphur Camp to
Hoodoo Basin) (14.5 mi.)

Hoodoo Basin Trail from Sunlight Basin is one of the most spectacular high-mountain trails to be found anywhere in the Yellowstone country. (Hoodoo Basin also may be reached via the Lamar River and Upper Miller Creek at a distance of 24 mi.; see p. 210.) The trailhead for this hike is located on the Sunlight Creek spur road off Sunlight Basin Road, which roughly connects Cooke City with Cody. Note that much of Sunlight Basin Road north of Sunlight Creek is paved; to the south, it is not, though it probably soon will be. The Sunlight Creek spur road is maintained to Sulphur Camp, 8 mi. beyond Sunlight Ranger Station. By mid-July a four-wheel-drive vehicle should be able to reach the Sunlight Creek crossing at Lee City, 4.3 mi. beyond Sulphur Camp, and by late summer, when the streams are low, possibly Painter Cabin, 7.3 mi. beyond Sulphur Camp. (Note that all mileages listed assume Sulphur Camp as the starting point.) It is recommended that you obtain for this hike a copy of the USFS map "North Half, Shoshone National Forest" from the Forest Supervisor, Shoshone National

Forest, P.O. Box 961, Cody, Wyoming 82414, and the USGS topo map of Sunlight Peak.

There are several mining claims in this region that date back to the turn of the century. Many people have held some sort of interest in these claims and have done extensive exploration work. All have believed that a rich deposit exists there somewhere, but none ever has been located.

You will pass a pile of debris referred to on your topo as Hardee's Cabins. Homer Hardee was a speculator and promoter who held an interest in some of the claims, and supposedly sold a lot of stock around the country for development. He built the Hardee Cabins for a base of operations and also built the road in the Upper Sunlight drainage.

At Painter Cabin you will have reached the end of the old road. Notice the trees growing right out of the foundation of the old cabin. J.R. Painter built this cabin for use while doing some exploration work at the Novelty Mine and others. He used to pack out ore samples by mule to Red Lodge, Montana, for assay. He never discovered anything of real value. When he left the region he blasted the drift shut to keep trespassers out.

Just beyond Painter Cabin you will notice a trailhead sign that reads "Yellowstone Boundary—5 miles." Another mile brings you to the entrance to the North Absaroka Wilderness Area and a trip registration box. If you plan to stay overnight in Yellowstone, you must have a backcountry use permit in addition to registering there, so be sure to obtain the permit in advance at a park ranger station.

From Lee City to Painter you have been traveling along Sunlight Creek through a lush forest of spruce and fir mixed with lodgepole and nice stands of cottonwood and aspen. The trail now turns north through mostly lodgepole and begins a 2,600-ft. climb to the park boundary. As you approach timberline notice the forest transition to whitebark pine. Above timberline you enter a magnificent alpine setting carpeted with flowers in July—white, yellow, and deep blue colors dominate. At the 12.3-mi. mark, the park boundary is reached at an elevation of 10,470 ft. The views are spectacular in all directions, particularly the Beartooth Mountains to the north and the craggy Absarokas to the east and south. Below you to the northwest is Hoodoo Basin, which is excellent habitat for elk, coyote, and grizzly; look for these animals and their signs. From the park boundary the trail continues 3 mi. through rolling alpine country before dropping several hundred feet to the "hoodoos" below Hoodoo Peak (see p. 210). Parker Peak is reached at the 18-mi. mark.

Canyon to Lake Trail (14.5 mi.)

Canyon to Lake Trailhead to:

Wrangler Lake Trail Junction	2.5 mi.
Cottongrass Creek	3.5 mi.
Buffalo Ford	9.5 mi.
LeHardy Rapids	11.5 mi.
Fishing Bridge	14.5 mi.

Start from the Chittenden Bridge parking area on the Artist Point spur road. Although this section of the old Howard Eaton Trail basically parallels Canyon–Lake Road, the opportunities for viewing and photographing wildlife and a tremendous variety of bird life are outstanding. The trail, which may be hard to follow in places, skirts the east edge of Hayden Valley through many open meadows along the meandering Yellowstone River. The LeHardy Rapids offers a spectacle during mid-June as thousands of cutthroat trout attempt to jump the rapids to reach their spawning grounds. This region has also experienced significant uplifting during the 1970s and 1980s, sometimes at the rate of about one inch per year!

Warning: This is prime grizzly country. Travel may be restricted. Check at Canyon Visitor Center before embarking on this trip.

HIKES FROM CANYON VILLAGE AREA

Crystal Falls Trail	0.6 mi.
Canyon Rim Trail	2.0 mi.
Ribbon Lake–Clear Lake Loop Trail	4.2 mi.
Glacial Boulder to Seven-Mile Hole	5.5 mi.
Mt. Washburn Trail	3.0 mi.
Mt. Washburn to Glacial Boulder	12.0 mi.
Wrangler Lake Trail	3.0 mi.

The Canyon Village area offers the best range of short hikes available to the day hiker anywhere in the park. Both rims of the Canyon itself contain trails that offer breathtaking views. An easy trail of only 0.1 mi. runs to the brink of Upper Falls. A short spur road leads there, beginning from Canyon–Lake Road about 2 mi. south of Canyon Junction. There are also trails to the brink and foot of Lower Falls, but they are quite strenuous. The short hike to the brink of Lower Falls begins from the one-way loop road on the north rim, and consists of a number of switchbacks. Uncle Tom's Trail, which begins from the Artist Point spur road on the south rim, leads to near the foot of Lower Falls, and provides a wonderful view of the falls from the bottom of the canyon. This particular trail was originally built in 1903 by Thomas Richardson, at which time it

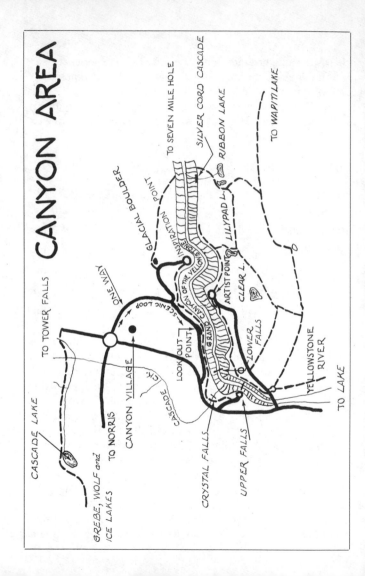

consisted of a number of rope ladders and was quite dangerous. A handy guide to the Canyon area may be obtained at the
Canyon Visitor Center.

Crystal Falls Trail (0.6 mi.)

Start from the parking lot on the Upper Falls spur road. There
you will find a bridge across a small stream; the trail begins
on the northwest side of the stream (trailhead not marked). The
first 200 yds. brings you to the edge of the canyon that Cascade Creek flows through and a fine view of Crystal Falls (129
ft.), discovered and named by members of the Washburn Party
in 1870. There the trail forks; the left fork is North Rim Trail,
leading to the edge of the Grand Canyon and around to the
Lower Falls brink trail; the right fork continues to an overlook
of Crystal Falls and ends. The left fork of the trail leads to a
small footbridge that crosses Cascade Creek above Crystal Falls.
Throughout the little gorge between the bridge and falls you
may be able to spot the aquatic water ouzel, one of the most
fascinating birds to be found anywhere. After plunging over
Crystal Falls, Cascade Creek flows only a short distance farther before it empties into the Yellowstone River, easily visible
below you to the east.

Canyon Rim Trail (2.0 mi.)

Most folks who come to the canyon view Lower Falls at one
of the main lookout points and leave. To get away from the
crowds and congestion and truly experience the canyon, take
this trail beginning from either Artist Point on the South Rim
or Inspiration Point on the North Rim. The trail will take you
past glorious views of both Lower and Upper falls. During June
over 64,000 gallons of water per second plunge over the brinks
in a seemingly slow-motion action. This flow is reduced to 5,000

gallons per second by autumn. In winter the falls are still active, but are often hidden behind a large ice-and-snow cone extending from brink to foot. The distance from Inspiration Point around to Artist Point is 2 mi. one way.

Ribbon Lake–Clear Lake Loop Trail   (4.2 mi.)

Try to visit the area several times — at sunrise, midday, sunset, and by moonlight. In this way you will really come to know the beauty of Lower Falls and the canyon. Indians referred to this section of the Yellowstone River as "the river with yellow, vertical walls." The park's name evolved from the name "Yellow Rock" River. Basically the canyon is composed of rhyolite softened by water and hot gases, and therefore more easily carved than unaltered rhyolite. The Yellowstone River channel is being deepened continually by the forces of the raging river, which carries silt and stones to accelerate the cutting process.

The Lower and Upper falls were created because the layers of basalt and extremely hard rhyolite at the lips of these cataracts have yielded very slowly to erosion as compared to the softer rhyolite. The yellows and oranges of the canyon's walls and pinnacles are the result of the oxides of various minerals contained in the rhyolite.

Start from Artist Point at the end of the spur road. From there, the trail follows the rim of the canyon for 0.5 mi. before bending off into the forest. If you are fortunate enough to be along this stretch at sunset, you will see an unforgettable sight. The flaming reds of the canyon on the north side are particularly striking. You can spot Mt. Washburn on your right (10,243 ft.) with its fire lookout tower on top. The next peak west from Mt. Washburn (to your left) is Dunraven Peak (9,900 ft.), named in honor of the Earl of Dunraven, who visited the park

Lower Falls of the Yellowstone
(Photo by Tom Caples)

in 1874 and published many works abroad about Yellowstone. To the left of Dunraven Peak is Hedges Peak, named after Cornelius Hedges, the member of the 1870 Washburn party who first proposed that Yellowstone be established as a national park. West of Dunraven is Observation Peak (9,397 ft.).

At 0.75 mi. you come to Lilypad Lake, where you will notice a sulphureous odor from the small outlet at the southeast end of the lake. Just beyond Lilypad Lake there is a trail junction. The left fork leads to Ribbon Lake, 1.3 mi. away, the right to Clear Lake and out to the Artist Point spur road. The 1.3-mi. walk to Ribbon Lake is through a forest where wildflowers abound. There are also a number of small ponds.

As the trail nears Ribbon Lake, you are above it. When you descend to the lake, you reach another trail junction, having come 2 mi. It is possible to follow this trail and loop back to the Chittenden bridge on the Artist Point spur road, but this is not recommended for a day hike because beautiful Clear Lake is bypassed. The trail to the left continues along Ribbon Lake, crosses its outlet (which flows into the Grand Canyon as Silver Cord Cascade), and terminates along the canyon rim. Ribbon Lake contains a growth of brown algae, hence the rusty color. After crossing this stream, the trail winds up to the canyon's edge for another spectacular view of the Yellowstone River below, several mountain peaks to the north and northwest, and a partial view of Silver Cord Cascade. Extensive meadows border both Ribbon Lake and the unnamed lake just to its northeast. Chances of sighting moose and elk in these meadows are excellent during early morning and later afternoon. There are some rainbow trout in Ribbon Lake.

From Ribbon Lake you follow the trail 1.3 mi. back to the trail junction near Lilypad Lake. As you proceed on the left fork (heading south), only a few hundred yards from the trail junction you will notice considerable thermal activity to the left of the trail. As there is a boiling mudpot here, be very careful not to approach it too closely. From this point on to Clear Lake (0.5 mi.), you will pass a number of boiling mudpots, hot springs, and fumaroles.

Clear Lake is fed by cold springs and contains no fish. After passing the lake, the trail emerges from the forest into an extensive open area that lasts the rest of the way. Just above Clear Lake the trail forks; there will probably be no sign here, but the left fork continues out to near the Chittenden bridge, and the right fork takes the shorter route out to the Uncle Tom's Trail parking lot on the Artist Point spur road. After turning right at the junction, you will come upon yet another lovely view of the canyon and of the familiar mountain peaks in the distance (left to right: Observation Peak, Hedges Peak, Dunraven Peak, and Mt. Washburn). You may spot an osprey soaring over the canyon. Look for osprey nests atop the pinnacles.

The wildflowers along this route, particularly in June, are spectacular. You can pick out the glacier lily, shooting star, balsam root, mariposa lily, harebell, and bitterroot, to mention only a few. The area is also ideal habitat for both grizzly and black bear. The grizzly will often spend hours digging for rodents and for the bulbous roots of glacier lilies and spring beauties.

The trail continues a short way farther before the Artist Point spur road comes into view below you. You emerge opposite the Uncle Tom's Trail parking lot. For additional maps and information, be sure to obtain for a nominal charge at the Canyon Visitor Center a copy of "Guide to the Canyon Area."

Glacial Boulder to Seven-Mile Hole (5.5 mi.)

The starting point is Glacial Boulder on Inspiration Point spur road, located on the north rim of the Grand Canyon. Although

the destination is Seven-Mile Hole, the total distance is only
5.5 mi. if you begin from Glacial Boulder, a huge mass of stone
deposited by moving glaciers during the Wisconsin Ice Age.

The first 1.2 mi. of this hike are highly recommended, as
there are splendid views into the Grand Canyon, and also of
Silver Cord Cascade, which plunges some 800 ft. down the
south wall of the canyon; the falls are in a crevice partially hidden from view except from directly across the canyon at this
point. Beyond, the trail swings away from the canyon's edge
for another 1.3 mi. before beginning the sharp descent to the
bottom. It winds all the way down to the Yellowstone River
at the foot of the canyon where Sulphur Creek empties into it.
Along the way you will notice signs of thermal activity. Be sure
to take plenty of water along with you. The climb back out
on a warm summer's day is strenuous.

Mt. Washburn Trail   (3.0 mi.)

The top of Mt. Washburn can be reached by trail either from
the Dunraven Pass Picnic Area (5.6 mi. from Canyon Junction
on Canyon–Tower Road) or along the old Chittenden dirt road
that begins about 5 mi. north of Dunraven Pass. General Henry
D. Washburn climbed the peak in August 1870 in a successful
attempt to locate the best route to Yellowstone Lake. The Chittenden Road opened in 1990 for bicycle use (see p. 259), but
check at the Canyon Ranger Station before using it. The best
hiking route is from the Dunraven Pass Picnic Area. Much of
Mt. Washburn burned in 1988, but this did nothing to hurt
the spectacular wildflower displays during late July and early
August. Considering the relatively small investment in vertical
climb (about 1,400 ft.) the payoff on the summit is spectacular.

Mt. Washburn, which rises to 10,243 ft., is composed largely
of breccia. Its slopes are summer home for a large number of

bighorn sheep, frequently spotted as you near the top. From the summit you will have a view of the Grand Canyon of Yellowstone (east), steam rising from Josephs Coat Springs and Whistler Geyser, and Hayden Valley and Yellowstone Lake to the south. Also visible on a clear day are the Tetons, Absarokas, and Gallatin Range. Near the summit, you may notice glacial grooves and scratches caused by sheets of ice 800 ft. thick scraping against the mountainside. Notice how the high altitude disfigures the whitebark pine. A lookout is stationed atop the summit during the summer months. The observation room even contains a pay telephone, where you can truly make a "long distance" call.

Mt. Washburn to Glacial Boulder (12.0 mi.)

Dunraven Pass Picnic Area to:

Summit of Mt. Washburn	3.0 mi.
Junction with Howard Eaton Trail	5.5 mi.
Washburn Hot Springs	7.5 mi.
Junction with Seven-Mile Hole Trail	9.5 mi.
View of Silver Cord Cascade	11.0 mi.
Glacial Boulder	12.0 mi.

One of the best day hikes available in the park is up to Mt. Washburn from Dunraven Pass (see p. 232) to the Washburn spur trail to Glacial Boulder. From the summit the trail descends down the southeast shoulder of Mt. Washburn, which did not burn in 1988. Of the three routes to the summit this trail is the least used. The views along the way are magnificent, especially of the Grand Canyon of the Yellowstone below. Once below the 8,400-ft. level the trail winds through flower-laden meadows through which sparkling streams course. This is prime grizzly country, so make noise when appropriate and stay alert.

When you join the old Howard Eaton Trail be sure to take the right (west) fork toward Canyon. The east fork travels through Antelope Valley to Tower but is usually closed as a bear management area. The Washburn Hot Springs area contains some very interesting thermal features, including Inkpot Spring, which is appropriately named. There are also some mudpots here. After leaving the thermal area the trail goes through lodgepole forest to the rim of the canyon, where some fine views of Silver Cord Cascade are obtained. The trail ends at Glacial Boulder on Inspiration Point.

Wrangler Lake Trail (3.0 mi.)

The trailhead is located at the Chittenden bridge parking area on the Artist Point spur road. The trail traverses open sagebrush terrain, marshy meadows, and lodgepole forest to reach this 35-acre lake. Sour Creek, a sluggish stream that drains several thermal basins upstream, is crossed along the way. Don't expect to find wranglers (or fish) at the lake, but there are usually plenty of mosquitoes.

TRAVEL BY
CANOE, BIKE, & SKI

Pacific Creek put-in, Snake River

Canoeing the
Yellowstone Backcountry

One of the best ways to leisurely explore the wild Yellowstone country is by canoe. Some backcountry travelers like to combine a backpacking trip with a canoe trip, especially from the arms of Yellowstone Lake. Although canoeing opportunities in Yellowstone are "limited" to Yellowstone Lake, Shoshone Lake, Lewis Lake, and the 3.5-mi. Lewis River Channel from Lewis Lake, these areas encompass a great deal of wilderness. (See topo map and maps on p. 84 and p. 122.)

Canoeing is not permitted on any other Yellowstone streams in order to afford protection to nesting waterfowl and other wildlife. Some paddlers object to this policy, but if the streams of the park were open to boating, dozens of outfitters would soon be shuttling thousands of visitors down the rivers and much of the wildness and serenity that now exist along Yellowstone's streams would be lost.

Yellowstone Lake alone contains 110 miles of shoreline—over 75 miles of which are away from the park's road system. There are also some fine canoeing trips available just south of Yellowstone in the Grand Tetons.

Before entering any waters in Yellowstone or Grand Teton, you must register your canoe and obtain a nonmotorized boat permit (nominal fee) in Yellowstone at Lake Ranger Station or Grant Village Visitor Center or in the Tetons at Colter Bay Visitor Center or Moose Visitor Center. Although the permit fee is good for both Yellowstone and Grand Teton parks, you must still register your boat in the park in which you will be using it. A ranger will need to inspect your PFD (personal flotation device) before your permit will be issued.

WARNING

Safety considerations are imperative when canoeing waters in Yellowstone and Grand Teton. *Note this well:* Survival time in the icy waters of Yellowstone and Shoshone lakes is but a few minutes—stay close to shore at all times! It may be tempting to paddle directly across a bay rather than follow the winding shoreline, and you may save 15 minutes; but ask yourself if it is really worth the risk. Yellowstone and Shoshone lakes are famous for their sudden winds and storms. Even on a clear and calm day I have observed sudden gusty winds quickly transform placid waters into raging four-ft. waves, spelling potential tragedy for canoeists venturing more than a quarter mile from shore. As additional precautions, be sure to bring along a bailer (a bleach bottle with the end cut off works well), an extra paddle, a large sponge, and a flotation device, such as an old truck inner tube. Please, before going into the backcountry thoroughly familiarize yourself with the dangers of hypothermia; too many tragedies have occurred on Yellowstone's lakes over the years.

CANOEING SHOSHONE LAKE
(VIA LEWIS LAKE AND LEWIS RIVER CHANNEL)

Note: Read the warning above before taking this trip.

Put-in & take-out: Boat dock at Lewis Lake Campground.

Former Yellowstone Superintendent Lemuel A. Garrison served the park well from 1956 to 1964. He possessed the character and courage to place the protection of park resources ahead of short-sighted politicians and the powerboat lobby. Thanks to his dedicated efforts, Shoshone Lake and the tips of the arms of Yellowstone Lake are protected wilderness today. Backcountry lakes the size of Shoshone (it is 7 mi. long) are indeed a rarity in the lower 48 states! (See the Bechler Region map on p. 84.)

Be sure to begin this trip from the boat dock on the south end of Lewis Lake near the campground, rather than from the east shore. Beginning from the boat dock adds about a mile to your trip, but you will normally find calmer waters along the west shore of Lewis Lake. Paddling along the north shore exposes you to the prevailing southwest winds, which can sweep across the lake and produce dangerous choppy conditions. Look for moose along the west shore.

Once you enter the Lewis River Channel the forest closes in from both sides and provides protection from winds. There are some nice rock formations along the way. The first 2 mi. of the channel contain very little current, since the elevations of the two lakes vary by only 12 ft. Most of this drop occurs along the last mile to Shoshone Lake, and since it will be necessary to pull your canoe most of this distance, be sure to bring adequate ropes. You will also need some good shoes you don't mind using on the river bottom. Motorboats are prohibited in the channel.

During early to mid-June the waters in the channel are high, swift, and cold, so plan accordingly. A wet suit to protect your lower body would come in handy under these conditions.

It takes about five hours to reach Shoshone by canoe, depending on experience, load, weather, and season. Keep this in mind when you request campsites and select a departure time. If you plan to paddle from the east to west shore of Shoshone Lake, be sure to depart very early to avoid the prevailing southwest winds that tend to whip up by mid-morning.

According to park ranger Lee Whittlesey, who has researched and authored an excellent book on Yellowstone's place names, Shoshone Lake bore six different names before Park Superintendent P.W. Norris named it during the late 1870s for the Indians who occasionally visited the lake during the summer. Fur trapper Osborne Russell described a journey up Lewis River to Shoshone Lake and Shoshone Geyser Basin in 1839 in his journals.

Shoshone Lake provides fishing opportunities for lake and brown trout and a few brook trout. The lake trout, or mackinaw, was first planted in 1890 in Lewis and Shoshone lakes, whose waters were originally barren of fish due to waterfall barriers along the Lewis River. Today's park distribution of lake trout, which may reach a weight of more than 30 lbs., is limited to Lewis, Shoshone, and Heart lakes and their primary tributaries. In the summer months, mackinaw remain in the deep cold waters of the lake, but they come into the shoal areas during October to spawn. If possible, plan to spend several days exploring the wilderness of Shoshone Lake, which covers over 8,000 acres. Various kinds of waterfowl are found on the lake, particularly in the swamps and backwater marshes. Some nice gravel beaches are located along parts of the eastern shore, formed by the prevailing southwest winds building strong waves that tear down the rocks. Shoshone Geyser Basin is a fascinating area to explore (see page 102), but it is very fragile. Please help protect this area (see page 18). In recent summers Shoshone Lake has begun to receive very heavy use. Backcountry rangers are reporting increased abuse of the resource, such as illegal cutting of trees and littering. Unfortunately, this type of abuse will probably lead to further restrictions, such as prohibiting fires in campsites. It is sad to see "light campers" penalized for the abuse of "heavy campers." Please treat the resource with all the respect it deserves, and if you observe someone abusing the land get a complete description of the party, site location, and time of incident and report this to a ranger as soon as possible.

The trip back out to Lewis Lake will be a lot easier and faster since the current will be with you during the first mile. There are nice views of Mt. Sheridan as you leave the channel and enter Lewis Lake.

CANOEING YELLOWSTONE LAKE

Note: Read the warning on p. 238 before taking this trip.

Put-ins & take-outs: For exploring Southeast Arm, put-in and take-out at Sedge Bay, located 8 mi. east of Fishing Bridge on East Entrance Road. For exploring Flat Mountain Arm and South Arm, put-in and take out at the Grant Village boat ramp. If time permits, and you wish to explore all three arms, it is possible to put in at Sedge Bay and take out at Grant Village, or vice versa. A portage between the lower ends of South and Southeast arms is possible, but not highly recommended unless you are traveling extremely lightly (unusual for canoeists).

Perhaps one of the best ways to see and enjoy Yellowstone's wilderness is to explore the far reaches of Yellowstone Lake. There is probably no more beautiful sight in all Yellowstone than the lake at sunset viewed from the east shore. F.V. Hayden wrote of Yellowstone Lake in 1871: " . . . a vast sheet of quiet water, of a most delicate ultramarine hue, one of the most beautiful scenes I have ever beheld. . . . The great object of all our labors had been reached, and we were amply paid for all our toils. Such a vision is worth a lifetime, and only one of such marvelous beauty will ever greet human eyes." Southeast, South, and Flat Mountain arms represent some of Yellowstone's finest wilderness scenery.

Early park explorers compared Yellowstone Lake to the

shape of a man's left hand, although there are only three "fingers," or arms, to the lake. West Thumb derives its name from this early description. It is in these three arms of the lake that canoeists can best explore Yellowstone's wilderness scenery. There are several designated campsites along the shores. Motorboats are restricted in the South and Southeast arms to 5 mph and are not allowed to operate at the arms' tips. Many people believe they should be disallowed altogether. The reasons are clear.

Of Yellowstone Lake's 134 sq. mi., only 19 sq. mi. are set aside for hand-propelled craft; of the 110 mi. of shoreline, only 13 mi. are protected from powerboats. If you feel that this represents a disproportionate total set aside for canoeists, consider writing to the appropriate authorities. South, Southeast, and Flat Mountain arms represent very wild portions of Yellowstone's wilderness. At the southern tips you are 12 to 16 mi. from the nearest road, yet the incongruous drone of motorboats is often part of the experience. Hopefully, in the near future powerboats will be prohibited from the arms of Yellowstone Lake so that those who hike or canoe into this magnificent wilderness will find the natural setting undisturbed.

From Yellowstone Lake the skyline will vary constantly with such backdrops as the mighty snowcapped Absarokas, Promontory, Flat Mountain, Mt. Sheridan, Chicken Ridge, and Two Ocean Plateau. A canoe trip up Flat Mountain arm is recommended, since the marshy meadow at the extreme tip is usually teeming with birdlife. Among the waterfowl you may expect to observe on Yellowstone Lake are the trumpeter swan, great blue heron, pelican, caspian tern, Canada goose, cormorant, and many species of duck, gull, and other birds. Bald eagles and ospreys are commonly observed as well. Flat Mountain rises some 1,500 ft. from the arm's south shore. There are some beautiful points, sandbars, and lagoons along the northern shore of

Flat Mountain arm. Unfortunately, for unknown reasons, there is no 5 mph zone in this arm, though the lower 1.5 miles are limited to hand-propelled craft.

South Arm also provides excellent sightseeing and exploring. The most beautiful scenery lies near the lower southern tip. There are several sloughs in this region that invite further exploration. Peale Island is particularly beautiful. (Camping is usually allowed on the island; check at any backcountry permit office. There's also a cabin used for administrative purposes.) The fishing, as in all the arms, is good for Yellowstone cutthroat trout. The mouth of Grouse Creek is an attractive area to explore, with a sizable meadow that often contains big game. About one mile west-northwest of Peale Island is a small island not shown to exist on some topo maps. This is because recent uplifting at LeHardy Rapids near Fishing Bridge has caused some tilting of the lake. This island used to be a peninsula. Also notice trees standing in the water at the South Arm's southern shore.

Several of the extensive meadows along the western shore of South Arm provide spectacular wildflower displays during midsummer. Portions of the shoreline burned in 1988 are now carpeted with fireweed, arnica, and lupine. Alder Lake, just inland along the east shore of South Arm, provides an interesting sidetrip. The 123-acre lake contains a good growth of lilypads. The drainage from the lake has the appearance of green pea soup due to the abundant nutrients and aquatic growth.

Southeast Arm is the largest arm of Yellowstone Lake, and perhaps the most beautiful—with the Absaroka Range in the background. Terrace Point, located on the east shore about two-thirds of the way up the southern tip of the arm, contains geological evidence of an earlier Yellowstone lake, which at the height of the Ice Age melt-off covered 310 sq. mi. (twice its present area), extended across much of Hayden Valley clear to the base of Mt. Washburn, and was approximately 160 ft.

higher than it is at present. Located on Terrace Point is a series of former shoreline beaches that extend up the hillside; the highest shoreline mark is 160 ft. above the present beach. The presence of multiple old beaches indicates that the lake did not drain continuously, but in stages during which the water level remained stationary. It took 15,000 years for the lake to lower 160 ft.

About 1 mi. south of Columbine Creek along the east shore is a prominent point (unnamed) opposite the tip of The Promontory. This point is a delightful stopping place as it contains a beautiful gravel beach with large cottonwoods along the shore. Just inland is a small pond that will probably contain some ducks and perhaps a moose. Bald eagles are occasionally spotted here.

Park Point with its extensive meadows is another beautiful spot to visit along the east shore. Nearby Park Point patrol cabin is periodically utilized by backcountry rangers on lake patrol. Depending on the wind direction you may notice the smell of rotten eggs while paddling between Park and Terrace points; there are several thermal features in the Brimstone Basin that emit this sulphureous odor. The basin, which contains mostly steam vents, can be seen if you are paddling along the west shore of the arm.

The most beautiful section of Southeast Arm is undoubtedly the southern tip, where the Upper Yellowstone River enters the lake. In this delta region, extensive meadows abound in wildlife. The area surrounding the mouth of Beaverdam Creek contains a great deal of willow brush, which moose favor. Of particular interest are the Molly Islands, located in the southwest end of the arm. The two islands, known as Sandy and Rocky, are little more than scraps of sand and rock. The combined areas equal only about 1 acre—certainly not much of a nesting space. Nevertheless, here is the only breeding colony of white pelicans in Wyoming, and the only one in a national park. The birds start arriving in April and May with snow and ice still present, and then begin to reproduce despite the ordeals of a cold, blustery spring. The hazards the young chicks must face are numerous; of every five eggs laid, only one will hatch and reach maturity. The pelicans fly for the first time in August, and begin their fall migration in September. Studies involving banded birds show that pelicans from the Molly Islands fly across southwestern America to spend the winter in Mexico along the Pacific Coast. Pelicans consume thousands of cutthroat trout every year from Yellowstone Lake. Boats are not allowed to approach the islands—regulations specifiy that boaters stay at least 0.25 mi. away—since the pelicans depend upon the remote conditions here for their successful breeding.

If you are paddling along the west shore of the arm you may want to consider a side trip to the top of The Promontory. The highest point is the middle summit (8,517 ft.) and can be reached by beginning from a meadow that extends to the shore. The meadow leads to a steep forested climb to the base of a rocky ridge. From here, animal trails climb gradually around the steep ridge to the summit. The views from this point (784 ft. above the lake) are spectacular. When paddling along the east shore of The Promontory, you will be able to enjoy a fine view of the Tetons to the south.

For those planning extensive trips into all the arms of Yellowstone Lake, it is advisable to allot eight or nine days to two weeks as adequate time. Obtain current information on the lake at the Lake or Grant Village ranger stations before departing. Following is some general information for your canoe trip.

On Flat Mountain Arm, prevailing winds usually funnel up the arm each afternoon and create choppy conditions. Keep in mind when planning a trip into the lower arms (South and Southeast) that the journey to the mouths is a lengthy one. There are usually smooth water conditions for easy paddling before

10:00 A.M. and after 7:00 to 9:00 P.M.; the lake's waters are frequently too choppy during midday. Rather than paddle up the east shore of South Arm (which often receives strong afternoon winds) around to Southeast Arm, you may want to beach at the *mouth* of Chipmunk Creek and portage across the meadow down to the trail that leads over to it. This portage is recommended *only* if you are traveling light. (Boating upstream is discouraged to protect an abundance of nesting waterfowl, as well as numerous beaver.)

Be content to take what the lake gives you. If the wind becomes prohibitive, enjoy exploring the shoreline. You may find yourself waiting for the moon to come up, or getting up at 4:00 A.M. It's all part of the game.

The prevailing wind direction is from the southwest, which means that while Flat Mountain Arm will develop a good chop, the west shores of the other two arms will normally be calm enough for safe passage. However, sudden changes in wind are to be expected and require the paddler to be adaptable and to exercise good judgement. In calm water, two paddlers can count on making 4 mph with ease.

Canoe Trips
Adjacent to Yellowstone

Note: For the following canoe trips in the Tetons be sure to obtain a USGS topographic map of Grand Teton National Park.

RIVER RATING DEFINITIONS

PADDLER DESCRIPTION

RIVER DESCRIPTION

Beginner: *New paddler or someone not familiar with river canoeing.*

Easy: *Slow river speed, with an easy course and small, regular waves; minor obstacles easily avoidable.*

Novice: *Knows basic river canoeing strokes and can handle boat in slow river currents.*

Medium: *Fairly frequent rapids with regular waves and easy eddies and bends; course easy to recognize.*

Intermediate: *Can use effectively all basic whitewater strokes in bow and stern of a canoe; can read water effectively and negotiate medium rapids with assurance.*

Difficult: *Characterized by numerous rapids and high, irregular waves; course not easily recognizable; requires maneuvering in rapids.*

Advanced: *Can negotiate rapids requiring complex maneuvering; is proficient in both bow and stern of a canoe and solo in difficult rapids.*

Very Difficult: *Long, powerful rapids with irregular waves, dangerous rocks, and boiling eddies.*

Expert: *Has proven ability to run very difficult rapids in both bow and stern of a canoe.*

Extremely Difficult: *Many long, violent rapids with high, irregular, unavoidable waves and holes.*

THE SNAKE RIVER

The Snake River is one of the nation's largest and most famous riverways; over 40 miles of it flow through Yellowstone Park. The Snake's source is near the Continental Divide on Two Ocean Plateau deep in the park's southeastern corner. By the time the Snake reaches the park's South Entrance it contains enough water through the summer for floating. But the Snake River can be a very treacherous and dangerous river for floating purposes, especially during late spring and early summer. For this reason I do not recommend canoeing the Snake until about mid-July or when the peak snow melt has subsided.

Please note the difficulty ratings for each section of the river. The level of difficulty will vary according to the river volume.

Yellowstone South Entrance to Flagg Ranch   (3.5 mi.)

Put-in: Just south of the entrance gate there is a dirt road that provides access to the river.

Take-out: Flagg Ranch bridge, 3 mi. south of Yellowstone's south gate.

Once the Snake River's flow subsides, this stretch provides a short but enjoyable run for the intermediate paddler. The narrow section of the canyon provides some nice whitewater. Be sure to check the river conditions report at the access point along the river (just west of the bridge at Flagg Ranch).

Flagg Ranch to Lizard Point   (10.0 mi.)

Put-in: The access point is located just south of the Flagg Ranch service station (3 mi. south of Yellowstone's south gate).

Take-out: Lizard Point, which is located in Lizard Creek Campground.

Canoeing the Snake River

The 10-mi. trip from Flagg Ranch to Lizard Point is ideal for paddlers who possess intermediate skills in river canoeing. (Do not take this trip if your paddling experience is limited only to calm lake waters; join your local canoe club to receive instruction on how to maneuver in river currents.) This section of the Snake does not contain any significant rapids, but there may be a few logjams and the current is quite swift, especially in early summer during the snow melt. There are numerous turns and bends in the river, which the paddler will be required to negotiate. This trip can be taken as a day trip, or as an overnight trip if at Colter Bay or Moose Visitor Center in the Tetons you obtain a backcountry use permit for the campsite at Wilcox Point across the bay from Lizard Point. In either case you will need to arrange for a shuttle between Flagg Ranch and Lizard Creek Campground or utilize two vehicles. Before beginning this trip be sure to register your boat at Colter Bay or Moose Visitor Center and also obtain a trip permit at the registration box located at the Flagg Ranch put-in on the river.

The views to the south of the snow-clad northern Tetons are spectacular. There are also some fine views of the southern edge of Yellowstone's Pitchstone Plateau, where volcanic lava flowed some 70,000 years ago. The river occasionally divides into channels. If you stay river-right, you will pass directly under a large cliff that contains hundreds of cliff swallows. The last 2 mi. flow through a delta area teeming with birdlife before the Snake empties into Jackson Lake. Look for osprey nests in the tops of dead trees. This is also moose country. The grassy banks rising above the river provide excellent habitat for elk. As you begin to enter Jackson Lake the current slows and your easy river trip becomes a lake trip. A headwind is common here, so the last 3 mi. may be a good workout for your upper body!

If you plan to stay overnight at Wilcox Point, veer to the right shore as you enter Jackson Lake. If you are day tripping, follow the left shore to Lizard Creek Campground. The shore-line may be marked by cobbles, dead snags, and stumps due to fluctuating water levels caused by the Jackson Lake dam. You may spot some old sawed-off tree stumps in this area. Constructed in 1916, the dam raised the water level of the lake by 39 ft. and increased its length by 5 mi. In fact further recent construction on the dam has increased the water level further, which has eliminated some of the beach areas. Depending on water levels you may have to negotiate a lot of blowdown and trees along the lakeshore when you beach your canoe.

The Wilcox Point campsite is located in a beautiful setting with fine views of the rich delta region to the north. Wilcox Point (and Fonda Point across the bay) are named for two early Grand Teton park rangers who tragically died while on a winter snowshoe patrol in this area. They broke through the ice while crossing the lake here. Plan for an early departure for the 1-mi. trip across the bay to Lizard Point in order to avoid the normal midday winds.

Some backcountry travelers choose to combine this canoe trip with a backpack loop hike around Moose Basin Divide via Webb and Owl creek drainages. This trip is best in August after the snow in the high country has subsided.

Jackson Lake Dam to Pacific Creek Landing (5.0 mi.)

Put-in: About one mi. south of Jackson Lake Junction is located a dirt road that provides access to the river below the dam.

Take-out: Pacific Creek Landing, located about 0.5 mi. north of Moran Junction.

The Snake River from below Jackson Lake Dam to Pacific Creek Landing near Moran Junction provides a very pleasant 5-mi. canoe trip appropriate for the paddler with novice skills. The current is slow and there are few, if any, obstacles. The

Oxbow Bend area is particularly beautiful, with splendid views of Mt. Moran and The Grand. The area is rich in waterfowl; please enjoy them from a distance and respect their home.

Pacific Creek Landing to Deadmans Bar (10.0 mi.)

Put-in: Pacific Creek Landing, 0.5 mi. north of Moran Junction.

Take-out: Deadmans Bar, reached via a rough spur road, about 9.5 mi. south of Moran Junction.

This section of the river is suitable for intermediate-level paddlers once the water level has stabilized at a reasonable flow in mid- to later summer. I have found a flow of about 2,600 cubic feet per second (cfs) to provide ample volume without being too "pushy." There may be a few logjams, especially in the first few miles from Pacific Creek. Be sure to read the river report at the put-in for current information on the cfs and obstacles to avoid, such as logjams.

Most of the trip to Deadmans Bar consists of wide channels. Spectacular views of the entire Teton Range are enjoyed at several spots along the way. You may see bison, pronghorn, and moose along this stretch of the river, as well as eagle and osprey nests. Please note that regulations prohibit stopping your canoe or traveling on foot in the eagle-nest areas (signs should be posted to this effect). After about 2 mi. you will note several impressive springs flowing into the river from the east bank. As you near Deadmans Bar there are some nice standing waves. The takeout road at Deadmans Bar is quite rough, but most two-wheel-drive vehicles can negotiate it.

Deadmans Bar to Moose (10.0 mi.)

Put-in: Via a steep and rough gravel road that leads to the west from Moran Junction–Moose Junction Road about 8 mi. north of Moose Junction.

Take-out: At Moose, prior to reaching the bridge. Be sure to stay river-right to avoid missing the takeout lagoon.

This section of the river is for the advanced paddler. The current is swifter, there are several stretches with standing waves, and the odds for obstacles in the river are greater. Read the river report carefully before putting in. The Deadmans Bar to Moose section is the most heavily traveled portion of the river, especially by float companies, so expect to see some other folks; however, the river can absorb quite a bit of use if proper river manners are used. Be sure to maintain an adequate distance from craft that are up- or downstream from you, and avoid loud or boisterous behavior. The Snake River is a place for enjoying nature's tranquil moods.

Just below Deadmans Bar are some nice standing waves. The Grand Teton looms overhead so close it almost seems as if you should be able to reach out and touch it. An impressive view of Cascade Canyon is enjoyed, and Buck Mountain dominates the view as you near Moose.

All along the Snake is substantial evidence of beaver cuts. In fact, when entering some of the narrow channels, be alert for fresh-cut cottonwood trees that may block your passage. There are more eagle-nest areas along this stretch.

It is possible to shorten the trip about 3 mi. by taking out at Schwabacher Landing. If you wish to do this you need to catch the proper channel. About one hour beyond Deadmans Bar you will see a very large bank, known as Otter Bank, on the right side of the river. After you pass this bank look for the first channel bending off to the left. In mid- to late summer the channel will not contain a great deal of water, but it should be sufficient to get you to the take-out at Schwabacher Landing. If you continue to Moose be careful to stay in the main river channel since some of the side channels are narrow and may be partially blocked by fallen trees.

JACKSON LAKE

Lizard Point to Spalding Bay   (20.0 mi.)

Put-in: Lizard Point, located in Lizard Creek Campground.

Take-out: About 1 mi. south of Deadmans Point, at a primitive dirt road that leads up to the paved road near North Jenny Lake Junction.

Although powerboats are allowed throughout Jackson Lake, most do not venture along the western shore, especially in the north end of the lake. Although more boat traffic is found around Moran Bay, a canoe trip from Lizard Point along the western shore and out at Spalding Bay provides for a beautiful and memorable journey. If you are an experienced river paddler you can begin at the Flagg Ranch put-in on the Snake River and add 10 mi. to your expedition (see p. 248). There are several backcountry campsites located along the west shore of Jackson Lake and in Moran Bay. Many people view the beauty of the Tetons from the east shore of Jackson Lake, but relatively few obtain the close-up views from the west shore. All along the west shore you are treated to spectacular views, especially when you enter North Moran and Moran bays. (Moran Bay would be an ideal area to designate as hand-propelled craft only.) From the north end of Moran Bay you will enjoy a fabulous view of the north face of Mt. Moran. Grassy Island provides a nice spot to stop, stretch your legs, enjoy the views, and perhaps eat lunch.

The more hardy and adventurous may enjoy extending this trip by canoeing into Bearpaw Bay and portaging to Bearpaw Lake to Leigh Lake and ending the trip at String Lake. However, the portage from Bearpaw Bay to Bearpaw Lake is rather tough since you must carry your boat uphill through a relatively dense forest (no trail) for a distance of about half a mile, so consider this option only if you are traveling extra light.

A LAKE-TO-LAKE TRIP

String Lake to Leigh Lake

Put-in & take-out: At the String Lake Picnic Area, just north of Jenny Lake.

Many cover photos and calendars reproduce the magnificent view of The Grand from String Lake. The 1-mi. trip from String Lake to Leigh Lake (easy portage required) provides a most enjoyable outing, but expect some company. From the outlet it is a 3.2-mi. trip along the east shore to the north end of Leigh Lake. Over the years powerful storms blasting down Leigh and Indian Paintbrush canyons have ground portions of the eastern shoreline into some nice beaches. From the north end of Leigh Lake be sure to beach your canoe and stroll the 0.5 mi. over to scenic Bearpaw Lake, formed as a result of ice and glacial action. As you paddle the 2.5 mi. along the north shore to the Leigh Canyon inlet, the views of Mt. Moran from Leigh Lake are just superb. Early in the summer the drainage from Leigh Canyon enters the west end of Leigh Lake with such force that large boulders can be heard to tumble down the stream! From the west end of Leigh Lake it is about 4.5 mi. back to the String Lake Picnic Area. An overnight stay on Leigh Lake is very rewarding, but good luck in reserving one of the campsites!

Exploring Yellowstone by Bicycle

Given the growing popularity of mountain bikes, many visitors to Yellowstone inquire about bicycling possibilities. In general, bicycles are not allowed on hiking trails in the park. However, there are some very nice designated routes (closed to motor vehicles) available for use by bicyclists. Also, several off-the-beaten-path roads (open to motor vehicles) provide pleasant bicycling opportunities. So bring your bikes with you (if you can fit them in along with your backpacks and canoe)! A pamphlet, "Bicycling in Yellowstone National Park," is available at all visitor centers.

Bicycling through Yellowstone on the park's Grand Loop Road is not recommended, especially during the heavy visitation season of June through August. Sharing the narrow roads with numerous oversized RVs is just not worth the risk. A summary of bicycling opportunities in the park follows.

OLD FAITHFUL AREA

Kepler Cascades to Lone Star Geyser   (5.0 mi. roundtrip)

This route follows an old paved road along the Firehole River to Lone Star Geyser. The scenery consists of lush forest, meadows, and the clear, flowing waters of the Firehole River. This area was not touched by the fires of 1988. If you are pedaling this route early or late in the day, look for elk in the meadows. The road ends at Lone Star Geyser, which ranks with Castle

Lone Star Geyser

Geyser as having one of the largest geyserite cones (over 12 ft. high) in the park. Lone Star erupts about every three hours, with splashing from the cone preceding the eruption by about an hour. The eruptions are over 25 ft. high and last about 20 minutes, followed by a noisy steam phase.

Upper Geyser Basin Trail (3.0 mi. roundtrip)

A paved trail leads from Old Faithful Visitor Center to Morning Glory Pool. Along the way you pass Castle Geyser and Riverside Geyser. A short side trail leads up to Daisy Geyser and

Punchbowl Spring. Before heading out from the Old Faithful Visitor Center, be sure to obtain a map of the Upper Geyser Basin and geyser prediction times. Bicycles are not permitted on boardwalks in the basin or on unpaved trails that continue beyond Morning Glory Pool and Punchbowl Spring. However, bike racks (and trees) are available so you may lock up your bikes and explore these areas by foot. A 1-mi. spur trail from Daisy Geyser to Biscuit Basin is also open to bikes. This trail leads through a forest, most of which burned in 1988, and some meadows. The trail is not paved and is sandy in spots, so only try this one if you have wide tires.

Fountain Freight Road (5.0 mi. roundtrip)

This route begins about 5 mi. north of Old Faithful (look for the "Trailhead" sign on the west side of the road). Or you may begin your trip at the locked gate at the end of Fountain Flat Drive, which is located 10 mi. north of Old Faithful. The route consists of an old dirt road that skirts Midway Geyser Basin. Much of the forest in this area burned in 1988. You may want to combine this trip with a hike into Fairy Falls, since you will pass right by the beginning of the 1.5-mi. foot trail (see page 108). Fountain Flat Drive itself, which is paved and open to motor vehicles, provides a very nice bike trip in the early morning and evening when traffic is light. The road traverses large meadows that are habitat to elk, coyote, bison, and sandhill crane. Also look along the banks of the Firehole River for duck and Canada geese.

MAMMOTH AREA

Abandoned Railroad
Along Park Boundary (10.0 mi. roundtrip)

This route begins at the east end of the town of Gardiner and follows the old Northern Pacific railroad bed 5 mi. to Reese

Creek. The scenery consists of open country with views of the Yellowstone River below you to the north and Sepulcher Mountain and majestic Electric Peak to the east. Plan on taking this trip early or late in the summer, since this route is at a low elevation (under 5,300 ft.) and is thus quite warm most of the summer.

INDIAN CREEK CAMPGROUND VICINITY

If you happen to be camping at Indian Creek Campground, there are two short trips available. About 1 mi. north of the campground is the old Swan Lake Service Road, which consists of a 2-mi. roundtrip route. Leading south right out of the campground is a short (1 mi. roundtrip) dirt road known locally as the Superintendent's Picnic Road.

TOWER–CANYON AREA

Chittenden Road to Mt. Washburn   (6.0 mi. roundtrip)

If you have a mountain bike (with good brakes) and desire a hearty workout, this may be the trip for you. You begin at the Chittenden Road parking area (located about 5 mi. north of Dunraven Pass) and follow a dirt road to the summit of Mt. Washburn, climbing approximately 1,443 ft. in 3 mi. If the weather is in your favor, this is a spectacular trip as the views (and wildflowers in July and August) are stupendous. Also you stand a good chance of viewing bighorn sheep. Once you are on the summit keep in mind that bicycles are *not* permitted on the wide trail leading down to Dunraven Pass. (For more information on the Mt. Washburn area, see page 232.) It is a good idea to check with rangers at Canyon Visitor Center to ascertain conditions before embarking on this strenuous trip.

Chittenden Service Road
to Tower Falls Campground (2.0 mi. one way)

This trip begins from Grand Loop Road about 3 mi. south of Tower Falls Campground. The route drops about 500 ft. in 2 mi., so if you can arrange the logistics, it is best to make this a one-way excursion. The first mile passes through lodgepole pine while the last mile is through a Douglas fir forest burned in 1988. Spectacular views of the Washburn Range and the Tower Creek drainage are enjoyed. This trail is occasionally closed due to bear activity, so check with a ranger before departing.

LAKE AREA

There are two bicycle routes available near Bridge Bay Campground: Natural Bridge Road (2 mi. roundtrip) and the old roadbed near the campground. However, check with a ranger before using either one since they are frequently closed due to bear activity. The 1-mi. road into the Natural Bridge area leads through a lodgepole forest with Bridge Creek nearby. Natural Bridge is a span of rock about 150 ft. high that arches above a tumbling stream.

LAMAR AREA

Rose Creek Service Area (2.0 mi. roundtrip)

This pleasant trip begins behind the Lamar Ranger Station and passes through open country along Rose Creek.

OFF-THE-BEATEN-PATH ROADS

Although the following routes allow motor vehicles, the traffic tends to be light, especially early and late in the day, thus providing for an enjoyable bicycling experience. All but one of the following trips consist of one-way roads.

Bunsen Peak Loop Road   (6.0 mi. one way)

This trip is excellent for mountain bikes (with good brakes), but keep in mind that it is usually closed following rain. Also it is a good idea to arrange for a shuttle for this bike trip. This one-way road begins 5 mi. south of Mammoth on Mammoth–Norris Road. The first 3 mi. are fairly level and pass through open sedge meadows and sage flats dotted with small ponds favored by ducks. Stands of aspen and Douglas fir populate the forest here. Quite a bit of this area burned in 1988, but the vegetation is recovering nicely. (Aspen actually depend on fire for effective regeneration.) The road begins a steep drop as it passes by the Osprey Falls trailhead (see page 181 for information on this hike). Just beyond the trailhead the road comes to a spectacular overlook of Sheepeater Canyon and 150-ft. Osprey Falls in the distance. From the overlook the road continues through a series of steep, hairpin switchbacks as it descends about 800 ft. in only 2 mi. The road passes through a government maintenance and residential area before rejoining the main road. As you enter this government area you may want to make a left turn on the dirt road in the maintenance area; it leads 0.7 mi. to beautiful Joffe Lake.

The Old Gardiner Road   (5.0 mi. one way)

The one-way dirt road begins behind Mammoth Hotel, climbs about 50 ft. around a ridge for a very nice view down to the Mammoth area and old Fort Yellowstone, then begins a pleasant and gradual descent of about 900 ft. toward the North Entrance. This is open sagebrush country with wonderful views of Sepulcher Mountain and Electric Peak to the west and Mt.

Everts and Gardner Canyon to the east. About halfway along your journey you will pass a small drainage that leads over to scenic Slide Lake about 0.25 mi. east of the road. Pronghorn antelope are frequently spotted along this section of the road. Old Gardiner Road comes out right at the North Entrance, about 0.5 mi. from the town of Gardiner. Early morning or late evening are the best times to find wildlife and to keep cool; this area is quite warm in midsummer. This road is usually closed after a rain. Obviously, a shuttle is recommended for this trip.

Blacktail Plateau Drive (8.0 mi. one way)

This one-way dirt road begins from Mammoth–Tower Road about 8.5 mi. from Mammoth. It traverses grass and sage hills and passes in and out of lodgepole pine and Douglas fir forests, punctuated with aspen groves. The area is particularly beautiful in early summer when the yellow balsamroot is in bloom. The road gradually climbs about 600 ft. to a narrow canyon known as The Cut, and then descends 450 ft. back to the main road near the Petrified Tree spur road. Along the descent you will cross lovely Elk Creek. This area burned in 1988, but much revegetation and colorful flowers have appeared since the fire. This road is closed after a rain. A shuttle should be arranged.

Upper Mammoth Terrace Loop Drive (1.6 mi. one way)

This narrow paved one-way road begins 2 mi. above the main Mammoth area and provides a very enjoyable bicycle trip in the early morning or evening when traffic is light. The road makes a complete loop, so no shuttle is needed. You will pass around the Narrow Gauge and New Highland Terrace, where the travertine has deposited at a rapid rate in years past. Unlike the geyserite in the geyser basins, which build at the slow rate of only one inch per 100 years, the travertine here has deposited at the rate of up to 20 inches per year. What better place to see living geology before your very eyes? Look for deer early in the morning and listen for the variety of birds in the area.

Gull Point Drive (6.0 mi. roundtrip)

This route begins near Bridge Bay and consists of a level, two-way road, so you don't have to arrange a shuttle for this trip. The road offers quiet forest scenery with water in sight most of the way. The backwater areas provide good habitat for waterfowl. Gull Point itself offers a spectacular view of Yellowstone Lake and the Absaroka Range to the east. There are nice sandy beaches all around as well. Plan to take this trip early in the morning or evening to miss the traffic. You will be glad you did for this area is quite beautiful.

Firehole Lake Drive (3.0 mi. one way)

This level one-way paved road begins from Old Faithful–Madison Road 8 mi. north of Old Faithful and takes you through much of the Lower Geyser Basin. There are numerous beautiful hot springs to view just off the road as well as geysers. The Great Fountain Geyser, one of Yellowstone's most spectacular, erupts about every 11 hours. It will overflow for about 70 minutes prior to erupting, so if the crater is full and you see water seeping out, by all means wait to see the eruption. Just beyond Great Fountain is White Dome Geyser with its very large and impressive geyserite cone. White Dome erupts fairly frequently, about every 30 to 60 minutes. Beyond White Dome you continue to pass thermal features, such as Pink Cone Geyser, which erupts rather infrequently, and Firehole Lake, which deserves an exploration along its boardwalks. The Firehole Lake area contains some large meadows that may contain such wildlife as coyote, bison, and sandhill crane. If you take this trip in early morning or evening when the traffic is light, you may want to bicycle down Old Faithful–Madison Road another mile to the point where you started.

Cross-Country Skiing

Some of the finest ski touring in America can be found on the high, gently rolling plateaus of Yellowstone. Sufficient snow for ski touring is usually present in the park's high elevations by the first of December, and good conditions typically exist through mid-April. If you plan an extended trip, February and March are usually ideal due to snow accumulation and condition and longer daylight hours. In early winter the days are short and snow accumulation may not be suitable, though conditions vary considerably each winter. During April, spells of warm weather may cause poor snow conditions, although at higher elevations it may be possible to ski as late as early June; this is especially true on Pitchstone Plateau and in the Beartooths outside the Northeast Entrance.

The only park road plowed during the winter lies between the North Entrance and Cooke City, just outside the Northeast Entrance. The rest of the park's roads are open to over-the-snow vehicles. Lodging is available at Mammoth Hot Springs and at Old Faithful. Mammoth Campground remains open during the winter, and its restrooms are heated. Concession snowcoaches provide service from Flagg Ranch near the South Entrance, West Yellowstone, and Mammoth. If you are new to ski touring and do not own skis, rentals are available at Old Faithful and Mammoth. Mammoth also provides such amenities as sleigh rides and ice skating.

There are some fine ski trails in the Mammoth area, and the plowed road from Mammoth to Cooke City provides access to some excellent skiing possibilities as well. The National Park Service and the park concessioner have produced a series of pamphlets that provide maps showing the location and rating the difficulty of ski trails. These pamphlets are available at visitor centers and warming huts, or write the National Park Service, P.O. Box 168, Yellowstone National Park, WY 82190. Skier shuttles by snowcoach may be available from Mammoth and Old Faithful; inquire at a visitor center. Some shuttles provide dropoffs at trailheads so skiers can enjoy pleasant, slightly downhill trips back to developed areas.

Some of the easy ski trails recommended in the Mammoth area include the Upper Terrace Loop; portions of Snow Pass, Bunsen Peak, and Sheepeater trails; and Bighorn and Indian Creek loop trails. In the Tower area there are four nice trails: Lost Lake, Tower Falls, Blacktail Plateau, and Chittenden Loop. Check at the Mammoth Motor Inn to see if shuttle service to the Tower area is available.

Near the Northeast Entrance two easy ski trips are available: the Bannock and Barronette trails. The Bannock Trail leads 2 mi. from the Warm Creek Picnic Area to the small town of Silver Gate just outside the Northeast Entrance. The Barronette Trail follows 3.5 mi. along the west side of Soda Butte Creek. You may begin from either the upper Soda Butte bridge (3 mi. from the Northeast Entrance) or the lower Soda Butte bridge (6.5 mi. from the Northeast Entrance). This trail provides some beautiful views of Barronette and Abiathar peaks. For longer excursions the 13-mi. trip up Slough Creek Valley to the northern park boundary is highly recommended, especially in late winter as an overnight outing. Another possible overnight trip for experienced skiers is the 13-mi. Pebble Creek Trail, which begins near the Northeast Entrance.

The Grand Canyon of Yellowstone area offers three pleasant trails. The Cascade Lake Trail winds 3 mi. through lodgepole forests and meadows over gentle terrain to ice-covered Cascade Lake, where there are some nice slopes on which to practice your downhill skiing skills. Before venturing up these fine slopes in the Washburn Range, check at the Canyon warming hut to determine snow conditions and avalanche danger. The Canyon Rim Trail begins from the warming hut and leads to Inspiration Point and along portions of the north rim of the Grand Canyon of the Yellowstone River. If you venture out to the actual viewpoints, take off your skis and walk out to the overlook. Fun for more experienced skiers is Roller Coaster Trail, which also begins from the warming hut. The trail is about 2 mi. in length and contains a string of ups and downs to spice up your skiing enjoyment.

The Old Faithful area provides over 40 mi. of ski trails, many winding through steam columns rising from geysers and hot springs. Upper Geyser Basin is also a wildlife spectacle during the winter. Elk and bison are drawn for food and warmth to the thermally warmed waters of the Firehole River. Places where the ground is thermally heated (thermal burns) are also attractants for animals. On clear and cold days the basin takes on an ethereal appearance. Steam columns from erupting geysers rise hundreds of feet into the air. The droplets of water quickly freeze into ice crystals and remain almost suspended in midair. The crystals act as miniature prisms, reflecting various colors from the sun's rays against a deep blue sky.

Another recommended ski trip includes Biscuit Basin via Morning Glory Pool. This trail is fairly level and provides a very pleasant 5-mi. roundtrip loop. If you ski into Mystic Falls from Biscuit Basin you add about 2 mi. onto your trip. A longer trip suitable for intermediate skiers takes you to 200-ft. Fairy Falls, which contains a marvelous encrustment of ice at its base. This trip can be completed as a 16-mi. roundtrip from Old Faithful, or you may be able to obtain a dropoff at the freight road, which would cut your total distance in half. Other relatively short trips include Lone Star Geyser, Spring Creek, and

Mallard Lake. Be sure to obtain at the visitor center a copy of the pamphlet *Old Faithful Ski Trails*.

For those interested in planning extended overnight winter trips, full consideration should be given to the severe elements. The Yellowstone country is often the coldest in the nation—lows of −30°F are not uncommon (the record low is −66°F!). Once while on an 18-day backcountry ski trip in the park during late February and early March, I found out just how rapidly the weather conditions can change. The first three days of our trip we enjoyed perfect snow conditions with temperatures ranging from a high of 20°F to a low of −20°F. Then the temperature soared to the high thirties and a heavy wet snow began to accumulate. It snowed 10 ft. over the next eight days!

It is essential that persons entering the winter wilderness be properly equipped and have adequate experience and training to withstand excursions under arduous conditions. A backcountry use permit is required, and you should be prepared for an equipment check and discussion of your trip plans with a ranger. It is important to carry emergency provisions, such as extra clothing (adjustable layers work best), extra food, and equipment repair parts and tools (see The Backpacker's Checklist on page 42). A map and compass and the know-how to use them are essential; most of Yellowstone's trails are identified by international orange metal markers located well above snow level, but whiteout conditions can obliterate visibility. On longer overnight trips expect to do a lot of trail breaking. A group of at least three persons is recommended for trail breaking in shifts. It is also a good idea to arrange to do most of your skiing between the hours of dawn and early afternoon for best snow and ski conditions.

Appendix

ADDITIONAL INFORMATION

Publications

For information on other publications pertaining to the natural and human history of Yellowstone write the Yellowstone Association, P.O. Box 117, Yellowstone National Park, WY 82190. The Yellowstone Association was founded in 1933 to assist with educational, historical, and scientific programs for the benefit of Yellowstone National Park and its visitors. The Association sells a large variety of educational materials about Yellowstone via mail order and in the park's visitor centers.

Activities

The National Park Service offers a wide variety of interpretive walks and programs, especially during the summer months. For information contact the Division of Intepretation, National Park Service, P.O. Box 168, Yellowstone National Park, WY 82190.

The Yellowstone Institute was founded in 1976 and offers many different courses on the park's natural and human history. For information write The Yellowstone Institute, P.O. Box 117, Yellowstone National Park, WY 82190.

Concessions, Supplies and Medical Service

Numerous types of facilities, services and supplies are available both inside the park and in the gateway communities outside Yellowstone. In order to obtain lodging in the park you should make reservations several months ahead of your planned visit. Call or write the National Park Service in Yellowstone for current concession information.

Index

Field Notes

Field Notes

Field Notes

Field Notes

Field Notes

Field Notes